E3

REIMAGINING INDIAN COUNTRY

REIMAGINING

 # INDIAN

FIRST PEOPLES New Directions
in Indigenous Studies

COUNTRY

Native American Migration & Identity

in Twentieth-Century Los Angeles

NICOLAS G. ROSENTHAL

THE UNIVERSITY OF NORTH CAROLINA PRESS
Chapel Hill

Publication of this book was made possible, in part, by a grant
from the Andrew W. Mellon Foundation.

Designed and set in Miller with TheSerif and Chase by Rebecca Evans
Manufactured in the United States of America

The paper in this book meets the guidelines for permanence and durability
of the Committee on Production Guidelines for Book Longevity of the
Council on Library Resources.

The University of North Carolina Press has been a member of the
Green Press Initiative since 2003.

Library of Congress Cataloging-in-Publication Data
Rosenthal, Nicolas G., 1974–
Reimagining Indian country : native American migration and identity in
twentieth-century Los Angeles / Nicolas G. Rosenthal.
p. cm. — (First peoples : new directions in indigenous studies)
Includes bibliographical references and index.
ISBN 978-0-8078-3555-5 (cloth : alk. paper)
1. Indians of North America—California—Los Angeles—Migrations.
2. Indians of North America—Urban residence—California—Los Angeles.
3. Indians of North America—California—Los Angeles—Social conditions.
4. Rural-urban migration—California—Los Angeles. I. Title.
E78.C15R67 2012
307.76'2'08997079494—dc23   2011047233

Portions of this work have appeared previously, in somewhat different form,
as "Repositioning Indianness: Native American Organizations in Portland,
Oregon, 1959–1975," *Pacific Historical Review* 71 (2002): 415–38, and
"Representing Indians: Native American Actors on Hollywood's Frontier,"
Western Historical Quarterly 36 (Autumn 2005): 328–52, copyright by the
Western History Association, and are reprinted here with permission.

16 15 14 13 12   5 4 3 2 1

CONTENTS

ILLUSTRATIONS & TABLES

ACKNOWLEDGMENTS

Reimagining Indian Country has come about because of the support of many people to whom I am indebted and grateful. It began to take shape within graduate programs at the University of Oregon and the University of California, Los Angeles (UCLA). Jeffrey Ostler was my undergraduate and graduate advisor and has remained a mentor. Every time I read his work I am reminded from whom I learned to think and write like a historian. Peggy Pascoe taught me how to be a professional academic. Her generosity in developing my work and helping me navigate academia explains how I got to where I am today. Melissa Meyer played a major role in the intellectual maturation of the project. She was a staunch advocate who worked tirelessly to help me secure internal and external funding, fellowships, and a tenure-track job. Sadly, Peggy and Melissa both passed away before I completed the book. I miss their counsel and warm presence. Henry Yu provided excellent professional advice and influenced the writing and framing of the book. Matthew Dennis, Julie Hessler, Shirley Hune, Jan Reiff, and Kevin Terraciano also were important mentors. Fellow graduate students fostered a sense of community and an atmosphere of intellectual exchange. John Bowes in particular remains a colleague, critic, and friend.

A postdoctoral fellowship at the University of California's Humanities Research Institute and an appointment in the Department of History at Loyola Marymount University (LMU) allowed me to continue researching, writing, and revising the work. The Bellarmine College of Liberal Arts at LMU provided support for faculty research under Deans Michael Engh, Michael O'Sullivan, and Paul Zeleza. Department of History chairs John Grever and Cara Anzilotti deserve special mention for their focus on junior faculty members. Teresa Hackett keeps daily life running smoothly. My colleagues eased the transition into the life of a teacher/scholar, and I have come to rely on them as friends.

The generosity of the American Indian people who have shared their stories with me has greatly enriched this work. Michael McLaughlin was especially important in contacting potential interviewees and discussing the project as it developed. Dennis Tafoya provided superb images from his family's photo collection. Glenda Ahhaitty, Glenna Amos, Mark Banks, H. Brown, Randy Edmonds, M. M., Dave Rambeau, John Spence, Sidney Stone, Dennis Tafoya, Marjorie Tanin, and Vincent Wannassay sat down with me to discuss a wide range of issues related to their lives and the experiences of their families and communities.

A project such as this one cannot be done without the dedication and hard work of archivists and librarians. Those who contributed their expertise to this project include Peter Blodgett at the Huntington Library; Marva Felchlin at the Autry National Center; Michael McLaughlin at the American Indian Resource Center, Los Angeles County Public Library; Ken Wade at the American Indian Studies Library, UCLA; Kim Walters at the Braun Research Library, Autry National Center; Paul Wormer at the National Archives and Records Administration, Pacific Region; and the staffs at the Chicago Historical Society; National Archives and Records Administration, Pacific Alaska Region; Newberry Library; Oral History Library, California State University, Fullerton; Stanley Parr Archives and Record Center; Seaver Center for Western History, Los Angeles Natural History Museum; Shield's Library, University of California, Davis; Southern California Library; and the institutions listed above.

Fellowship support also made this work possible. The American Philosophical Society, Andrew W. Mellon Foundation, Autry National Center, Historical Society of Southern California, Immigrant and Ethnic History Society, LMU Bellarmine College of Liberal Arts, LMU Department of History, Newberry Library, University of California Humanities Research Institute, UCLA Department of History, UCLA Graduate Division, UCLA Institute of American Cultures and American Indian Studies Center, University of North Carolina Press, and University of Oregon provided crucial funding.

Several scholars read part or all of the work and were generous with their time and insight. They include Carl Abbott, Ned Blackhawk, Matt Bokovoy, John Bowes, Dan Cobb, Matt Garcia, Brian Hosmer, Frederick Hoxie, Adria Imada, David Johnson, David Rich Lewis, Colleen O'Neill, Lorena Oropeza, Paige Raibmon, Robert Self, Michelle Raheja, Allison

Varzally, Penny Von Eschen, Mark Wild, and two anonymous manuscript readers.

The University of North Carolina Press proves that academic publishing can persevere and adapt in these challenging times without sacrificing important principles. Mark Simpson-Vos has been both a responsive editor and a mentor who has shaped the project with his thoughtfulness and steady hand. The staff at UNC Press has been a pleasure to work with at every stage.

My family and friends have also contributed to this project. Lauren has supported me in innumerable ways. Jane provides daily perspective. This book is dedicated to my parents, Michael R. and Linda G. Rosenthal, who have always worked for my success and happiness.

REIMAGINING INDIAN COUNTRY

REIMAGINING INDIAN COUNTRY

P awnee tribal members John and Lois Knifechief lived most of their lives in and around Pawnee, Okla., until 1954. Born in the late 1920s, they attended public schools and earned high school diplomas. When World War II came along, John served oversees in the U.S. military. John got a job driving buses for a local company on his return, the couple married, and they began having children. Over several years, however, the Knifechiefs became frustrated trying to make a living and raise a family in Pawnee. Widespread discrimination against Indians made it unlikely that John would ever receive a promotion. Lois hoped to work someday, and the prospects in town were slim. With four small boys between the ages of one and seven, these challenges became more crucial. Despite a deep attachment to the community, the Knifechiefs resolved to move on. They took advantage of a new federal program and accepted $50 from the Bureau of Indian Affairs (BIA), piled into their car, and made the long three-day trip to Los Angeles. John and Lois hoped to find the kinds of opportunities that would allow them to provide a better life for their family, once in the city.

After a shaky start and with much effort, Los Angeles proved to offer the Knifechiefs what they sought. They first drove to the BIA's Los Angeles Field Relocation Office, where the staff directed them to a hotel near downtown's Skid Row. The office rented them a two-room apartment later meant to house all six family members. John was dismayed and angrily informed the BIA, "We didn't have much where we came from, but we had better than this, and we were supposed to come out here to improve ourselves." John began operating a streetcar for Los Angeles Transit thereafter, which allowed the Knifechiefs to move into a bigger house. John got a better job operating rides at Disneyland in Anaheim a few years later and moved up to performing in the park's Indian Village. He eventually left for a managerial position with a county bus company. Lois worked part-time when the children got a bit older, both as a motel manager and as a cook at a private day school. The boys attended local public schools through the 1960s. The two oldest had graduated from high school and were attending college nearby in Long Beach by the early 1970s.

Whereas their lives in the city could be understood as a move away from a tribal community and toward mainstream American life, the Knifechiefs continued to identify as Indians, albeit in some new ways. Every summer they returned to Pawnee to renew connections with friends and relatives and because they wanted their children to know their heritage. They continued to vote in tribal elections through absentee ballots. While working at Disneyland, John joined an intertribal Indian dance group called the Road Runners, which performed at area schools, at shopping centers, and for various organizations. John also was well known as a singer of "Southern style" powwow songs and recorded an album as the lead vocalist of a group of Pawnee singers. In 1968 the Knifechiefs became charter members of the Orange County Indian Center, an organization that sought to provide a network of support and a basis of community for other Indians in the Los Angeles area. With John as president between 1968 and 1970, the Indian Center provided material assistance to needy Indian families, helped Indians negotiate the city's social services network, and held powwows, dances, and holiday parties that involved hundreds of Indians throughout Greater Los Angeles.[1]

The Knifechiefs' experiences were not unusual, resembling those of many other Native people who made their way to American cities over the course of the twentieth century. Federal census takers counted 27,000 Indians (8 percent of the Indian population) in U.S. cities in 1940, a number that then steadily increased to 56,000 (16 percent) in 1950, 146,000 (28 percent) in 1960, 356,000 (45 percent) in 1970, and 807,000 (53 percent) in 1980.[2] These migrations occurred all over the country, but American Indian urbanization has been greatest in the nation's largest metropolitan areas, such as New York, Chicago, Seattle, the San Francisco Bay area, and especially Los Angeles, which by 1970 was second only to the Navajo reservation as the largest concentration of American Indians in the country. Indians have also long maintained a presence in smaller cities close to large rural Indian populations, such as Buffalo, N.Y.; Minneapolis; Oklahoma City; Phoenix; Albuquerque; and Portland, Ore. In every case, migration to urban areas has been accompanied by the formation of highly diverse urban Indian communities that have maintained connections to reservations throughout the country.

While these are nationwide trends, this study focuses on Greater Los Angeles as the "urban Indian capital of the United States" and the home of the largest and most diverse urban American Indian population in the country.[3] Los Angeles is at the center of this book and the site for much of the narrative, analysis, and discussion. Studying Los Angeles, however, has wider implications—the city also is meant to stand as a model that can illustrate larger, national patterns of Indian urbanization. Toward that end numerous examples from other cities are brought into the discussion throughout the chapters. There are certainly variations of urban Indian experience from city to city and region to region, which subsequent studies may highlight. Nonetheless, this work shows that it is possible "to argue from Los Angeles outward," in order to understand both the broad contours and the specific experiences of American Indians in myriad relationships with cities over the last century of U.S. history.[4]

This book attempts to put the story of the Knifechiefs in a larger context through the prism of Los Angeles, by telling a social and cultural history of American Indians and cities in modern America. The book connects American Indians to larger discussions about mobility and migration, racialized power structures, and individual and community agency that have helped scholars make sense of a country becoming increasingly urban, multiracial, national, and transnational over the twentieth century. I argue that the frequent movements of American Indians throughout the cities, towns, and rural spaces of the United States call for "reimagining Indian Country" beyond the reservations and rural communities where scholars, policymakers, and popular culture tend to conceptualize it. In fact, much of this book is about how American Indians themselves have long been actively reimagining and defining an Indian Country that includes cities, towns, rural areas, and reservations. By following Native people's cues and taking the basic but crucial step of reimagining Indian Country, scholars can begin to see that cities have played a central and defining role in twentieth-century Native American life. Reimagining Indian Country reveals how American Indian experiences complemented, complicated, and contradicted patterns of racial oppression and subaltern resistance in America. This book shows that American Indian lives in urban America have been structured in ways that resemble the experiences of other racialized groups, but that they also have differed because of both the singular relationships American Indians have had with the federal government and

Native people's unique place within American popular culture. American Indian efforts to operate within and transcend or overturn racialized hierarchies also have been similar to those of other subaltern groups, even as Native people have negotiated U.S. society and culture by drawing on their political and cultural exceptionalism and a proximity to their established homelands. This overlooked history of American Indians in cities both complements and expands ongoing discussions about race in twentieth-century urban America.

The pace and scope of American Indian migration to cities—again, a reimagining and defining of Indian Country by American Indians themselves—should in itself be cause for scholars to also reimagine Indian Country and consider what these movements might mean for both Native people and the cities of the United States. Yet, scholars and especially historians have often missed these trends. Over the past thirty-five years, there have been revolutionary advances in scholarship on Native peoples, often referred to under the rubric of the "New Indian History." Moving away from studies that tended to cast Native people as savages, noble or otherwise, swept aside by the forces of Euro-American progress, New Indian historians sought Indian perspectives, stressed Indian agency, took a critical view of U.S. colonialism, and argued for the central place of Indian people in the development of North America.[5] Except for a brief flurry of work by urban anthropologists in the 1970s, however, only a handful of scholars have worked to examine the relationships between American Indians and cities.[6] With so much of the American Indian population affected by urban areas, especially in the twentieth century, it is crucial that historians of American Indians reimagine Indian Country, or take urbanity seriously, as they continue working to move the field forward.

While each chapter that follows is concerned with how reimagining Indian Country can shape the field of American Indian Studies, this book also engages broader scholarly conversations that bridge gaps to other historical fields. At times, this will mean focusing less on established ways of understanding Native people's experiences popular within American Indian Studies, in favor of analytical frameworks that connect American Indians to more broadly understood historical trends and narratives. For example, in arguing for an expansive Indian Country, this book is particularly influenced by the work of historians and American Studies scholars who have emphasized migration and especially *mobility* as a defining and consistent feature of modern America. These scholars recognize that migration only sometimes occurs as a simple process that transplants people from one location to another, where they lay down roots and live out their lives. Especially in the twentieth century, all of the "push and pull" factors commonly treated in studies of immigration (e.g., the development of transportation systems, political unrest, economic crises) have been seen to have combined with the formulation and workings of immigration policies, the tenacity of migrants in circumventing immigration laws, the industrializing or economic restructuring of parts of the third world, and the globalizing of systems of labor and capital, to encourage migrations that over a lifetime encompass frequent movements, numerous locations, the repeated crossing of national borders, and the development of transnational identities. Scholar Henry Yu, in an essay focusing on Los Angeles (but meant to suggest a larger, urban experience), suggests conceptualizing the city as "an intersection on a larger grid" that encompasses, for his purposes, the entire Pacific Rim. Migration, in this provocative formulation, is "a process without end, comings and goings rather than the singular leaving of one place and arriving at another by which we mythically understand the immigrant's story."[7]

This interpretation of modern American history is crucial for conceptualizing the history of American Indians and cities over the course of the twentieth century. Los Angeles, for instance, was a singular point, albeit an especially important one, on a network of places visited by Native people that extended throughout Southern California, the American Southwest, and the rest of the United States. Although some American Indians did indeed leave reservations, settle in Los Angeles with their families, and live out the rest of their lives—a trend that will also be treated by this work—this was far from the only pattern. Other Native people traveled to Los Angeles seasonally to find work, visited the city for leisure and recreation, took special advantage of something particularly unique to the Los Angeles area, attended Los Angeles area universities, after some period moved on to a job or opportunity in another urban area, and/or returned to the reservation after retirement, among additional lines of experiences and uses of the city. This book explains these patterns by showing how American Indians used Los Angeles and other cities throughout the twentieth century and how these uses fit into their larger social, cultural, and economic strategies rooted in migrant networks. Furthermore, it draws connections between American Indian mobility and shifting conceptions of American Indian identity, cultural life, and community, based on the findings that such tremendous and varied movements, as well as extended contact with diverse and dynamic urban areas, have destabilized what it means to "be

Indian" in modern America. In other words, this book explores how Native people lived as American Indians when they were in the city; their conceptions and expressions of American Indian culture; how tribal identities persisted in urban areas, sometimes in tension with the development of "pan-Indian" perspectives; and how "city Indians" drew connections to tribally based, primarily rural communities on reservations, and vice versa. These discussions are meant to deepen our understanding of what mobility has meant to American Indians and more generally to all peoples traveling the well-worn and crisscrossing paths that make up migration networks.

By focusing on American Indian movement and the reconceptualizations of identity and community, this book also interprets Native people's responses to the pressures and limitations of living as members of an aggrieved and racialized group in modern American society. Like the New Indian historians, scholars more generally emerged from the 1960s ready to critique both structural racism and racist practices on the one hand, while on the other they worked to produce histories that emphasized the perspectives of racialized and oppressed groups. More recently, historians, many of whom are situated within the field of American Studies, have deepened the discussion of agency by expanding discussions of resistance beyond the overtly political. I have found especially useful anthropologist James C. Scott's theories on subaltern resistance and studies by historians who have subsequently addressed and developed Scott's work, as well as that of Antonio Gramsci, to whom Scott is indebted. Especially in his 1990 volume, *Domination and the Arts of Resistance: Hidden Transcripts*, Scott theorized that a range of activities aside from political protest might be considered authentic forms of resistance, because of their power in shaping both the consciousness and the lives of the actors.[8] For some scholars, expanding the boundaries of what constituted resistance and opposition helped make sense of activities that centered on fundamental "nonmaterial" issues such as culture, dignity, and identity, but which nevertheless disrupted the status quo and empowered subaltern actors. Major studies by scholars such as Robin D. G. Kelley, George Lipsitz, and Matt Garcia interrogated cultural forms and social activities to help understand the wide range of possibilities for resistance.[9] At the same time, these scholars kept sight of the fact that this opposition, although fashioned by the actors, was nevertheless shaped by the very real constraints imposed by structures of power. Indeed, a critique of past studies that highlight subaltern agency and the perspectives of oppressed people is that there has been too little conception and analysis of how various forms of cultural and political resistance have been channeled by hegemonic forces.

Delving deeper into the complex relationships between power and agency, scholars can learn more about how hegemony works and the fashioning of counterhegemonic strategies. In the case of American Indians in cities such as Los Angeles, scholars should keep in mind this *tension* between power and agency and how it has come to characterize much of modern, urban life. At the turn of the twentieth century, American Indians had already endured a long and devastating history of European and American colonialism that had made Indian communities among the poorest and most neglected in the country. Coming to the city, Native people faced a racialized hierarchy that limited their opportunities for work, housing, public services, education, and recreation. While their experiences resembled those of other racialized groups, especially Latinos (with whom they were often conflated or confused), American Indians differed in that they had a unique relationship with the federal government. Based on treaty obligations and Native people's legal status, the federal government continued to operate institutions and programs in the city that sought to discipline American Indian behavior and eliminate cultural forms of expression. These efforts ranged from the "outing" programs at federal boarding schools to the urban "relocation" and vocational programs of the post–World War II era. At the same time, somewhat conversely, American Indians faced expectations that they behave according to the derogatory stereotypes and caricatures that appeared throughout popular culture. This was especially true for Native people who tried to make a living as performers, educational lecturers, or Hollywood entertainers, but American Indians also faced cultural stereotyping every day in advertising, schools, museums, films, literature, television, amusement parks, and civic festivals.

These limitations profoundly shaped American Indian lives in the city, but they did not determine them. Native people settled throughout various parts of American cities, from vibrant, multiethnic working-class neighborhoods to industrial and waterfront districts, to truck farms on the city outskirts, to impoverished and plagued areas such as skid row. Like other peoples of color, they worked in the fields and in the factories, raised families, attended schools and universities, and made inroads into the middle class, even as they suffered in disproportionate numbers from poverty and related conditions largely brought on by racism and discrimination. Efforts to "be Indian" in the city faced special challenges, but nonetheless took form in various new and developing cultural expressions, urban clubs and organizations, a wide-ranging political activism that shifted within the larger context of civil rights movements in the United States, and changing relationships with both reservation and urban American Indian communities throughout the country. This book elucidates these efforts by American Indians to negotiate racism and discrimination in the urban setting, by exploring the racialized structures of power that American Indians faced in the city and their responses; how American Indian "culture" functioned as a site of resistance; in what ways American Indians engaged in more "traditional" forms of opposition tied to political organizing and protest; and how this range of responses compared with those taken by other racialized groups.

In the first decades of the twenty-first century, significant challenges remain for Native people invested in American cities. Historical patterns of colonialism and racialized discrimination lay at the roots of many contemporary issues, but Native people also face a lack of visibility that can be equally nefarious. More than any other ethnic group, American Indians are forced to confront racialized caricatures embedded within larger patterns of cultural appropriation and commodification. Whether they serve as sports mascots, advertising icons, or stock characters in Western films, popular images of Indians have become so pervasive, time-honored, and familiar that they serve to relegate Native people to a distant past and to obscure the realities of modern American Indian life. Indeed, among the most crucial issues for Native people are the ways that erroneous cultural perceptions obscure the formulation of effective public policy. Without adequate assessments of American Indians and the relationships they have to cities, policy serving American Indian populations is bound to be ineffective, whether it is formulated on the local, state, or federal level, by government officials or by Native people themselves. Even by scholarly accounts, American Indians seem to have little to do with major currents of contemporary culture and society. The fact that American Indian stereotypes are so cherished and clung to with such tenacity is problematic on a number of levels and should start a larger, self-conscious conversation among educators, scholars, and cultural critics. In the end, stories like the Knifechiefs' and those of other American Indians who have been incorporated into cities and participated in the currents of modern American life over the past 100 years need to play prominent roles in people's conceptions of Indians, superseding tales of savagery on the nineteenth-century Great Plains. The first step is but an intellectual one, yet it is crucial. It involves reimagining Indian Country to include the cities and towns of the United States. With this book I hope to begin that project, by examining the history of American Indians and cities through the twentieth century, showing how Native people themselves have reimagined and defined an Indian Country in which urban areas play a central role.

CHAPTER 1

SETTLING INTO THE CITY

*American Indian Migration and
Urbanization, 1900–1945*

Romaldo LaChusa was born in 1883 and raised on the Mesa Grande Indian Reservation, an impoverished rural farming community in northern San Diego County. LaChusa attended a government-run day school on the reservation as a child and then at the age of sixteen transferred to the Perris Indian School for the next four years. LaChusa enrolled at the Sherman Institute in 1902, a new federal Indian boarding school just east of Los Angeles in the town of Riverside. LaChusa graduated from the eighth grade and took a job on the school's instructional farm, leaving a few years later for the city. LaChusa had no trouble finding steady work once in Los Angeles, especially as the population of the city grew and its economy expanded to create thousands of jobs in the industrial and service sectors. LaChusa was living near downtown and working as a landscape gardener by 1917. Two years later LaChusa married his first wife, Annie, who was a California Indian. The couple relocated to Torrance, an ethnically diverse industrial area near the coast, where LaChusa worked as a laborer at Llewellyn Iron Works alongside Mexican immigrants and several Indians from Arizona. By 1924 LaChusa had married his second wife, Margaret, a California Indian who was born on the Torrez-Martinez Reservation. The two moved to Hollywood, and LaChusa returned to work as a gardener. In 1950, at the age of sixty-seven, LaChusa retired to the city where he had spent most of his life.[1]

Most American Indian Studies scholars who have recognized the migration of Native people to cities in the twentieth century have characterized Indian urbanity as a post–World War II phenomenon. Historians have referred to the dislocation of the war years and postwar federal relocation programs in particular and argue that they sparked the first significant movements of Native people to urban centers. Others have noted the presence of a prewar population, or even suggested that postwar migration was an intensification of earlier trends. These scholars have proceeded to focus on the postwar era and provide little sense of what Indian life in the city was like before 1945, and how these migratory patterns might have shaped Indian Country as a whole.[2] Scholars also have missed the presence of American Indians who often traveled, lived, and worked alongside other peoples of color in the burgeoning cities of North America.[3]

The stories of Romaldo LaChusa and thousands of others illustrate a longer history of American Indians reimagining Indian Country to include the cities of the United States. Throughout the first half of the twentieth century, the American Indian population of urban areas throughout the country steadily increased. American Indians traveled to cities and their surrounding areas for thousands of new jobs in the agricultural, industrial, and service sectors. This migration was often regional, as Native people were most likely to take advantage of economic opportunities in the towns and cities closest to their established lands and communities. Built on decades of participation by wage laborers, these movements were often a logical extension of Native people's more established social patterns rooted in tribal life. American Indians in towns and cities tended to be concentrated in domestic service and unskilled occupations, as they were in rural areas, and these occupations offered the lowest pay under the least favorable of working conditions. Native people also found more skilled and better-paying positions, however, enabling them to settle into the multiethnic, working- and middle-class neighborhoods that came to characterize many U.S. cities. When great numbers of Indian people traveled to urban areas for defense work and military service, there was already a long history of urban American Indian migration. The history of American Indians in American cities from 1900 to 1945 is marked by migrations in correlation to urban expansion. Seen in this light, Indian migration was part of the development of urban America in this era, as well as the foundation for the expansion and development of American Indian communities in cities after the war. American Indians were finding and settling into the cities of the United States as early as the first decades of the twentieth century, beginning a long process of reimagining Indian Country.

❖ ❖ ❖

American Indians have always lived in the towns and cities of North America to some extent.[4] In Southern California, the Spaniards who ventured north to Alta California in the late eighteenth century relied on Chumash,

Serrano, Gabrielino, Cahuilla, Cupeño, San Luiseño, and Kumeyaay Indians to build and maintain the missions, pueblos, and presidios of the region. In places such as San Fernando, San Juan Capistrano, San Luis Rey, San Gabriel, San Diego, and Los Angeles, Native people served as masons, carpenters, plasterers, soap makers, tanners, shoemakers, blacksmiths, millers, bakers, cooks, spinners, shepherds, and vaqueros, among other occupations. During the remainder of the Spanish period (1769–1821) and through the Mexican period (1821–48), Native people from throughout the region came or were coerced to live in these population centers, often working for wages or forced into labor by indebtedness and legal codes that institutionalized Indian slavery. After the U.S. conquest of the American Southwest in 1848, much of the land that had been granted to Indians in California was claimed by new settlers, especially along the coast and in the immediate interior valleys. Some Indians stayed in the coastal regions and continued to farm, raise livestock, gather traditional food resources, and fill the region's labor needs, while others retreated to the interior and intermingled with other bands.[5] After decades of investigations, surveys, commissions, and debates, Congress passed the 1891 Act for the Relief of the Mission Indians, which paved the way for the establishment of reservations managed by the Office of Indian Affairs (OIA). These reservations existed throughout San Diego, Imperial, Riverside, and San Bernardino counties, along the periphery of the region's population centers and east over the mountains and into the desert. Although most reservation boundaries incorporated the primary lands of individual bands as understood at the time, some bands relocated entirely to other territories, and others remained outside the reservation system. Still others refused to move onto nearby reservations and continued to reside on their settled lands.[6] The OIA founded the Sherman Institute in 1902 as a federal boarding school for Indians. In 1920 the OIA also consolidated the jurisdictions of various Indian superintendents to create the Mission Indian Agency, with subagencies on the Pala, Morongo, and Torrez-Martinez reservations. Working out of offices in Riverside, the Mission Indian Agency administered all reservations in Southern California.[7] After the establishment of these reservations and the rationalization of their bureaucratic structures, American Indians in Southern California continued to cross reservation boundaries with regularity to interact with cities and towns throughout the region.[8]

The process of Indian removal, combined with the establishment of reservations in Southern California and other parts of North America, can be understood as a latter stage in the colonization of the continent and the shift of control over enormous areas of land with vast natural resources. With these losses in political authority, insufferable hardships, and drastic population losses, however, Native people did not vanish quietly into the past, nor did they live out diminished lives confined to reservations, as so many popular and scholarly understandings of history would have one believe. Over the first few decades of the twentieth century, Indians often engaged the territories that had come under the influence of Euro-American settlers. These lands were not as Native people had left them, for settlers had rapidly transformed them into farmland, towns, and cities. Indians from surrounding regions and Native people from farther away played a role in this development. Some worked for wages and returned to reservation communities, while others settled in cities and towns to add to the social and cultural landscape.

The movement of Indians back to the growing cities and towns of North America is explained by the harshness of reservation life and the dispossession of Native land and resources. In Southern California, reservations existed on marginal lands isolated from population centers and subject to extremes of weather. Agriculture was often risky and the only economic prospect at hand. These conditions only worsened over time, due to long droughts and because non-Indian farmers and ranchers siphoned off local water supplies. The availability of traditional foods, historically gathered from nearby areas, also decreased in the face of rural and urban development. An almost total lack of developed roads, utilities, and other basic services created unsanitary and dangerous conditions and could make day-to-day life a struggle to maintain a decent standard of living or to even survive.[9]

A small sample of reports from Southern California reservations illustrates some of these difficulties. Between 1921 and 1922, several reservations sent local news and conditions to the Mission Indian Federation, an Indian-run advocacy group for Southern California Indians. The La Jolla Tribe noted that the drought of 1921 had caused the failure of the reservation's 300 acres of crops and led many to look in the surrounding area for work.[10] This drought was followed by one of the worst winters in many years. On the Cahuilla Reservation several cattle and horses were lost to fall and winter storms. The Morongo Reservation reported that "cold blizzards did great damage to our stock and fruit trees. Ten head of stock died for lack of pasture feed. . . . Our fruit buds were damaged by the freezing cold, and we face a shortage of fruit this season. The people will not be able to put any fruit in great quantities for winter's use."[11] The following spring, the secretary for the Soboba Tribe wrote that the lack of work at the reservation had made life dreary. Tribal members looked forward to the fruit season and travel to the Hemet Valley to pick in the orchards. At the same time, on the Campo Reservation, a "sickness" spread and caused the death of several reservation residents, while many more were taken ill.[12] Such illness and premature death were common. A tribal member from the Los Coyotes Reservation lamented that his sister had fifteen children and all had died in infancy.[13] These types of conditions alarmed the San Diego branch of the Bureau of Catholic Charities, which began a collection of money, food, and clothes for Southern California reservations.[14] It is not surprising that many Southern California Indians—and Native people in other parts of the country, who faced similar hardships—would search off the reservation in the hopes of obtaining better standards of living.

Many Indians first looked to nearby rural areas and towns, where they found seasonal jobs as migratory laborers. This work could provide Indian people with crucial sources of income and also presented possibilities for integrating wage labor into social, cultural, and economic strategies rooted in tribal lands and communities. Historian Eric Meeks has argued that the participation of Tohono O'odham Indians in the federal and corporate industrialization of southern Arizona was a case of "resistant adaptation," because the Tohono O'odham engaged in cotton picking, mining, domestic service, and railroad work to complement their seasonal subsistence patterns. Historian Colleen O'Neill has shown how Navajos similarly absorbed wage labor on and near the reservation into a diverse, household-centered economy that included domestic production and sheepherding. Both authors have stressed how Native cultural and social values filtered their participation in the capitalist market, even as wage labor transformed Indian people and communities.[15] Native experience resembled that of other rural Americans who confronted the integration of the lands and resources they depended on into larger markets and found new values attached to their labor. Early American historian Christopher Clark has examined the processes in rural New England that drew it into the industrial orbit of late-eighteenth- and nineteenth-century America. It was a comparable process whereby rural residents gradually engaged in market capitalism grounded in the values of their local exchange economies.[16]

Cases abound of Indians participating in labor markets that grew rapidly in rural areas around Indian reservations throughout the United States and Canada. During the 1920s, in Needles, Calif., on the Arizona border, about 300 Mojave Indians from nearby Fort Mojave Reservation found jobs alongside European Americans, African Americans, and immigrants from Mexico and Japan, as casual laborers for the Santa Fe Railway. Mojave Indians also worked paving streets, building roads, and constructing houses, and on area farms. In Arizona, Apache Indians from the San Carlos Reservation spent part of the year in the nearby towns of Globe and Miami, employed in mining, road construction, railroad work, domestic service, and the production of Native crafts. Members of the Hualapai tribe similarly worked for wages in Kingman, Ariz., just outside the reservation's western boundary.[17] Throughout British Columbia and Alaska, Indians served as loggers, longshoremen, teamsters, cowboys, miners, fishermen, and cannery workers.[18] In the Northern Plains and Upper Midwest regions, Indians worked both in the timber industry and on farms and ranches. Menominee Indians were employed in the forests and sawmills, while Ho-Chunk Indians picked strawberries, cranberries, cherries, corn, peas, and potatoes. Outside the Pine Ridge Reservation in South Dakota, the town of Rapid City maintained a population of approximately 3,000 migratory Sioux Indians who mostly worked cutting timber.[19] In the 1920s, in northern Maine, Mi'kmaw, Passamaquoddy, Penobscot, and Maliseet Indians were recruited as migratory laborers on the region's growing potato farms.[20] Indians filled labor needs on the farms and ranches of Northern California, both as field hands and domestic servants.[21]

Southern California emerged as another site of Indian migratory wage labor. As early as 1909, most "young people" at the Rincon, La Jolla, and Pechanga reservations spent all but a few weeks away from the reservation, because their jobs were either on area ranches or in cities.[22] The superintendent of the Malki Agency in the desert town of Banning wrote in 1919: "Many of the Indians belonging in this jurisdiction do not live on the reservation, but in nearby towns and on ranches where they find ready employment at good wages. It is also true that the majority of those living on the reservations are employed in the towns or in the white ranchers' orchards adjoining the reservations, going to their work early in the morning and returning late in the evening." The superintendent lamented that "the demand for labor and high wages paid has taken many of our Indians" from the "gardens" and "home work" that were part of the government's assimilation program.[23] Several more cases illustrate larger patterns of Indian migration and labor. Every autumn during the first decades of the twentieth century, Indians from San Diego County traveled to El Cajon, east of San Diego, to work in the grape fields.[24] In November 1921, several families from the Soboba Reservation worked in the walnut groves near the town of Walnut, while the men living at the Cahuilla Reservation were away picking oranges or building roads.[25] Early in 1922, Indians from Southern California could be found in the vicinity of Riverside, where the orange groves were expected to provide steady work for months.[26] A number of families from the Campo Reservation traveled to Brawley, to work in the cotton and corn fields and on small ranches. Two men from the Pala Reservation, meanwhile, spent the late winter traveling a circuit to shear sheep.[27] Indians from several reservations had migrated to Hemet by summer, in time for fruit season. Others were camped in the Palomar Mountains, north of San Diego, where there was great demand in the apricot orchards for pickers and pitters.[28] Work in the walnut and fruit groves and packinghouses continued well into the fall throughout the region.[29] After living in cities throughout the American West and settling in Los Angeles, Martina Costo, a Cahuilla Indian who was born in 1910, remembered growing up in the town of Hemet, where her parents were employed year-round by a citrus-growing colony.[30]

Wage labor can be understood as a pragmatic adaptation that helped offset the loss of indigenous lands and resources and also as the source of considerable hardship for Native peoples. In Southern California, wage work often meant moving seasonally throughout the rural areas of the region, camping out in the open, and laboring arduously in the fields. Mr. and Mrs. Manuel Largo, a couple from the Soboba Reservation, spent the winter of 1922 traveling with their two daughters. The Mission Indian Federation described their plight: "Under all sorts of weather this family has been away from home seeking work, the method used by many of the reservation people to earn money to keep the wolf away from the door. It seems impossible that they can make these long journeys under such severe winter weather, but they do it for the sake of their children, to keep them fed, clothed and warm."[31] A member of a Southern California tribe wrote from the San Fernando Valley, just north of Los Angeles, relating similar experiences: "There are many other families here beside mine, picking olives. The cold blast, gale, rainy days we are having prevent us from working. We are earning enough to live on. We are very much exposed to the weather [and] subject to colds. But we feel certain someday we will be content to stay at home, housed comfortably."[32] Through the 1930s and into the 1940s, Indians faced similar circumstances, as they continued to participate in the region's agricultural economy. Migratory labor made sense to and became necessary for many Indian people during the first half of the twentieth century, but these types of conditions and the role of non-Indians in defining them often differentiated wage labor from earlier subsistence strategies based on greater degrees of Indian agency and autonomy, during times when natural resources were more abundant and available to Native people.

Considering how difficult migratory wage labor could be, it is not surprising that many Indian people sought better work and living conditions in the burgeoning cities of the United States, even if it meant moving farther away from tribal communities. Urban areas around the country went through a period of tremendous expansion around the turn of the last century, as the U.S. economy, driven by new industries, created thousands of jobs, many of which were filled by immigrants and rural migrants. Los Angeles County experienced particularly explosive growth, as its industrial and agricultural economy swelled and its population soared, making Los Angeles the preeminent urban center on the Pacific Coast. By 1880, Los Angeles had already outpaced San Diego as the capital of Southern California. Although its economy was based mainly on farm exports, Los Angeles also established a modest industrial sector around foundries, slaughterhouses, and lumberyards. A sometimes chaotic real estate market was fueled by rising populations from both natural growth and increasing migrations. Civic boosters aggressively touted the city as a "garden paradise" suitable for farming, but turn-of-the-century travelers to Los Angeles also included health seekers, retirees, artisans, merchants, manufacturers, and workers. After World War I, the city expanded more rapidly; the population of Los Angeles County rose from 504,000 in 1910 to 936,000 in 1920. Two industries in particular, oil and motion pictures, brought tremendous wealth to the city. Other companies came to see Los Angeles as their West Coast headquarters, and they built rubber, automobile, furniture, and clothing factories.[33]

The boom that began in Los Angeles after World War I continued at a rapid pace through the 1920s. In addition to the expansion of the oil and motion picture industries, Los Angeles became the aviation capital of the United States, as many airplane manufacturers established production facilities in the city. Also experiencing growth were older industries such as iron, steel, and rubber, as well as industries new to the city, such as electronics and chemicals. To support the thriving economy, private business and public officials worked to build infrastructure throughout Los Angeles County, by constructing highways, securing water supplies, and carving subdivisions out of rural lands. By 1930 the county's population had skyrocketed to more than 2 million, including new waves of Latino,

African American, and Eastern European migrants.[34] Robert M. Fogelson, pioneering historian of Los Angeles, described the tremendous pull of the city: "The appeal of Los Angeles and environs was almost irresistible during the 1920s, and, as immigration to southern California gained in momentum, it perpetuated the very conditions which attracted newcomers . . . the mild climate, exotic landscape, and suburban environment still so intrigued those in quest of a new life."[35] Los Angeles in the 1920s was a "metropolis in the making." The city came to stand for a burgeoning metropolitan region composed of the city limits, several independent municipalities, and agricultural areas interspersed throughout the county and along the urban fringe.[36]

American Indians took notice of this rapid urban growth and development that occurred in some form all over the country. A handful of studies have provided a few glimpses into what was a much larger phenomenon of Indians' participation in the migration, urbanization, and industrialization that characterized early-twentieth-century America. Railroads and commercial ships hired Indians as traveling laborers, so that places such as Chicago, the San Francisco Bay area, and other regional transportation centers became familiar places to Native people.[37] Indians took a variety of mill, construction, and factory jobs in expanding industrial areas such as Minneapolis–St. Paul, Milwaukee, Detroit, Phoenix, and Seattle-Tacoma.[38] Beginning in the 1920s, Mohawk Indians from reservations in New York and Canada worked in New York City's high steel industry, constructing many of the high-rise office buildings that came to dominate the city's skyline, while shuttling between reservations and an Indian neighborhood in Brooklyn.[39] Laguna Pueblo people worked for the Santa Fe Railway, building and maintaining the tracks all the way from their lands in New Mexico, through the American Southwest, to the San Francisco Bay area–city of Richmond, where they established an enclave.[40] Some cities were home to small communities or populations of Native people who were alumni of nearby Office of Indian Affairs boarding schools. A 1928 government survey in Phoenix, Ariz., found about forty Indian families and thirty single Indian women who were either graduates or current students on a work program from Phoenix Indian School.[41] Indian women who attended federal boarding schools were likely to find jobs as domestic servants in non-Indian homes.[42]

Los Angeles exerted a strong pull on Indian migrants, with its rapid economic expansion and its proximity to Indian communities throughout the American Southwest. Native people from Southern California reservations saw new opportunities in the urban areas and farmlands of the burgeoning region. A total of 704 California Indians declared their home addresses within Los Angeles County in 1928, when registering in a special census to settle California Indian land claims. These residents of Greater Los Angeles were mostly from reservations or traced their lineage to missions closer to the city, such as the Cahuilla, Pechanga, or Agua Caliente reservations, Mission San Gabriel or Mission San Juan Capistrano, as opposed to those farther away or in the northern part of the state. This was an overwhelmingly young population, with the potential for rapid growth in subsequent years. About 40 percent (300) were under the age of eighteen, and approximately one-half (178) of adults (404) were between the ages of eighteen and thirty, with about two-thirds (271) of adults married. Intermarriage with non-Indians also was common, which could have been a result of increased contact with other ethnic groups within the city, or intermarried couples may have been more likely to seek opportunities off the reservation. More than 45 percent of adult California Indian men and 67 percent of California Indian women were married to someone "not of Indian descent."[43]

Most California Indians during this period found jobs as laborers in agriculture and industry alongside other people of color and European immigrants, or, in the case of Indian women, as domestic servants in the homes of the middle class and wealthy. Helena Macara's experience was typical of other Indian women who were young and single. Macara was born in California in 1877 and was able to speak, read, and write English, perhaps as a result of attending government schools. By 1900 she worked as a maid and lived with her employers, a couple with two young children, in a native-born, middle-class neighborhood. Other Indians working as domestic servants might have been from outside California, and they came to Los Angeles through the Sherman Institute in Riverside. Ethel Rogoff was born in Laguna Pueblo in 1910, then went to Sherman for high school. After returning home to New Mexico and not being able to find work, she moved to Los Angeles, where the Office of Indian Affairs placed her with a family as a live-in maid.[44] California Indians who worked in agriculture lived among ethnic Mexicans, ethnic Chinese, African Americans, and poor whites. In the township of Ballona, forty-three-year-old Tomas Ramirez, a Spanish-speaking Indian born in Temecula, lived alone in a shack and worked as a farm laborer. Ella Verdugo and her husband, Jalino, a California-born ethnic Mexican, resided in a house they owned in San Gabriel. Besides their two young sons, they lived with Ella's sixty-year-old mother and her two brothers who were farm laborers. Indians also were drawn to the industrial areas of the city. Juana Campadona was married to an Italian immigrant, and she stayed with her four young children in Wilmington Township, in the harbor area, among families of Italian, Mexican, and Portuguese immigrants, most of whom were laborers and ship carpenters. Mariano Reis, a sixty-five-year-old Indian born in California, lived in the same neighborhood, where he worked as a day laborer. Reis and his wife, Ramona, a fifty-nine-year-old Indian born in California, had five children between the ages of twelve and thirty-one living at home.[45]

Indians from outside California also came to reside in Los Angeles during the early decades of the twentieth century. Although their numbers were relatively small, they increased gradually in the years up to the outbreak of World War II. In 1920, for instance, 183 Indian adults living within Los Angeles County were registered by the federal census. Of these, 31 percent were from California, and 36 percent came from Arizona and New Mexico, states relatively close to California.[46] Simon J. Ortiz, an Acoma Pueblo writer and poet, remembered a song from his childhood in New Mexico that translated as "California! Let us go!" According to Ortiz: "That's a song my beloved late mother sang a number of years ago when she was telling about the time quite a while back—probably around 1910 or 1911—when Acoma men and boys were going to California to look for work. It was a hard time then, very hard; the people didn't have much of anything, she said, and the beloved men and boys had to leave Aacqu to look for work so their families could be provided for. So that's what the song says: 'California! Let us go!'"[47] Other Indians traveled to Los Angeles from farther away, from such places as Oklahoma (9 percent), the American South (6 percent), and the American Midwest (5 percent).[48] Over the next ten years, the adult Indian population of the city increased to 246. The number of Indian children spiked to 133, up from just 35 in 1920, perhaps as a reflection of the predominance of young married couples. Approximately 25 percent of Indian adults in Los Angeles still came from California, and another 29 percent were born in the Southwestern states of Arizona and New Mexico. The population of Indians from Oklahoma increased to 20 percent of the Indians in the city. With a slight increase in adult Indians born in Texas, Arkansas, and Missouri (7 percent of the 1930 population), it is likely that these were migrants who lost lands or otherwise found hard times in the preceding and early years of the Great Depression and by environmental devastation brought on by the Dust Bowl.[49] Brenda Underwood's Cherokee-Comanche family first came to Los

Angeles in the 1930s after her grandparents lost their small farm in Texas. As a child her mother grew up in the city and eventually married another Cherokee, Brenda's father.[50] Oil found on Indian lands in Oklahoma in the 1920s and 1930s brought sudden wealth to a handful of tribes. Some newly wealthy tribal members moved to Los Angeles, hoping to experience the glamour and leisure for which the city had become famous.[51]

Indian migrants to the city in this period continued to be affected by factors that concentrated them in the lower tiers of the city's economy—lack of education, the training provided by federal boarding schools, and race and gender discrimination—but Indian men were gradually finding their way to more diverse occupations. Approximately 28 percent of Indian women worked as servants, and 53 percent listed their occupation as "none" in 1920. Ten years later the figures remained fairly steady at 39 percent and 56 percent, respectively. Occupations held by Indian men, however, showed greater change. More than 50 percent of Indian men in Los Angeles County were still laborers, and almost all others worked in unskilled professions in 1920. The number of Indian men who were laborers had dropped to 38 percent, and unskilled workers constituted 11 percent of the population (another 18 percent did not specify their occupations) in 1930.[52]

These better-paying and higher-status occupations varied greatly. They included hairdresser, stenographer, store clerk, nurse, civil engineer, printer, writer, electrician, police officer, mechanic, truck driver, blacksmith, plasterer, bookkeeper, carpenter, artist, public utilities supervisor, cabaret entertainer, actor, prizefighter, boilermaker, fireman, railroad foreman, night watchman, butcher, seamstress, lunch-stand proprietress, assistant postmaster, and horse salesman. They offered greater opportunities and supported Indian individuals and families to settle into the multiethnic, working-class neighborhoods throughout Greater Los Angeles. Historian Mark Wild has pointed out that, "From Lincoln Heights to Watts, working-class Angelenos of various ethnic backgrounds built up, worked in, and moved through a collage of industrial, commercial, and residential spaces at a time when the city was poised to vault into the ranks of the most powerful metropolises in America."[53] Native people also were part of this process, not only in the central city, but also in the harbor and coastal areas in the southwestern part of Los Angeles County. Joseph and Ethel Mills, two Indians born in Oklahoma, lived with their nine-year-old son Anthony in a predominantly white, middle-class neighborhood while Joseph worked as an auto mechanic. Several streets over, in a white and Latino working-class neighborhood, two families of California Indians—Robert and Lizzie

Hood and John and Nell O.—worked as railroad machinists and shared a house with their children, their landlady, a second-generation Russian street laborer, and a Russian immigrant couple. Mary L Frontierhouse, a twenty-four-year-old Indian born in Oklahoma, worked as a waitress in a teahouse, while rooming in a boardinghouse run by a Russian immigrant in a Latino and white working-class neighborhood. Etta Sarracino, a single, forty-two-year-old Indian born in New Mexico, shared a house with three other single women while working as a nurse in a local hospital. Carlos McPherson, a veteran of World War I and a driller for Standard Oil Company, headed a home in a white, working- and middle-class neighborhood. Chief Jack, a Winnebago Indian born in Wisconsin, owned his own shoemaking shop and lived with his wife, Little Bird, an Indian born in Oklahoma, in an ethnically Russian, working-class neighborhood.[54]

It is also likely that the ethnic American Indian population in the first decades of the twentieth century was somewhat greater than is indicated by decennial census figures. This point is evident from a few comparisons between individual entries on the regular 1930 decennial census, based on data collection by census workers going door-to-door,[55] and the special 1928 census of California Indians, in which Native people self-registered.[56] Carolina Burbee was enrolled in the 1928 census as a forty-two-year-old Pechanga Indian of "one-half Indian ancestry." In the 1930 census, Burbee is listed as "white" and married to Charles Burbee, a white man born in Connecticut, of parents born in Canada. It is not hard to imagine that a census taker visiting the Burbee home might identify Charles as white, then without even seeing Carolina, or with prompting from Charles, also list her as white. Julia Chappell, a Pauite Indian of one-quarter Indian ancestry, was recorded similarly in the 1928 census as Indian, then in the 1930 census as the white wife of a white man. The possibility of Chappell having a Euro-American phenotype increases the chances that a census taker would see her as non-Indian. Other California Indians were assumed to be Mexican immigrants or Mexican Americans. Belva Helm King registered in 1928 as an Agua Caliente Indian of one-fourth ancestry, with her two children of one-eighth ancestry. In the 1930 census she was listed as Mexican, of a Mexican-born father and California-born mother, and married to a Mexican-born man. The family also lived in a predominantly ethnic-Mexican neighborhood, making it unlikely a census taker would classify her as anything but Mexican.[57]

Other personal circumstances help explain why some California Indians might have intentionally passed as white, or, conversely, insisted on their

Indian identity. Nelson Smith registered in the 1928 census as one-fourth Agua Caliente Indian, but then he was recorded as white in the 1930 census. As city fire chief, a homeowner, and husband to a white woman, Smith could have felt his social and economic position compromised, should he identify primarily or too strongly as an Indian. Thomas Largo, meanwhile, a Cahuilla Indian, is in the 1920, 1928, and 1930 censuses as Indian. In 1920, Largo was working at the Lomita Iron Works and living in a boardinghouse with ethnic Mexicans, native-born white Americans, and immigrants from Italy and Armenia. Ten years later, in 1930, Largo was married to a Papago Indian woman born in Arizona and working as a landscape gardener, while living in a neighborhood of Italian and Russian immigrants, ethnic Japanese, and native-born whites. An informed census taker may have identified Largo's phenotype, or may have been more apt to question ethnicity when working in such diverse surroundings. Largo, however, also was an activist for Indian civil rights, making it more likely that he would be frank about his Indian heritage and offer it without qualms to any federal officials.[58]

During the 1930s, the turmoil of the Great Depression halted the economic expansion of urban areas, but migrants of all ethnic backgrounds still traveled to cities, particularly residents of Dust Bowl states who lost their farms and moved west. Some 250,000 migrants left the states of Oklahoma, Texas, Arkansas, and Missouri between 1935 and 1940, and 38 percent of them settled in Los Angeles.[59] Urban populations surged again during World War II, when factories ramped up to wartime production and thousands of soldiers moved through cities for military service. The population of Los Angeles in this period grew even faster than it had during the boom of the 1920s. Between 1940 and 1943, the metropolitan area saw half a million new people, so that one in every forty Americans in the United States resided in Greater Los Angeles. Many new arrivals came to work in the defense industries that revived the economy and produced 10 percent of all the nation's war goods, driving an employment rate that was four times the national average. As in earlier decades, a few large industries, in this case aircraft and shipbuilding, existed alongside smaller manufacturing, including aluminum, rubber, machine tools, ordinance, oil refining, and tank assembly. Los Angeles also was home to large military installations such as the U.S. Naval Drydocks at Terminal Island, the U.S. Naval Supply Depot at San Pedro, and the Long Beach Naval Hospital.[60]

American Indians were drawn into the trends and patterns that defined America during World War II, with their enthusiastic participation in the

U.S. war effort. Approximately 25,000 Indians entered the armed forces, and approximately 40,000 worked in armament plants.[61] A historian of the Umatilla Reservation in Oregon vividly conveyed the scope of Indian involvement, stating, "So many reservation men [were] part of the war effort that when they return[ed] home deer and elk [were] crossing the reservation roads in their plentifulness."[62] Indians from Southern California reservations were particularly active as soldiers and defense-plant workers. As of January 1944, 239 Southern California Indians enlisted in the U.S. armed forces and were deployed to U.S. military installations all over the world and throughout the Pacific and European theaters of the war, including Australia, England, Guam, Hawaii, Iceland, Ireland, India, North Africa, Panama, the Philippines, the Solomon Islands, Wake Island, and Alaska. A total of 149 Southern California Indian women and 175 men were employed by war industries in Riverside, Los Angeles, San Diego, Escondido, and Palm Springs. In July 1945 the number of Southern California Indians in the military increased to 340, including 243 soldiers in the army, sixty-three sailors in the navy, twenty-eight marines, three women in the Women's Auxiliary Corps (WACS), one in the merchant marine, and two members of the coast guard. A Mission Indian Agency official reported that, because of the military and defense work, there was "no Indian unemployment"—a remarkable statement, considering the poverty that had for so long prevailed on Southern California Indian reservations.[63]

Practically all Native people involved in the war effort experienced life in an urban area, whether laboring in a factory, training for the military, serving at a military base in the United States, or deployed overseas. Indian migration was particularly acute in places with war industries and military installations. The small prewar Indian population of Portland, Ore., expanded to include new arrivals during the war. Indians came to Portland in part because of encouragement by federal officials. As the United States mobilized for war in 1941, the National Youth Administration (NYA) trained young Indian women and men for work in wartime industries. Under the auspices of the National Defense Program, the Oregon branch of the NYA helped establish a curriculum at the Eugene Vocational School, in Eugene, Ore. It worked to recruit Indian students from area reservations and from the Chemawa Indian School, a federal boarding school in the Oregon town of Salem. The school offered free full-time training in fields such as radio and electrical work, machine shop, foundry, welding, and aviation sheet metal. By the summer of 1942, forty Indian students had come through the Eugene Vocational School and were working in Portland, primarily in the three shipyards established by the Kaiser Corporation.[64] The NYA also set up courses under the National Defense Training Program at Chemawa that sent graduates to work in Seattle, Portland, and other cities.[65]

Indian people increasingly joined the crowds of Americans who were attracted to Portland's defense industries from various places around the county. Government contracts for iron, steel, aluminum, shipping, and assembled war materials spurred 260,000 people to move to the Portland area and led to the creation of 140,000 jobs in wartime industry.[66] According to Aletha White, a Umatilla woman whose family moved to Portland for employment during the war, "Many Indians came to Portland during those years to work in the shipyards."[67] A few more individual cases help to illustrate what were wider patterns. Helen and George Reifel were Indians from Oklahoma who were teaching on the Navajo Reservation when the United States entered World War II. So many of the Reifels' students left to join the armed forces that they decided to take their two sons to Portland, where Helen found work as a welder and George became a shipwright with Kaiser's Oregon Shipbuilding Corporation.[68] Lewis Tomahkera, a Comanche Indian, arrived from Lawton, Okla., to work at Kaiser. Inspired by a contest to bring new recruits, he convinced seven tribal members, six of them women, to come to Portland and join Kaiser as welder trainees.[69] Ernest Peters, aged sixty-three years and an Indian, found work as a swing shift worker at Kaiser's Swan Island shipyards. He settled down in southeast Portland, where he lived in a five-room house with ten family members: his wife, six children, and three grandchildren.[70] Joe Bergie came to Kaiser via the Carlisle Indian School in Pennsylvania and Stanford University, where he was a football star. At the Vancouver yards across the Columbia River from Portland, he took a job working on the ventilation systems of ships.[71] A great deal of work remains to be done on Indians in cities during World War II, but there are indications that similar patterns of Indian urbanization occurred in other centers of wartime mobilization, such as Seattle, the San Francisco Bay area, Detroit, Chicago, Oklahoma City, and, of course, Los Angeles.[72]

Los Angeles was a city with which Indian people became intimate during the war, as a crucial site for major military installations and defense industries. The U.S. government played a more direct role in this migration than in previous decades as in Portland. One source for the increasing Indian presence in Los Angeles throughout the war was the Sherman Institute, the federal boarding school in Riverside, Calif. As residents of a government-run institution that emphasized industrial trades and the

Americanization of Native peoples, Sherman students were uniquely positioned to take up the war effort. Beginning in 1940, the school lost a steady stream of students to both the military and defense industries. By September 1940, six students had been hired to work at the Douglas Aircraft Corporation in Santa Monica, Calif., and another five were employed at an airplane plant in San Diego.[73] The following month, draft registration began on the Sherman campus.[74] In February 1941, three Sherman students boarded a train for Los Angeles, where they were to report for the U.S. Army, the latest of thirty boys from the school who had recently joined the armed forces.[75] That spring several recent graduates were placed in defense industries in Los Angeles, including two mechanics at Solar Aircraft, two welders at Northrop Aircraft, one worker at Pacific Wood Products, one employee at Douglas Cement, and two sailors on a Union Oil tanker ship.[76] In November, Douglas Aircraft featured four Sherman alumni in its corporate magazine. Clifton Ignacio Martinez was a Comanche Indian who worked as a welder. Ferris Paisano, a Pueblo Indian born in New Mexico, spent four years at Sherman before going to work for Douglas. Victor Irving Crutchfield, a Klamath Indian, worked as a U.S. Forest Patrol scout and professional truck driver, trained at Sherman, and then got his job at Douglas. Wallace Edwards Leeds began work at Douglas in 1937, as one of the first four Indians to be employed by the company. After training at Sherman and taking night classes at Santa Monica Technical School, Leeds was promoted to supervise dimpling and riveting machines.[77]

In the weeks leading up to United States entry into the war in late 1941, Sherman moved to more closely coordinate its training program with the war industries in Los Angeles, by training students for defense plants and by working to recruit additional trainees. The day before the Japanese attack on Pearl Harbor, a Sherman official wrote to reservation officials and superintendents at Indian schools in Arizona, New Mexico, Colorado, Nevada, and California: "Located in the center of an active industrial development in defense production [Sherman Institute] has integrated its training program closely with the needs of these plants. The demands for skilled craftsmen are such that Sherman students in welding, sheet metal work, and other branches are being snapped up . . . because they are considered superior to the average applicant. . . . As a result of this rapid turn-over . . . Sherman is in a position to accept other older students interested in securing placement in the defense industries."[78] The following month, after the United States joined the Allied forces, Sherman expanded and formalized its defense training program. The school newsletter reported that corporations such as Solar Aircraft and Vegas Air Craft encouraged Sherman officials to place female Indian students in the program, as they had previously employed women and expected to hire more as men left for military service. Sherman officials responded enthusiastically and said, "Sherman is favorably located and equipped to give training to girls who have the ability and talent to profit by this type of training." So great was the demand for defense workers that Douglas Aircraft Corporation officials decided that the company would hire eighteen-year-old students, despite their eligibility for the draft at age nineteen. Prior to the start of classes, all qualified Sherman students were placed "in good jobs in San Diego, Los Angeles, and nearby" in the "aircraft industry, shipyards and other factories."[79]

The defense training classes held from 1942 to 1943 provided intensive training in electric welding, gas welding, machine shop, auto mechanics, and wood shop to young Indian women and men from the ages of eighteen to forty.[80] After the first few months, twenty-two welding graduates were placed in defense work, and four more were employed building ships.[81] The chronicling of events at Sherman began to occur less frequently, perhaps as a result of wartime rationing or shifting wartime priorities. Nevertheless, a few reports of Sherman's involvement in the war effort trickled out. Solar Aircraft Company published an article on its cooperative relationship with Sherman in training and employing workers.[82] The welding training program began accepting female students sixteen and over, because male students had become eligible for the draft at seventeen. Of the thirteen new enrollees in the program that month, ten were women.[83] Sherman also reported that thirty students had recently entered the armed services.[84] Enrollments at the school were lower and younger than during peacetime, as "Sherman's older students [were] either working in defense industries or [had] been called to the colors."[85]

American Indian civilians and other Native people outside of Indian boarding schools also chose Los Angeles as a destination during the war. According to the U.S. Bureau of the Census, there were 1,378 American Indians in Los Angeles County in 1940 and then 1,671 in 1950, but, because of the errors associated with the census, the actual numbers are likely to have been much greater.[86] Some cases can illustrate what were probably much wider patterns. Richard Gibbs, an Oglala Sioux Indian, recalled how his mother, who had a high school education and had previously spent some time in Los Angeles as a governess, moved from South Dakota to Long Beach when war broke out, to work in the California Shipyards as an electrician's helper.[87] Patricia Mae Wills was a young child when her parents left her on the Rosebud Reservation in South Dakota during the war, to go and work for Douglas Aircraft in Santa Monica.[88] Considering that Indian migrations to Los Angeles had always followed the expansion of the city's economy, it is likely that many more Indian people traveled to Los Angeles for jobs during the boom of the war years.

A substantial portion of Indian migrants to U.S. cities as well as servicewomen and -men went back to their reservations and rural communities after the war, especially as the troops were brought home and defense plants returned to peacetime production. Indians who traveled to U.S. cities such as Los Angeles and areas overseas were changed by World War II in profound ways that would continue to resonate thereafter. Native people who served in the military, worked in defense plants, or even followed the progress of U.S. troops on the radio significantly widened their horizons and altered their visions of the world. Purcell Rainwater, a Sioux Indian living on the Rosebud Reservation, recalled what happened when his daughter came home after serving for three years in the WACS: "She went, come back and stayed for, I don't know, a week or two. Then she says, Dad, there's nothing around for me. Well, I said, that's all right, I said, I know it's hard for you. And so we helped her get ready and she left." By the 1960s, Rainwater's daughter had settled in Los Angeles, where she worked and had a family, after stints in Indiana and Chicago.[89] Similarly, Simon Ortiz remembered:

> And then in World War II, young men and women went to California for U.S. military training . . . and then they were shipped out from California seaports. . . . I recall myself as a boy waving to "soldier boys" on troop trains headed west, passing through the Acoma reservation. And, of course, numbers of our own service women and men home on leave in uniform were seen at tribal ceremonial activities, social events, and church services.
>
> When our military service people came home, their stories of the Philippines, Guadalcanal, Iwo Jima . . . abounded. . . . So there were stories of a world beyond the reservation back home, and that world always seemed to feature California prominently because it was a place you went to on the way to a destination—or it was the destination itself?[90]

For Indian people like Rainwater and Ortiz, reservations and rural Indian communities after the war seemed much smaller places, isolated from the experiences that could be found in larger towns and cities or overseas.[91]

Native people struck out from reservations for new destinations such as Los Angeles in greater numbers than ever before in the following years.

Although wartime experiences influenced these subsequent migrations, American Indian postwar urbanization was also predicated on decades of earlier experiences in the urban areas of the United States. Throughout the first half of the twentieth century, Los Angeles and other cities throughout the country were places where Indian people participated in the expansion and development of urban America, one of the broadest and most defining features of American life. Against a backdrop of reservation poverty and dispossession of tribal lands and natural resources, Indian migrants found jobs alongside immigrants and other rural migrants, settled into multiethnic, working-class neighborhoods to build a foundation for the expansion of American Indian urbanism in the postwar period, and more broadly began the process of reimagining Indian Country to include the cities of the United States. The story turns now to how the earliest Indian migrants negotiated the demands of living as a racial minority in cities where racism and discrimination could be a daily reality, where the majority of non-Indians had such a long and complicated history with Native peoples.

CHAPTER 2

REPRESENTING INDIANS

American Indian Performance and
Activism in Urban America

Richard Davis Thunderbird, a Cheyenne Indian, left his home in Los Angeles one day in 1936 and joined director and movie star Buck Jones in scouting movie locations throughout the American Southwest. Thereafter, the pair began filming *For the Service*, a Western tale that followed a group of U.S. soldiers chasing a gang of outlaws. A press release by Universal Studios claimed that Thunderbird, who appeared as Chief Big Bear, had "exchanged war paint for grease paint" and "traded his wigwam for a Hollywood bungalow" to take part in the picture.[1] As often was the case with studio dispatches, this was not quite true. At the time of the film's production Thunderbird had lived in Los Angeles for more than twenty years and had built a successful career as a leader of a Cheyenne dance troupe, lecturer on American Indian history and culture, and actor and technical advisor for Western movies. Through his public appearances, writings, and work with national organizations, Thunderbird also served a variety of American Indian causes, especially those that defended the cultural prerogatives of Native peoples. Thunderbird lived in Los Angeles as a performer and activist until he passed away in 1946 at the age of 80. After his death he was laid to rest at Forest Lawn Memorial Park, a cemetery favored by Hollywood actors.[2]

Thousands of American Indians like Thunderbird traveled to cities throughout the United States and Europe in the late nineteenth and early twentieth centuries for careers as entertainers and performers. With the end of hostilities between Native peoples and the U.S. government, Americans developed nostalgia for the nation's Western past and a fascination with the "disappearing" cultures of American Indians. Non-Indian entrepreneurs and American Indian performers capitalized on this interest, by producing and taking part in a variety of traveling shows, exposi-

Richard Davis Thunderbird in a publicity photo taken in the Santa Monica Mountains, ca. 1945. Courtesy of the Braun Research Library Collection, Autry National Center; P.36272.

tions, and tourist attractions that became immensely popular both in the United States and abroad. Beginning in the 1910s, the cultural production of America's Western past shifted to Hollywood, where Western movies drove the rapid development of the nation's film industry, aided by American Indian actors, stunt persons, animal wranglers, and technical advisors. Especially with the addition of film work, many American Indians were able to assemble entertainment careers centered on displays of Indian culture and popular ideas about "Indianness" that encompassed several venues of performance and took them to cities around the world. American Indians chose this life of performance because of the prospects for good pay, travel, new experiences, and cultural expression, especially in contrast to the poverty, isolation, and paternalism that could mark reservation life, or the kinds of arduous, unskilled labor that were otherwise most available to them. In the course of their work, many Native performers settled in American cities, where they helped establish and contributed to the development of some of the earliest urban American Indian communities. Los Angeles particularly drew Native performers, as it was a site for both live performances and the burgeoning film industry.

Although Native people found opportunities in performance, they also faced considerable limitations. American Indian entertainers frequently obtained minor parts and were supporting characters, but they were rarely featured in starring roles. Even in these positions they generally earned less than non-Indians for the same type and amount of work. Indians performing in traveling shows, expositions, and Western movies helped invent a mythic West that glorified the conquest and subordination of North America's indigenous populations. Almost without exception, the Indian characters portrayed by Indian entertainers conveyed unflattering portraits of Native people and distorted Indian history and culture. With little control over the content of these shows and the conditions of their work, Indian performers often confronted the stark choice between participating in such cultural productions and finding other ways to make their livings.

Numerous American Indian Studies scholars have addressed the ways that American Indians have been portrayed in film and live performances, by critically analyzing Indian imagery, then linking its production and popularization to larger mythologies and ideologies about America's past and its history of relationships with Native people.[3] Less attention, however, has been paid to the lives of American Indians who worked as entertainers, their motivations for participating in these cultural productions, and the ways that they worked to negotiate the terms of their performance. Focusing on Native people themselves can reveal new narratives of American Indian experience, while also contributing to wider conversations about the meanings of ethnic performance and the nature of subaltern resistance. Some scholars recently have sought to develop more nuanced understandings of ethnic performance by peoples of color, by acknowledging the power relations involved in entertaining a popular audience, while at the same time recognizing these exhibitions as arenas for resistance to the dominant culture. Some of these studies also have considered how ethnic entertainers sought to gain more control over their performances and to use their status for addressing individual and community goals.[4] This work merges with more than a decade of scholarship in ethnic studies that redefines political resistance to include "infrapolitics," or the struggles to oppose social and economic domination that can include but also transcend traditional political organizations and means of protest. Importantly, these battles tend to center on fundamental "nonmaterial" issues such as culture, dignity, and identity.[5]

American Indians waged these types of struggles as they participated in live shows and expositions, then intensified their efforts as they took part in the development of the film industry. Like other peoples of color, Native entertainers sought to reconcile the contradictions between the freedoms and the limitations found in performing for a popular audience. Using institutionalized methods, such as labor organizations, philanthropic work, and speeches and literary appeals to the public conscience, they sought a broad range of changes that addressed basic issues such as labor conditions and also nonmaterial concerns such as control over the production and articulation of Indian culture and identity. American Indian actors appearing in Hollywood films also worked to claim social and cultural space for Native people in the city that helped to nurture an emergent Los Angeles American Indian community. Although limited in important ways, these efforts led to meaningful change. In seeking to "represent" Indians, both in popular entertainment venues and throughout American society, American Indian performers helped initiate struggles over material rewards and larger issues of cultural identity. They also often reinforced ideas about Indians as rural and even "primitive" or "antimodern" peoples, even as they began to reimagine Indian Country as the urban areas in which they worked and lived.

❖ ❖ ❖

The first traveling Wild West show was created by Buffalo Bill Cody in the early 1880s, and it relied heavily on American Indian performers. Cody, a shrewd promoter and showman, took advantage of a growing interest in the "Old West." Wild West shows were performed for audiences in arenas throughout the United States and Europe, reenacting Western scenes that included bareback pony races, Indian attacks on stagecoaches, bison hunts, and famous battles. Cody aggressively recruited American Indian performers for the Wild West shows, relying on Native skills and knowledge and on the simple presence of American Indian bodies, both for the content of the shows and to attract patrons lured by promises of exoticism and authenticity. During its first season in 1883, Cody's Wild West show employed thirty-six Pawnee Indians from Indian Territory. A few years later Cody switched to hiring Lakota Sioux performers and held auditions near the Pine Ridge Agency in South Dakota that annually drew 500–600 Indian hopefuls.[6]

American Indians took jobs as performers with these Wild West shows because they understood them as good opportunities, especially in contrast to the crushing poverty and government paternalism that characterized Indian communities in the late nineteenth and early twentieth centuries. Those who ventured beyond Indian communities often did so with few job skills and encountered the types of racism and discrimination that made it difficult to find anything but unskilled work.[7] Historians L. G. Moses and Clyde Ellis have argued that in this context performing in Wild West shows gave Native people the chance to earn relatively good wages, travel around the world, and engage in the same types of singing, dancing, and other cultural activities that were actively being discouraged by federal officials on reservations.[8] For instance, Luther Standing Bear, a Lakota Sioux Indian, was in charge of the sixty-five Indian performers on Buffalo Bill's 1902–3 tour of England.[9] The salary that Standing Bear earned supported his wife and newborn daughter, both of whom came along and also appeared as attractions. Standing Bear noted that the "work was very light for my wife, and as for the baby, before she was twenty-four hours old, she was making more money then my wife and I together."[10]

Closely related to the Wild West shows were the jobs that American Indians took as performers for international expositions. A number of these fairs were produced around the turn of the twentieth century, to celebrate the "progress" of Gilded Age America. Ethnographic displays of American Indian people were prominent at these fairs, especially because organizers saw their presence as a contrast to the "civilization" that the expositions were designed to champion. Native people, as they did in the Wild West shows, took these ethnographic displays seriously as jobs and opportunities to validate their cultural practices. Historian Paige Raibmon has argued that the Kwakwaka'wakw performers from Vancouver Island, British Columbia, used their appearance at the 1893 Columbian Exposition to declare "both their cultural persistence and their political defiance." Sixteen Kwakwaka'wakw lived in a reconstructed Northwest Coast village on the exposition grounds for seven and a half months, where they each earned twenty dollars a month to dance and exhibit Native craft skills, such as wood carving and basket weaving. Raibmon notes that this work fit into larger patterns of wage labor the Kwakwaka'wakw had recently adopted that included fishing, canning, prostitution, washing clothes, picking hops, logging, and sealing. Raibmon also argues that the exposition became a chance for the Kwakwaka'wakw to "enact their rejection of assimilationist programs on an international stage." Native performers at the fair delighted in the opportunity to dazzle fairgoers with their singing and dancing, after years of struggling with Canadian government and Anglican Church attempts to eliminate Kwakwaka'wakw culture. The Kwakwaka'wakw even went so far as to save for the busiest days of the fair the most extreme, violent, and "savage" dances that elicited the greatest degree of objection from government and church officials, so they could be seen by the largest crowds and garner the most press coverage.[11]

Smaller entertainment venues also featured American Indian performers. Both Miccosukee and Seminole Indians worked in "Indian villages" that catered to Florida's increasing tourist trade in the early twentieth century. Miccosukee families appeared in camps and "commercial exhibition villages" located along state highways and in Miami, where motorists and tourists for an admission fee observed elements of Miccosukee life and bought locally produced arts and crafts.[12] Seminole Indians similarly began to market Native culture through tourist villages in Fort Lauderdale that combined demonstrations of older Seminole cultural practices with activities designed especially for the amusement of non-Indians, such as alligator wrestling.[13] Tourist villages also became popular in Hawaii, especially in Honolulu, where visitors could watch Native Hawaiians perform hula dances and harvest coconuts. Historian Adria Imada has understood hula and other cultural performance in Hawaii as an engagement with the modern economy that provided wages, an alternative to more arduous and less fulfilling labor, and a means for the preservation of Native Hawaiian culture. Imada also follows Hawaiian performers to New York City, where, beginning in the 1930s, they danced the hula in nightclubs. These Native Hawaiian performers experienced the glamour and excitement of the city, both in New York and in Hollywood, where several went on to appear in movies.[14]

Hollywood films came to dominate the market for Native perform-ers over time. Most American film studios operated out of Fort Lee, N.J., until several studios relocated west in the 1910s to avoid paying royalties to Thomas Edison, who owned the patent on the movie camera. Once in Southern California, they found the weather and physical environment perfect for shooting pictures. The mountains and canyons around the Los Angeles area seemed especially fitted to recreating the many unique loca-tions of the American West, and Western movies quickly became a favorite with the growing audiences of motion picture goers. Hollywood produc-ers and directors sought actors with the skills and knowledge to convinc-ingly depict frontier life, and the first place they looked were the Wild West shows, expositions, and other performance venues that preceded them. The Bison Life Motion Pictures Company relocated to the West Coast in 1910 and leased 10,000 acres in Santa Ynez Canyon, near Pacific Palisades, that it fenced off and patrolled to discourage patent investigators. During the winter of 1912, the company struck a deal with the Miller Brothers 101 Ranch Real Wild West Show (wintering in nearby Venice), which agreed to provide approximately seventy-five Indians and one hundred cowboys—in addition to oxen, bison, horses, tepees, stagecoaches, wagons, and cos-tumes—for use in the production of films under the Bison 101 label. The collaboration quickly churned out four two-reel Western movies titled *War on the Plains, The Indian Massacre, The Battle of the Red Men,* and *The Deserter.*[15]

When they could not find enough Indian actors in Los Angeles or from Wild West shows, Hollywood studios recruited Indians directly from reser-vations. Film director Thomas Ince traveled to the Pine Ridge Reservation in South Dakota in 1913 and convinced the Indian agent to allow thirty Sioux Indians to come to Los Angeles, provided that Ince assume guard-ianship for the period they were away. After arriving in the city, the Indians set up an encampment on the Santa Ynez Canyon property, now known as Inceville, and were dubbed the Inceville Sioux by studio employees. They remained in Los Angeles for six months, appearing in films and explor-ing the city.[16] This practice of recruiting Indian actors from reservations continued until at least 1941, when a Warner Brothers studio representa-tive traveled to South Dakota and found sixteen Sioux Indians to appear in *They Died with Their Boots On* (1941).[17] Indians performers also came from reservations to advertise Western films that featured Indian actors. The Famous Players–Lasky Studio shot *The Covered Wagon* on location in Wyoming in 1923, with the help of many Indians from the Wind River

Reservation. The studio then hired thirty-five Arapaho women, men, and children from Wind River to perform a live prologue before each showing of the film at Grauman's Egyptian Theatre in Hollywood. Two years later many of the same Indian performers were hired to perform another live prologue at Grauman's for the Western film *The Iron Horse*.[18]

Hollywood's allure cuts across demographic groups, but Native people in particular were attracted to film work for the same reasons that they embraced earlier chances to work as performers. For some Indians Hollywood could serve an alternative to the sense of confinement and oppression that often came with life on an Indian reservation. Many of the Arapaho Indians that traveled to Hollywood in the 1920s came of age in an earlier era before the United States established control over their lands. Goes-in-Lodge and Left Hand both fought against the U.S. Army as young men, then later served as army scouts. Charlie Whiteman was an Arapaho who was captured by Utes in the 1860s and lived with the tribe for some time, then was recaptured by his people. Lizzie Fletcher was born a non-Indian but was taken from her family in 1865, raised among the Cheyenne and Arapaho, and integrated into Arapaho society. These and the other Arapaho performers reveled in the spotlight while in Hollywood, and they delighted in going to the movies, attending banquets, and visiting the beach. They earned eight dollars a day plus expenses, far more money than they could have earned back on the reservation.[19] Andre De Rockbraine was among the sixteen American Indian performers who appeared in *They Died with Their Boots On*. He remembered taking the train from McLaughlin, S.D., to Butte, Mont., riding in a special coach to Los Angeles, and staying in a hotel in Hollywood. De Rockbraine and his fellow Indian actors earned approximately $900 each over seven weeks, which they considered "pretty good money." De Rockbraine also fondly recalled working with Errol Flynn, Olivia de Havilland, and Anthony Quinn, meeting Clark Gable and Gary Cooper, and spending some of his time off riding the roller coaster at the Santa Monica Pier. These and other American Indian performers and actors are sure to have missed their families and homes. Indeed, De Rockbraine noted, "Yeah it was a nice place down there, but too crowded, too many people down there." They nonetheless understood Hollywood as a place that offered freedom from government supervision and opportunities to escape the poverty that could accompany reservation life.[20]

Other American Indians gravitated to Hollywood after a stint at working in America's urban economy. Charles Bruner, a Muscogee Indian, was born in Indian Territory in 1893 and grew up attending federal boarding schools. After graduating from Bacone Junior College in Oklahoma in 1921, Bruner moved to Los Angeles, where he ran a grocery store in Bell, southeast of downtown. Within a few years Bruner quit the grocery store business and began appearing in Western films. He later recalled being part of a group of a dozen Indian actors who worked steadily by "making the rounds from picture to picture" and spending a couple of weeks on each set. As acting roles became harder to obtain, Bruner found that he could increase his chances of getting a job if he had his own clothes, so he began making outfits based on specific tribal traditions and wearing them in films. Bruner also sold these clothes to the studios and served as a technical advisor on several films and television shows.[21]

For some Indian performers Hollywood was part of a larger career centered on displays and performances of Indian culture and popular ideas about "Indianness." William Eagleshirt, a Sioux Indian, joined the 101 Ranch Wild West Show sometime in the late 1890s and began making pictures with Bison 101 in 1912. He appeared in and wrote the scenario for the first Bison 101 picture, *War on the Plains* (1912). He stayed on in Hollywood when the 101 Ranch Wild West Show went back on tour, appearing in films such as *The Indian Massacre* (1912), *Custer's Last Fight* (1912), *The Silent Lie* (1917), and *The Conqueror* (1917).[22] Charlie Stevens, grandson of the Apache leader Geronimo, also began performing with the 101 Ranch, after growing up in the small town of Solomonsville, Ariz. Stevens came to Hollywood in 1915 and appeared in D. W. Griffith's *Birth of a Nation*. Stevens befriended Douglas Fairbanks while working for Griffith, and he became part of a rowdy group of actors and stuntmen that socialized and worked with Fairbanks on dozens of films. Stevens went on to appear in more than 200 films and 30 television shows up to his death in 1964.[23]

Other Indian actors had even more complex and varied entertainment careers that encompassed several venues of performance and took them all over the world. Molly Spotted Elk was born Molly Nelson on the Penobscot Indian Reserve in Maine around the turn of the twentieth century. As a teenager Nelson played an Indian character for vaudeville shows throughout the Northeastern states. In 1926 she moved to New York City, where she worked as an artist's model, a chorus girl, and an "Indian dancer" at cabarets and nightclubs. Nelson's work in New York caught the attention of a film producer, who cast Nelson for *The Silent Enemy* (1930), a docudrama that focused on the struggles of an Ojibwa band to survive a harsh winter. Nelson later went to Europe as part of an Indian jazz band, then stayed on to play concerts, appear in cabarets, and give recitals and lectures. By the mid-1930s she had moved to Hollywood, where she roomed with Cherokee actress Ann Ross, granddaughter of Cherokee principal chief John Ross. She appeared in *Charge of the Light Brigade* (1936), *Ramona* (1936), *Last of the Mohicans* (1936), *The Good Earth* (1937), and *Lost Horizon* (1937).[24] Daniel Yowlachie had an equally wide-ranging entertainment career. Born on the Yakama Reservation in Washington State in 1891, Yowlachie was educated at government schools, then went on to study opera as a bass-baritone, and spent some time singing with an opera company. He broke into Western films as an actor under the name Chief Yowlachie in 1925, and for the next forty years appeared in more than seventy movies and a handful of television shows. Yowlachie also gave concerts and sang at various events, such as the 1928 Pacific Southwest Exposition held in Long Beach, Calif., the 1930 dedication of the Greek Theatre in Hollywood's Griffith Park, and programs at the Southwest Museum of the American Indian in Los Angeles.[25]

Native people also came to Hollywood after many years of following the paths laid out for them by the U.S. government and growing frustrated by their limitations. Richard Davis Thunderbird, a Cheyenne Indian, was born in 1867, shortly before his tribe signed a treaty to end military conflict with the U.S. government. Thunderbird joined the first class of students to enter Carlisle Indian School at the age of thirteen, and he spent the next eight years there. He then rejoined his people in Oklahoma and was favored with various government jobs. In 1903, Thunderbird began assisting anthropologists, from both the Bureau of American Ethnology and Chicago's Field Museum of Natural History, with their investigations into Cheyenne religion. This seems to have been a pivotal experience in which Thunderbird realized that he could make a living interpreting and performing Indian culture for a non-Indian audience. Thunderbird spent the next two decades traveling with the 101 Ranch Wild West Show, the Orpheum Vaudeville Circuit, and a troupe of Cheyenne dancers that he organized. By the 1920s, Thunderbird had settled in Los Angeles. He worked steadily as an actor and technical advisor in Hollywood and as a dance troupe leader and lecturer on Indian history and lore for schools, museums, historical organizations, the Boy Scouts, and other clubs and groups throughout Southern California. Until his death in 1946, Thunderbird owned a large brick house in the Pasadena hills that was known as a gathering spot and place of revelry for both Indian and non-Indian actors and entertainers.[26]

Thunderbird at home in Pasadena, Calif., ca. 1945. Courtesy of the Braun Research Library Collection, Autry National Center; P.36278.

Luther Standing Bear's story is remarkably similar. Born in 1868 in Nebraska Territory, Standing Bear also was a member of the first class at Carlisle Indian School. He returned to his people in 1885 and spent the next seventeen years working on the Pine Ridge and Rosebud reservations. Standing Bear joined Buffalo Bill's Wild West Show in the 1890s and traveled with the show to Europe. Then he moved to New York City, where he acted with a troupe of Indian performers, lectured, and appeared in theaters and sideshows.[27] Standing Bear found he could no longer tolerate the idea of going back to live on the reservation, where he would again be subject to the authority of government officials. He recalled, in 1907: "I made a trip back to the reservation to visit my folks and tell them what I intended to do. My brothers and sisters wanted me to remain, but I told them if we were free it might be different, but as for myself, I had come to the conclusion that the reservation was no place for me."[28] Standing Bear spent three decades acting and advising for Western films after settling in Los Angeles in 1910. He also opened an archery concession on the Venice Pier, where he challenged tourists and locals to test their skills. Standing Bear was a popular lecturer and teacher on Indian subjects like Thunderbird and billed himself as an "Official Sioux Authority." He wrote four books on Indian history and culture, and he taught Indian sign language at the Southwest Museum and the University of California, Los Angeles.[29] Reservation life offered relatively privileged positions in the way of jobs and favor from local officials for Standing Bear and Thunderbird alike. It did not, however, offer the freedom and the opportunities that they were able to find living and working in Los Angeles.

Notwithstanding all of its advantages, Hollywood presented formidable problems and challenges for Native people. Studio labor practices were particularly hard on Indian actors. Indians obtained bit parts and played extras, while starring roles went to non-Indians, even when the script called for Indian characters. Luther Standing Bear attempted to convince director Thomas Ince that Indians could play more substantial roles, and he offered to serve as a language coach for the Inceville Sioux. Ince, like many other early Hollywood directors, thought that Indians were incapable of serious acting.[30] As Westerns developed into a mainstay of the motion picture industry, more non-Indian actors competed with Indian people for Indian roles, going so far as to copy Indian dress and to learn necessary skills such as shooting arrows and riding horses. William S. Hart, a popular Western star and a friend to many Indian actors, reported in 1926 that "since the motion pictures have become controlled by business interests they do not go in for the real things so much. They use Mexicans for Indians and there are a great many Mexicans in this country."[31] In the 1930s, Native actors organized the Indian Actors Association, partially because of the "practice among some studios of engaging pseudo-Indians for leading roles" and the need to "try to displace the Syrians, Swedes, Aryans, and Latins who [were] being manufactured into Indians by sun-tan oil and braided wigs."[32] When Indian actors did find work, they were paid at disproportionate rates relative to their non-Indian counterparts, and such work often did not provide a regular living.[33] Shifts in the production of Westerns also negatively impacted Indian actors in Hollywood. Motion picture studios began shooting Westerns on location in the 1930s, and, instead of transporting a full cast of Indian actors from Hollywood, they began hiring only a few Hollywood-based Indian actors and recruiting the Indian extras they needed from nearby reservations for short-term work.[34]

Indians in Hollywood also were profoundly frustrated by the ways that Western films distorted Indian culture and history. The prospectus of the Indian Actors Association stated, "We cannot reconcile ourselves to . . . the practice among some studios of misrepresenting the actions of the Indian [and] faking his dialect." An association member elaborated, complaining,

"We Indians are made to talk and grunt like morons."[35] Chief Red Fox, a Sioux Indian who began appearing in westerns made by Thomas Ince in the 1910s, later recalled the anguish and sense of resignation his portrayal of Indian characters caused him: "Those pictures [I appeared in] were mostly two-reelers in which I engaged in savage attacks on wagon trains, ambushed White troops, set fire to the homes of White settlers. . . . I was pictured in war dances that a script writer must have dreamed up while in a nightmare. . . . There were times when I wanted to go down to a clean stream and wash away my duplicity, but I had been under the klieg lights a long time, and realized that I could do little to change opinions that were rigidly fixed from the preceding centuries."[36] Luther Standing Bear wrote in 1928: "I have seen probably all of the pictures which are supposed to depict Indian life, and not one of them is correctly made. . . . I have gone personally to directors and stage managers and playwrights and explained this to them, telling them that their actors do not play the part as it should be played, and do not even know how to put on an Indian costume and get it right; but the answer is always the same, 'The public don't know the difference, and we should worry[?]'"[37] Indian actors were both conscious of and troubled by Hollywood's distortions of Indian life and culture, even as they acted in the films that perpetuated the problem.

Considering studio labor practices as well as Native representations in film, it might make sense to think of Hollywood as part of a larger colonial system that used Indians for its own profit.[38] It may even be tempting to pass judgment on Native actors for contributing to the construction of such negative ideas about Indians that continue to permeate American culture and negatively impact Indian people.[39] Historian Matt Garcia has argued that such interpretations tend to be "narrowly functionalist," by denying people of color agency in the production and articulation of ethnic performance and limiting its larger meaning.[40] Both the freedoms and the limitations of ethnic performance have to be kept in sight in order to understand the experiences of Native actors in Hollywood. Furthermore, Indian actors and performers did not blindly follow the dictates of Hollywood directors and producers; they put up substantial resistance to these demands, often in the face of tremendous pressures to conform. This resistance and its long-term implications make the legacy of Indian actors on Hollywood's frontier far more complex and ambiguous than suggested by narratives of victimization.

This resistance by Indian actors addressed both immediate material conditions in Hollywood and wider issues of community development, federal Indian policy, and cultural identity. In 1926, Indian actors formed the War Paint Club, an organization meant to protect the rights of Native actors and establish a pool of "authentic" Indians for work in movies. It also sought to "keep the Indian character from defamation or ridicule . . . as often is the case when white men, who don't know what it's all about, are dressed up to represent Indians."[41] The War Paint Club gave way to the Indian Actors Association (IAA) in 1936. Bill Hazlett, a Blackfeet Indian and an actor and the IAA chairman, explained that "when [the studios] were casting *The Last of the Mohicans* [1936], some of us noticed that Indians were underbidding each other just so they could get work." A group of Indian actors then started the association to "stop the movie producers from encouraging and allowing this price cutting" and to replace non-Indians in acting jobs with Indians.[42] Hazlett went on to outline the IAA's accomplishments over its first three years:

> The Indian Actors' Association is [now] affiliated with the Screen Actors' Guild. We are protected by a Closed Shop Clause. . . . We are also protected by job preferences for our members, better salaries and working conditions. . . . We used to get $5.50 a day if we wore studio costumes. Non-Indian actors got $11 a day for the same work. Now that's no longer true. If we wear a studio costume and are on foot, we get $8.25 a day, on horseback $11 and if we supply our own costumes, $13.75 a day. By the way, to show what it means to be a member, on the *Man of Conquest* [1939] set some of our people were using sign language and wanted full speaking part pay for this. The producers refused and we took the matter to the Screen Actors' Guild and they ruled in our favor and our people got paid what they deserved. Now we are pushing for $16.50 a day if we wear our own costumes. And we're going to get it, too, because we've already got that rate for *Union Pacific* [1939].[43]

The IAA also functioned as a support group and provided subsistence funds for out-of-work Indian actors that it raised through membership dues, powwows, and performances for local clubs and organizations.[44]

Native actors also played an important role in helping to nurture and support a community of American Indians in Los Angeles by taking the lead to claim social and cultural space for the city's varied Native population. During the 1920s and 1930s, Indian actors held regular "powwows," or large parties attended by Indians and non-Indians from throughout the city. Luther Standing Bear hosted a powwow at his home in Culver City in

1926. It drew a crowd of more than 2,000, including "Indians from every part of Los Angeles," two Los Angeles County judges, and a delegation of Boy Scouts. The party lasted into the early morning and featured dances, songs, drumming, and a peace-pipe ceremonial.[45] Indian actors also organized annual Thanksgiving and Christmas powwows. Members of eleven Indian tribes gathered for Christmas carols, the exchanging of gifts, "Indian chants, [and] ancient Indian ceremonial dances" on Christmas Eve in 1932. One attendee dressed as Santa Claus led the group caroling through Hollywood, and the party broke up at dawn, after a singing of "Silent Night."[46] Many Indians gathered on a daily basis at the American Indian Art Shop, a store on Hollywood Boulevard that was opened in 1929 by White Bird, the wife of Chief Yowlachie. The store became a meeting spot where Indians could socialize and exchange news on jobs, and it provided a place for Indians in Los Angeles to sell their art and crafts.[47]

Alongside these gatherings for an emerging Los Angeles Indian community, Indians in Hollywood participated in advocacy and charitable efforts meant to serve the city's Indian population. Indian actors were among the founding members and ongoing supporters of the Wigwam Club, a group that raised money for welfare to needy Indians in Los Angeles. The club's most popular event was an annual Indian Day Picnic, held in Sycamore Grove Park. Beginning in 1928, the event annually drew thousands of Indian and non-Indian attendees who gathered for food, music, dancing, and speeches, with many of the performances supplied by Indian actors.[48] In 1935, Hollywood Indians were central to the organization of another group, the Los Angeles Indian Center. It became the primary meeting place and welfare agency for Los Angeles Indians over the next five decades. Indian actors served as a source of support for the center by taking leadership roles, donating time and money, and planning and participating in the center's programs and activities.[49] Individual Hollywood Indians also were active in using their resources and positions to assist Indians in Los Angeles. The actor Nipo Strongheart, a Yakama Indian, began opening his home in 1931 to students from Sherman Institute, an Indian boarding school in nearby Riverside, so that they would have a safe place to stay during weekend excursions to the city.[50]

Some Indian actors combined their work for Native people in Los Angeles with efforts to serve other Indian communities. These activists were particularly interested in defending the cultural prerogatives of Indian people and arguing for Indian civil rights more generally. In 1931, Richard Davis Thunderbird began a national organization for Indian people known as the "First Americans." It was designed to bring Indians of different tribes together so that they could "work in harmony along constructive lines [and] encourage studying the art and music of their forefathers."[51] The First Americans reflected Thunderbird's larger concern with the ways that Indians were depicted throughout society, and his efforts to convince non-Indians of the importance of Indian culture. He explained this view in the introduction to a manuscript he completed on Cheyenne religion, stating, "This book is written to help the white man try to understand the Indian. No matter what mistakes have been made in the past, it is still possible to do right in the future. . . . I wish only to prove to the white man that there is nothing essentially objectionable in the celebration of the tribe's rites and ceremonies and to show that the Indian's religion is the best one for him."[52] Nipo Strongheart was another forceful advocate for Indian civil rights and for the value of Indian culture, which he promoted as he traveled lecture circuits throughout the country. In 1932, Strongheart became secretary of the National League for Justice for the American Indians, a group formed to advocate for Native Americans and to encourage Native arts.[53]

There was a direct link between these types of advocacy and Indian participation in the motion picture industry. Filmic representations and the treatment of Indian actors could be a galvanizing force, motivating Indian actors to get involved in larger struggles over the construction of Indian culture and identity. Hollywood also provided crucial material support and the types of personal connections that helped ensure that Indian activists reached a wider audience. The prestige and recognition that came with being a Hollywood actor led to opportunities for the articulation of Indian culture and identity, by fostering connections to people and resources and increasing the influence of Indian activists. Considering the long American obsession with Hollywood personalities, it makes sense that participation in the film industry would lend Indian activists a degree of authority and an aura of celebrity that could help catch the attention of book publishers, museum curators, show promoters, philanthropists, and the general public.

The derogatory images and representations of Indians propagated by film and other venues of performance, with the help of Indian entertainers, have continued to maintain a profound hold over American culture. This point is made starkly clear by attendance at an Atlanta Braves baseball game or any of the hundreds of other professional, collegiate, and amateur teams that use Indians as monikers and mascots. Such cultural images are rooted in the nineteenth century, but there has been no greater influence in

Thunderbird and friends waiting for a streetcar in Pasadena, Calif., ca. 1945. Courtesy of the Braun Research Library Collection, Autry National Center; P.36279.

developing and sustaining them to the present day than Hollywood Westerns. Indians in Hollywood struggled to change filmic representations of Indians, and these images may well have been even more demeaning without their participation. Nonetheless, the failure by Indians in Hollywood to more profoundly influence portrayals of Indian culture and identity in movies sharply delineates the boundaries of their agency.

Condemning American Indian performers for their participation in these cultural productions or understanding them only as victims fails to understand the choices they made within their historical context. Native entertainers took the opportunities available to them in an American society that imposed profound constraints in the first half of the twentieth century. Their performances and work for Indian people in Hollywood, Los Angeles, and throughout the country—their efforts to "represent Indians," on their own terms—constituted active resistance to broader systems of power and racial discrimination. Such efforts to alter filmic representations of Indians often fell short, yet this resistance had additional impacts on Indian people by providing a range of material and cultural benefits. Efforts at labor organization provided tangible results such as the raising of Indian salaries. Indian entertainers offered critiques of federal Indian policy, recommendations for action, and arguments for the value of Indian culture. Finally, Indian actors helped establish a basis for a Los Angeles Indian community by organizing social and cultural spaces for Indians and providing for the neediest Indians in the city. In other words, through their complex negotiations with urban life, Indian actors began defining cities as Native space, thereby contributing to the reimagining of Indian Country in the early twentieth century.

CHAPTER 3

FROM AMERICANIZATION TO
SELF-DETERMINATION

The Federal Urban Relocation Program

Howard Yackitonipah, a Comanche Indian, was born on his family's farm in Lawton, Okla., in 1932. Yackitonipah moved to Wichita, Kans., as a child, where his parents found work during World War II. He joined the U.S. Navy in 1956 and spent some time in both Los Angeles and San Francisco. Yackitonipah returned to Oklahoma, where much of his family lived, after his discharge three years later. He took a job in a mobile home factory but began to think about finding something that offered better pay. Yackitonipah was perusing the job board at the tribal agency when he noticed a flyer for a federal program under the Bureau of Indian Affairs (BIA) Relocation Services called "Adult Vocational Training" (AVT). It promised to move participants for up to two years to a major urban center, where they would be enrolled in a vocational school. Yackitonipah applied and was accepted to attend barber school in Long Beach, Calif.[1]

Yackitonipah found himself chafing over the paternalistic aspects of the program immediately upon arriving in the city. A BIA relocation counselor accompanied Yackitonipah to look for an apartment near his school, and Yackitonipah remembered, "The counselor took me to this one rooming house and he said this little cubicle about six foot by ten was gonna be my room. All they had here was a wash basin and a bed and [he said the people here will] make my lunch and then I [will] pay them so much. . . . And I told him, 'That's half of my check already. . . . I don't think I want to stay,' I'd find another some place else. So we argued back and forth." After another day of searching they settled on the Long Beach YMCA, where Yackitonipah was satisfied with the clean rooms and the use of the pool and gymnasium for substantially less money. Yackitonipah and the counselor then had a longer conversation about what it meant to be in the program. When he was told that he would receive regular visits to monitor his progress and to ensure that he was meeting the program requirements, another argument ensued. Yackitonipah told the counselor: "'I don't need anybody to nurse-maid me . . . if I wanted that, well I would have stayed in the army or something,' and he said, 'That's the program.' I said, 'Looks to me like you're not helping any at all.'" Yackitonipah finished barber school in seven months, then had to wait a few weeks to take the state licensing exam, so he went home to Oklahoma for a brief visit. On his return a counselor informed him that it was against the rules to leave the city and he was thus disqualified from receiving any further assistance. "In other words," Yackitonipah said, "they just dropped you [and] you just got written off."[2]

Approximately 155,000 American Indian women, men, and children like Howard Yackitonipah struggled to negotiate both the policies of federal officials and the challenges of urban life as they came to live, work, and attend school in U.S. cities "on relocation" from 1948 to the 1970s. Relocation had deep roots in the history of both U.S.-Indian relations specifically and government-supported policies toward ethnic groups more generally. Beginning in the late nineteenth century, federal Indian policy was guided by the concept of "assimilation," or the idea that the nation would best be served if Native cultures were eradicated and replaced by American standards of "civilization." Assimilation policy drove legislation such as the Dawes Act of 1887 and led to the establishment of Indian boarding schools that sought to instill the principles of private property and manual labor, redefine gender roles, and suppress indigenous languages and religions. Meanwhile, as waves of immigrants made their way to America from around the world, the federal government expanded the practices of assimilation, alternatively referred to as "Americanization." Progressive Era settlement houses, "100% Americanism" campaigns, and the development of national education policy were all extensions of policies first tested on American Indians and designed to create a society based on common values, beliefs, and practices.[3]

The relocation program exemplifies the gap between scholars of American Indians and historians of both immigrant America and the twentieth-century United States more generally. These two sets of historians have described similar processes that go back to the same explanatory factors while employing different language and focusing on separate groups. They have talked among themselves but have failed to learn from each other, thus preventing the pieces of their stories from coming together to form a broader, richer, and more informed narrative. American Indian scholars have written about assimilation and government paternalism, while immigrant historians have charted efforts at Americanization. The two conversations ought to be merged as one.

Relocation policy can be understood as another chapter in the history of state-sponsored efforts at Americanization that for the first time sought to use cities as a way of integrating American Indians into the mainstream of American life. BIA officials at both the federal and local levels implemented policies designed to break down tribal ties and to assimilate Indian people into the nation's industrial and domestic economy. Officials worked to choose the candidates whom they thought had the best chance of becoming the idealized American citizens they envisioned. Relocation participants were held to notions of gender and family that favored men as primary breadwinners, limited married women to serving as housewives, and narrowly defined the experience of single women. Those enrolled in the AVT program also were circumscribed by ideas about people of color and their place in the American workforce. Federal officials attempted to condition Indians according to middle-class assumptions of proper social behavior and good citizenship through religious organizations, surveillance by local BIA employees, and disciplinary measures.

These policies often had unwanted implications for American Indian people. Some Indians on relocation found the city a lonely and alienating place that did not deliver on the promises made by relocation officials. Others were stifled by BIA oversight and ran aground of the program rules. American Indians who traveled to cities on relocation also skillfully negotiated federal policies in ways that confounded the plans of U.S. policymakers and officials and turned relocation policy around to serve their own needs. Many Indians on relocation eventually found the opportunities they sought and became satisfied with their lives in the city, adding to the diversity and complexity of the urban Indian populations that had been building for decades. Others used relocation as a way to gain experience that would serve them in the long run, contrary to the intentions of federal officials. Some relocation participants became involved with organizations that strengthened Indian identity and built Indian communities in the city, then used those groups as a platform for critiquing the relocation program or providing some of the services they felt the BIA had neglected. These critiques resonated with policymakers, so that Indian people eventually came to participate in the planning and implementation of relocation policy. By the 1970s the relocation program had become remarkably less a policy of "Americanization" and considerably more one of "self-determination," or a policy that enabled Indian people to identify and serve the needs of their community as they saw fit. This shift to self-determination was a manifestation of larger changes in both federal Indian policy and government antipoverty programs that occurred across the country and fundamentally altered the nature of U.S.-Indian relations. In this sense, the relocation program helps to illustrate what was happening, as urban Indian people and government officials struggled to define new relationships in a period marked by reservation-to-city migration, Indian activism, and an overhaul of federal Indian policy. Put more simply, federal officials were trying to erase the notion of Indian Country altogether through relocation. Native people meanwhile were building on the precedents established in the early twentieth century and more than ever before reimagining Indian country to encompass both reservations and cities.

◆ ◆ ◆

Federal officials understood relocation as a way to move Indians off tribal lands and to assimilate them into the larger society. The program began on a small scale when BIA officials sought off-reservation jobs for groups of Navajo and Hopi who had suffered through a particularly harsh winter in 1948. The BIA and the U.S. Congress then developed a more comprehensive program under the theory that reservations were scarce in natural resources and therefore would never support large Indian populations. In 1950 Dillon Myer was appointed the new Indian commissioner, based in part on his experience as the director of the agency that managed the relocation and internment of Japanese Americans during World War II. Myer saw relocation as a corollary to "termination policy," the federal government's efforts to end its government-to-government relationship with Indian tribes, to remove Indian land from trust status, and to cease providing services to Indian people. Myer called for a disbursement of Indians to cities throughout the country to integrate Indians into the economic life of the nation. Myer and other supporters of relocation also believed in depopulating reservations to the point that they would be "self-sufficient" and no longer in need of federal services. The BIA's new Branch of Placement and Relocation set up field offices in Chicago; Denver; Salt Lake City; Los Angeles; San Francisco; Oakland; San Jose; Portland, Ore.; Dallas; Oklahoma City; Tulsa; St. Louis; Cincinnati; Cleveland; and Joliet and Waukegan, Ill.[4]

Indians on relocation found their way to these offices, where they were given an orientation and placed in temporary housing such as a hotel or a boardinghouse in a low-income part of the city. The field office staff worked to find them permanent housing and employment during the first two weeks. Program participants could expect limited aid from the field office that included subsistence funds, adjustment counseling, stipends for tools and equipment, and basic health care.[5] In 1956 federal officials expanded relocation to include the AVT program. AVT participants could enroll in a number of two-year vocational courses at urban schools, with the understanding that the BIA would provide for the students' subsistence as long as the students continued to make what was deemed satisfactory progress.[6] Federal expenditures for both direct relocation and AVT continued to increase throughout the 1950s and 1960s, before tailing off in the 1970s. About 100,000 Indians participated in direct relocation, and 55,000 enrolled in AVT.[7]

Federal eligibility requirements and decisions made on the local level by employees at the field offices worked to identify the applicants with the greatest potential for making a clean break from the reservation and assimilating into the city. Regulations favored those applicants who seemed to have the best chances of finding a steady job, raising a family, staying out of legal trouble, and becoming self-sufficient so that they no longer needed assistance from the federal government. The application process could be initiated only by federally recognized and enrolled Indians living on reservations or in predominantly Indian rural areas (such as parts of Oklahoma that had undergone allotment). This meant that Indians already in the city were not eligible for relocation services. Indians usually heard about relocation from agency personnel, BIA employees who traveled promoting the program, or friends and relatives on relocation. Those interested could contact the local BIA agency, which often had hired relocation officers specifically to coordinate the program. The federal official and the potential participant filled out an application together that asked standard information such as name, address, age, sex, marital status, number of children, work record, education, degree of Indian blood, and tribe. Additional questions included knowledge of English, previous experience off reservations, number of relatives living near or at the relocation destination, amount of furniture and household goods, amount of continuing income, amount of debt, medical problems or handicaps, and social problems or other "special problems." The applicant was given a physical examination, and agency personnel performed a thorough background check by conferring with other agency employees, former employers, school officials, and local police. The application was forwarded to the field relocation office in the city where the candidate desired placement if agency personnel thought that the applicant was a good candidate for relocation services. Officials at the field office made the final decision by either rejecting the application or beginning the process to bring the applicant to the city.[8]

Federal officials from Washington, D.C., down to the field relocation officers in individual cities tried to define what made a good candidate for relocation, based on a subjective evaluation of the information revealed through the application process. Officials were primarily looking for Indians with the greatest chance of assimilating according to federal standards. The head of the relocation program sent a memo to all relocation officials in 1956, stating that it was time to tighten the requirements for acceptance. It suggested that a number of factors might limit the potential of a candidate for becoming a "success" and might disqualify his or her application for relocation, including advanced age, "physical defects and abnormalities," educational limitations, oversized families, degree of ability to speak and read English, penal records, dishonorable military discharge, history of excessive alcohol use, and heavy debts.[9] The director of the Los Angeles Field Relocation Office (LAFRO), Mary Nan Gamble, replied enthusiastically to these recommendations. A year earlier she had written to the national office complaining that all of the "undesirable Indians" with "no potential to be a success" were coming to Los Angeles and jeopardizing the whole program. She applauded the new initiative for being more selective in accepting program participants. Gamble argued that her staff could list names of people who had dropped out of the program for every consideration listed in the national office's memo. Gamble believed that there was no "sure formula" but that the individual's ability, past record, and chance for "success" had to be taken into consideration.[10]

The BIA framed the narratives and testimonies of American Indians on relocation to offer additional examples of what federal officials were looking for when they tried to identify good candidates. LAFRO officials kept a file full of "success" stories to advertise the program and as an instructional tool for new or struggling program participants. These stories emphasized middle-class American values—hard work, individual responsibility, and competitive spirit—as the keys to overcoming obstacles and turning one's life around. L. Bear in 1956 stated that in the course of his program he had realized that he was "not a baby or child . . . but a grown man and that [he had] to get out and grub for [himself]." He went on to argue that "Indians back home have a lot of dreams. They get a picture in their minds about how they won't have to put out any effort on their part if they decide they want to relocate. They think that success will just come to them through moving [to Los Angeles]." Bear lamented that "Indians jump onto the Relocation Program, or the [Indian] Agency for the predicament they are in. One of the most important things they need to learn," Bear claimed, was that "they are grown people and that sometime they are going to have to . . . learn to be responsible for themselves." Bear himself had found this through trial and error. He spent much of his time drinking and getting into trouble when he arrived in the city. Once he found a steady job he resolved to "quit carousing around because . . . it [was] more fun to be at home with [his wife and baby], to take [his wife] shopping, to go to movies with her, and to take [his] family to church."[11] Bear's story was the epitome of "successful" relocation for officials, because Bear had left the reservation, joined the low-wage work force, and become self-sufficient to relieve the federal government of its responsibility. The BIA's Portland Area Office (PAO) managed relocation services to Pacific Northwest cities and similarly asked certain relocation participants to write letters, to give interviews for BIA pamphlets, and to appear in filmed advertisements that were shown on reservations. Officials made a special effort to publicize the experiences of Sylvia Earling, a nineteen-year-old Umatilla Indian woman who graduated second in her class from Portland's Beau Monde Beauty College and found a job as a cosmetologist at a popular Portland shopping mall. Earling traveled around Oregon, Washington, and Idaho at BIA expense, appearing at state offices and Indian conferences to explain the relocation program and to speak of its potential benefits to Indian people.[12]

Eligibility requirements also showed the tendency of federal officials to use relocation for the promotion of nuclear, patriarchal families. Federal officials allocated women's benefits in relation to prevailing notions about their secondary positions within the American family. Specifically, many Indian women were denied opportunities afforded to men for vocational training and relocation services because officials regarded women as domestic caretakers dependent upon male breadwinners.[13] Applications for relocation services were limited to "Indian heads of households," meaning an Indian man in the case of a married couple and single people regardless of gender, so that Indian men would qualify for direct relocation and vocational training regardless of marital status or the ethnicity of their spouse. Indian women could come on direct relocation only if single or married to an Indian man and could get vocational training as a single person but not as a spouse.[14] Single women with children were discouraged from participating in relocation also because they were perceived as deviating from the kinds of nuclear patriarchal families federal officials sought to promote. All applicants were required to take a physical exam, and pregnant women were disqualified under the terms of a federal rule instituted in 1958.[15] Helen Sanger, a Spokane Indian, applied for relocation in 1960 and found out during the physical that she was expecting a child. The agency relocation officer rejected her application and suggested that Helen marry her boyfriend so that he could apply and receive training as a head of household.[16] Single women who already had children were also denied relocation services by local practice. An agency officer hesitated to recommend the application of a Snohomish Indian woman with two children in 1962 though he decided to go ahead and "keep an open mind about the situation."[17] Portland officials in 1964 decided that "training mothers with dependent children generally has been found to be impractical," and in 1965 it rejected an Indian woman with children from the Warm Springs Reservation by citing "child care problems that would arise."[18] A BIA official in Anchorage, Alaska, in 1963 wrote to LAFRO recommending an "unusually good young lady" with high scholastic standing and test scores for vocational training. A representative wrote back stating that from their experience a woman with children had "more problems than [could] be adequately met" and if the applicant really wanted training she would have to leave her children at home.[19]

Once they reached the city of relocation, those American Indian women who did meet the federal and local requirements for direct relocation and vocational training were confined to a range of employment and training options that corresponded to predominant notions about the place of ethnic women in the workforce. The experience of Indian women on relocation supports the work of scholars such as Evelyn Nakano Glenn who have charted the expansion of "racial-ethnic" women's work after World War II to include the lower levels of the service and clerical industries in addition to traditional sectors such as domestic service.[20] Ninety-eight women traveled to Portland, Ore., to participate in relocation's Adult Vocational Training program and about half took courses at one of four business colleges to learn general office, secretarial, stenography, and IBM key punch operation. Another one-fourth attended beauty school and studied cosmetology, while the remaining one-fourth received training to become practical nurses and dental assistants.[21] The American Indian women who traveled to Los Angeles by 1961 on relocation similarly were offered training that prepared them for jobs as beauticians, dental assistants, nurses, x-ray technicians, office clerks, and secretaries. Officials saw fit to skip training altogether in favor of employment as domestic servants in the case of

Graduates of the BIA's Intermountain Boarding School prepare to leave for jobs in Los Angeles, March 1956. Courtesy of National Archives and Record Administration Pacific Region (Riverside, Calif.), Record Group 75, Field Employment Assistance Office Los Angeles, Central Subject Files, Box 10.

some single women and especially graduates of federal boarding schools for Indians.[22] Those women who sought to break gender and racial boundaries by enrolling in training to prepare for more fulfilling or better-paid employment could be prevented from doing so. An Indian agent wrote to LAFRO in 1959 on behalf of an Indian woman who desired training as a nursery horticulturist, and the office wrote back that such training was available only for men.[23] A counselor from an art school in Minneapolis that same year contacted the PAO on the behalf of an Indian woman who was interested in attending and was told that the AVT did not promote that kind of training.[24]

Relocation policies also maintained practices that had long carved out distinct markets for the labor of ethnic men and denied them access to more highly skilled and professional occupations.[25] American Indian men participating in AVT primarily enrolled in technical schools that offered programs geared toward skilled and semi-skilled industrial jobs. Courses

Luke Notah, a Navajo man, is pictured in his Los Angeles residence a year after his arrival, in this 1955 BIA publicity photo. Notah worked at North American Aviation. Courtesy of National Archives and Record Administration Pacific Region (Riverside, Calif.), Record Group 75, Field Employment Assistance Office Los Angeles, Central Subject Files, Box 10.

preparing men for fields such as airplane mechanic, auto body repair, auto mechanic, machine shop work, sheet metal work, radio and television repair, truck driving, and welding were the most popular placements in Portland and Los Angeles through the 1950s and 1960s. Other men prepared for the lower tiers of business professions and the service industry by training to become barbers, beauticians, office clerks, bookkeepers, mechanical draftsmen, secretaries, nurses, and x-ray technicians.[26] As for women, for men, too, there were links between the types of work chosen by relocation officials and more widely held notions within the BIA about what was appropriate for Indians. BIA-run boarding schools emphasized vocational training to the exclusion of a more general academic education and began to work directly with the relocation program in the 1950s. A relocation officer was hired to recruit students at the BIA's largest off-reservation school, Intermountain School in Brigham City, Utah, and directed fifty male graduates to the relocation program by 1957.[27] Seventy more American Indian men from Intermountain went to Los Angeles alone over the next two years and took jobs as auto mechanics, mill apprentices, metal

*The Dodges, a Navajo family, arrive at the BIA's Los Angeles Field Relocation Office
and are greeted by employee Virginia Gomez, ca. 1955. The BIA's caption read: "It's good
to see a friendly person on your arrival in a strange place." Courtesy of National Archives
and Record Administration Pacific Region (Riverside, Calif.), Record Group 75, Field
Employment Assistance Office Los Angeles, Central Subject Files, Box 23.*

work helpers, upholsterers, welders, brick and cement finisher helpers, and
fry cooks.[28]

Field offices sought to further the process of Americanization through
paternalistic policies that had local officials and their allies moralizing,
monitoring, and disciplining relocation participants. The first visit relocation participants made to LAFRO included an orientation with filmstrips
advising Indians on subjects such as "personal appearance" and "keeping
up your home."[29] LAFRO officials also gave new arrivals a "community adjustment" booklet developed by office employees that began by stressing
the importance of sound work habits and the perils of excessive drinking.
It went on to provide blanks where new arrivals could fill in the addresses
for their local grocery store, bank, movie house, gas station, church, and
friends. It advocated good relations with neighbors by picturing a house
and warning that "[y]our neighbors judge you by the appearance of your
lawn and home." The booklet also had "hints for housewives" that advised
Indian women to keep their homes clean and neat, shop around for the
best deals in the grocery store, make stews and purchase less expensive

cuts of meat, pack nutritious lunches for children, and sew at home instead of buying new clothes. The booklet ended by listing a number of recommendations under the title "What It Takes to Succeed" that included the desire to get a job and keep it, efforts to make new friends, love of family, acceptance of guidance, industrious work effort, cleanliness, an ordinary educational background, no excessive drink, courage, and the will to learn.[30]

Relocation officers also teamed with local religious organizations in order to promote middle-class, Christian values of temperance and propriety. The Church Federation of Greater Chicago formed a Joint Committee on Indian Work that operated in conjunction with the BIA's Chicago Relocation Office. Relocation participants received a form from the Church Federation explaining that "Christian Churches are eager to welcome Indians into the Community and Church of their choice," followed by a request for personal information. A letter from the Church Federation followed if participants responded that they would like suggestions for a church in or near their neighborhood.[31] A study by the municipal organization, Los Angeles Welfare Planning Council, reported that it was the practice of LAFRO to give the names of recent arrivals to "responsible church groups . . . in order that they might aid in the orientation and assimilation of the Indian."[32] Several Christian denominations and organizations became interested in missionary work among Indians in Los Angeles, such as the Southern California Council of Churches, the Brighter Day Mission Church (which established an American Indian Baptist Mission group), St. Joseph's Catholic Church, the Presbyterian Church (which established the All Nation's Church), and the Church of Jesus Christ of Latter-day Saints. Other church groups formed specifically to work with this growing population, including the, San Creek Mission Indian Church, Indian Revival Center, American Indian Mission Church, First Indian Baptist Church, and Indian Church of the Nazarene.[33] LAFRO officers supported the work of Christian groups by recommending relocation participants, donating money and clothes, and referring members of the public who contacted LAFRO for recommendations on deserving groups for donations and charity work.[34] Director of LAFRO George Felshaw responded to a judge's suggestion in 1960 that "good, wholesome recreational opportunity for [Indians might] keep them away from the undesirable sections of the city" by pointing out that several local churches had developed such activities and that Indians might even be released on parole, provided they promise to engage in them.[35]

Federal officials turned to surveillance and discipline in their efforts to Americanize Indians after relocation participants were settled into their new homes, schools, churches, and jobs. Some of these efforts were in conjunction with local churches. Officials in Chicago from 1959 to 1961 relied on the Church Federation's Indian Ministry to run a home visitation program that welcomed "newcomer Indians" and reported back to the relocation office about such things as the condition of homes, dress of the relocation participants, languages spoken, and church attendance.[36] Relocation officials also made monthly home visits to program participants and consulted with vocational school officials to prepare progress reports on how participants were adjusting to the city. This process became more formalized for AVT in 1961 when the BIA's national office mandated that regular evaluations of each trainee be made in consultation with school officials and staff members, taking into consideration the trainee's personal habits, aptitude, interests, mental ability, and general interest in the course.[37]

Officials resorted to threatening program participants with expulsion from the program, the withdrawal of funding, and changing their methods so as to exercise more control when these home visits, formal evaluations, and informal observations and reports revealed behavior that did not meet BIA standards of what was proper. The LAFRO director wrote vocational trainees in 1959 to remind them that their subsistence funds would be garnished if they were absent from classes without permission.[38] The PAO director informed trainees the same year that they would be docked $4.00 for every absence from class not excused by relocation officials.[39] A written warning to a woman enrolled in the program in 1958 was typical of PAO threats and moralizing: "We have received a report from your landlady that your conduct came under criticism by her. She reports that you and your roommate have been entertaining gentlemen friends at a late hour and have done so repeatedly, even after a request by her to curtail these activities. . . We have contacted the school officials at the College of Beauty to advise them of your reported activities and to request that they counsel with you also."[40] This letter was mild in tone when compared to one sent by PAO officials the following year to a trainee residing at a boardinghouse run by Catholic nuns: "It has been reported to us by the authorities of the Joan of Arc that your conduct has been unacceptable to them as a resident. This is exceedingly embarrassing to us, as this is a Christian boarding home, and that you are reflecting discredit to yourself, to us, and to the Indian people. It is evident that your lack of application to your studies will have an adverse effect on your employment plans. Since your training is nearly completed we expect you to get down to business and behave yourself."[41] Local relocation officials could also be especially manipulative in their efforts to monitor and discipline relocation participants. Relocation workers made unannounced visits to participants' homes in Portland under the pretext of delivering a check or in order to obtain a signature, then used the opportunity to observe the appearance of participants and their homes and to note their attitudes and "progress." Portland officials removed an apartment complex from an approved housing list because the landlady allegedly was "covering" for program participants and refusing to report on their behavior.[42] A Los Angeles official convinced his superiors to change a group of young men's housing so that they were no longer clustered together after receiving complaints of loud noises, heavy drinking, and fighting from a hotel that housed a number of single Indian men. Officials also decided to have the men come in once a week to get their checks instead of having them mailed twice monthly so it would be easier to keep an eye on them and control their spending.[43]

The relocation program also discouraged the kinds of activities that might have facilitated the maintenance of Indian identity in the city as part of its Americanization program. Relocation was based on the idea that a separation from extended kinship networks and Indian communities was necessary to facilitate the assimilation of Indian people, much like the off-reservation boarding schools of the late nineteenth and twentieth centuries. Many relocation participants made trips back to area reservations to attend family, tribal, or intertribal events or simply to visit family and friends. Officials rarely excused such visits and added them to the individual's list of infractions or expelled the individual from the program.[44] Relocation officials also discouraged such visits and Indian gatherings less formally. A Umatilla woman was chosen to represent her tribe at an Indian Days celebration in British Columbia in 1960 and asked permission to attend. Portland officials "frowned upon it," so she agreed to stay in the city.[45] The PAO went so far as to adopt a policy of discouraging Indian interaction in Portland in 1962 by reasoning that "too much excessive drinking and unacceptable behavior [results] when Indian groups get together."[46] Relocation policy in Portland also mandated that new trainees be advised that program funds were never to be used for "the support of visiting friends and relatives."[47]

Indian experience on relocation often turned out to be very different from what relocation officials had in mind, despite the intentions and efforts of the BIA. Many program participants were not able to realize the middle-class life promoted by relocation officials and instead found the city difficult and alienating. Relocation records are filled with indicators that Indians often experienced life in the city as a great shock that could lead to feelings of loneliness and inadequacy. Ernie Peters relocated to Los Angeles in 1957 from the Lower Sioux Reservation in Minnesota and found that urban life was more daunting than he had been led to believe. He remembered, "Boy, I was expecting to come out here and live like a king, I mean the way [the BIA] talked about [relocation back on the reservation]." Peters stepped off the train at Union Station in downtown Los Angeles and began to wonder "when the next train left back for the reservation in Minnesota." He made his way to LAFRO, where he was received and placed in a room at a nearby skid row hotel. Peters experienced a sense of confusion and neglect that first night that stayed with him for the next several months. He said, "I didn't even know how to get down [off the third floor]. I didn't know where the stairs were, and there were elevators [but] I never rode one in my life. [I was so frightened that] I couldn't even speak up. You've got to be an Indian just to have that feeling." Officials moved him to an apartment in Echo Park soon after, and he began looking for work but found it difficult to compete in the city's deindustrializing economy with no training and few marketable skills. He worked a variety of jobs for six years, kept getting laid off, and returned to the reservation in 1963 after receiving word that his father had passed away.[48]

Other Indians on relocation were dismayed to find their lives in the city marked by poverty since they came to urban areas to escape it. M. M. relocated to Los Angeles from the Winnebago Reservation when he was a child and his family moved to a mostly poor white neighborhood on the south side of Glendale. His mother and grandmother found low-wage jobs that allowed them to get by, but without much left over. As he recalled: "It was like let's save enough to pay the rent, and if we had money left over, a big day out or a big night out was going to the Woolworth's Diner for a hot dog, that was extravagance. So it was very much [a] working class [life], going to school, coming home after work, watching TV, getting ready to go to work the next day. There were no frills, no movies."[49] This poverty was reinforced by BIA housing policies that tended to settle individuals and families in overcrowded, dilapidated, and cheaply furnished homes. The Fixicos came to Los Angeles in 1957 from the Rosebud Sioux Reservation as a family of two adults and six children. LAFRO officials placed all eight family members in a small two-room apartment.[50] Mahonta Bad Horse remembered coming to Los Angeles ten years later. She was given furniture so badly made that the surface of a table rolled up from the sun shining on it through her apartment window.[51]

One of the greatest obstacles for relocation participants was the discrepancy between the BIA's promises of economic opportunity and the realities of America's postwar economy. Indians and other ethnic minorities were often the first laid off as low- and semi-skilled manufacturing jobs declined in the late 1950s and early 1960s. Racial discrimination also barred their entry into the unions that were necessary for work in many professions.[52] Even those relocation participants who enrolled in AVT and obtained a degree often found that the experience had inadequately prepared them for steady work. A Navajo man received training as an auto mechanic in Seattle, Wash., and then he and his family were placed in Los Angeles in 1960. BIA officials reported that due to the "local labor market . . . it was impossible to locate an auto mechanics job," and he was forced to accept an unskilled position in a factory that manufactured wire products, where he was subjected to frequent layoffs of up to a week at a time.[53] Ernie Peters reported that the school he attended while in the AVT program studying auto body repair used tools and teaching techniques that were "20 years outdated."[54] One especially frustrated relocation participant complained bitterly of the gap between what the program advertised and what it delivered: "You look around and you realize that on the reservation, you have nothing going for you at all. The BIA tells you life will be better in the cities and that they'll train you and get you a job. Since nothing could be worse than the life they force on the Indian at the reservation, you take it. But then you get to Los Angles and all that training that is supposed to be waiting for you doesn't materialize."[55] These sentiments were echoed by other Indians who came to the city and struggled because of lack of work experience, inadequate training, or racial discrimination in the workplace.[56]

This combination of loneliness and alienation, urban poverty, and frustration over diminishing opportunities for work translated into great mental and emotional pain for some relocation participants. Some drifted into homelessness, addiction, and incarceration. These Indians spent time drifting between streets, Indian bars, hospitals, and local jails. Certain parts of cities, such as skid row in downtown Los Angeles, became known as gathering sites for these homeless Indians. H. Brown, a Winnebago Indian from Nebraska, remembered spending much of the 1950s in Los Angeles "running around" with a group of Indians that hung out in Indian bars such as the Ritz and the Columbine, took free meals at downtown missions, and slept on the streets.[57] Ed Goodvoice similarly lived among a community of homeless Indians for seventeen years around Chicago's skid row, performing casual labor and drinking on the streets and in Indian bars.[58] Some Indians ventured to "Hill X" in Los Angeles's Chavez Ravine or an area underneath the intersection of the 5 and 110 freeways known as "the Tombs" to drink, beat drums, sing songs, and generally socialize. These places offered a sense of community and familiarity for Indians brought to the city on relocation, but they also were frequently places of despair marked by alcohol, drugs, and violence.[59]

Indian people as a whole did not passively accept the policies of relocation, nor were they simply victims of its many inadequacies, despite all of the considerable difficulties they faced. Relocation participants adopted a variety of strategies designed to negotiate the program and use it to their own advantage. Many American Indians on relocation eventually benefited from their experiences with the program because of their willingness to struggle through the difficulties of urban life and cope with the shortcomings of federal policy.

Indian agency in shaping the terms of their own experiences began with the initiative they took in signing up for the program. Many Indians willingly chose to participate in relocation after coming to a realization that their economic choices would always be limited on the reservation. A theme running throughout the perspectives of Indians on the program is the desire to "create a better life" by obtaining a steady and secure job through a move to the city. Marlene Strouse, a Pima Indian, was a child when her family decided to relocate to Chicago in 1952 because "My dad could not support his family, which was six in number, not very well on what he made back home. And so when they heard about the relocation program, they jumped at it. To get away and to find better jobs to take care of their families. My dad used to move around with the people who combined wheat, you know [before that]. Traveled all over the wheat states like Nebraska and Kansas and be gone six months out of the year."[60] Caroline Martinez, a sixteen-year-old Pueblo Indian living near Taos, N. Mex., asked for relocation to Los Angeles in 1956 by explaining that her brothers had all married, her father was blind, and she now had no way to support herself.[61] During World War II, Joe (Whitecloud) Tafoya, from Santa Clara Pueblo in New Mexico, traveled to Europe, where he met and married his wife, Trudy. The two returned to Santa Clara, and Joe began working as an operations engineer at the Los Alamos atomic research facility. The Los Alamos workforce unionized in the early 1950s and crowded out local Indians and Latinos. Relocation seemed the only economic option, so Joe and Trudy contacted a BIA relocation officer and soon made the move to Los Angeles with their three children.[62] Benjamin James relocated to Los Angeles from Oklahoma in 1955 and wrote to the BIA officer back home soon after arriving in the city. He declared his family's intention to stay in the city by stating that he did not "believe [they would] ever go back to Oklahoma to chop cotton again."[63] Robert Lawrence, a Nez Perce man, went to see the agency relocation officer in 1963 a few days after he was married and explained that "he knew he needed training so that he could learn a trade and take care of his family."[64] LaNada Boyer left the Ft. Hall Reservation in Idaho for relocation to San Francisco in 1965 because "There were no jobs on the reservation, and the 'No Indians or Dogs Allowed' signs had barely been taken down in my home town of Blackfoot, Idaho. Poverty, hardship and despair had grown to be a way of life on the reservation."[65] The harsh conditions of reservation life and the prospects for economic mobility in the city largely explain why so many Indians embraced relocation.

Relocation participants often found they could take advantage of the program's benefits on their own terms. Many Indians became adept at abiding by the letter of the regulations while running against their spirit. Relocation services were available only to Indians who engaged the relocation office at their local agencies and were denied to Indians already living in cities. Francis Allen noted that his son lived in Los Angeles and wanted to get services through relocation, so he went back to the reservation and signed up for AVT, then traveled to Los Angeles, where he received training at BIA expense.[66] Glenna Amos, a Cherokee Indian, was born and raised in Los Angeles and married her husband, Will, a Choctaw Indian who had come to Los Angeles on relocation with his parents in 1954. Five years later the couple went to live with relatives in Oklahoma so that they could apply for relocation services and Will could enroll in vocational school upon their return to Los Angeles.[67] Russell Means grew up in the San Francisco Bay area and spent time living and working in Los Angeles. He twice traveled to the Pine Ridge Reservation and applied for relocation.[68]

Other Indians disagreed with the paternalistic rules and regulations and refused to yield to them, pushing to have things done according to their own needs and vision of life in the city. Russell Means constantly challenged the oversight of local relocation officials in Cleveland. He "possessed the verbal skills to demand a change" and was able to use BIA resources to secure a suburban home and white-collar job rather than settling his family in the urban slum and taking the factory position that was offered to him.[69] The Tafoya family is another example of this tenacity. The family took the first opportunity it could to drive out and visit the beach after settling into the hot and overcrowded hotel room chosen by the BIA. Dennis Tafoya remembered:

> [LAFRO] gave my mom and dad a map of the area, Los Angeles, and they said here's where you want to go and look for employment, here's where you're living, Hotel Los Angeles, here's various geographic areas, here's where the beaches are, and here's how you get out there. You go out to the beaches for your recreation and your enjoyment. . . . So when we got out there, we saw the ocean, it was wonderful, and the beach, and they looked around and they saw a little beach house, I think it rented for fifty dollars a month. They came back, and they were all excited, and my mom said we're going to live here. They went back to the BIA office and told them with excitement, that gee, we did something on our own. The BIA got kind of upset. They said, wait a minute, that's the place where you go for recreation. That's where we said you go to spend the weekend. That's not a place where Indians live. And my mom said the hell with the BIA at that point, we realized where this was going, and [my parents] actually stopped any contact with the local Bureau office after that. And we moved from an old dingy hotel off the Harbor Freeway here, to Hermosa Beach, of all places, [in] 1955.

This interaction led LAFRO officials to label the Tafoyas as "uncooperative" since they were acting outside the boundaries of LAFRO control. LAFRO officials changed their tune the following year. A LAFRO official came to the conclusion that the family had "done wonderfully well for themselves . . . due to their own determination" after observing the Tafoyas' new car and hearing about Joe's employment record and their plans to buy a new home.[70]

Accounts by federal officials that cite excessive drinking and "bad behavior," absences from school, and returns to the reservation can be similarly interpreted as Indian insistence on defining the terms of their own experience. One case that frustrated Portland officials was that of a young Navajo man named George Begay who came to the program in May 1958 from Chemawa Indian School and enrolled in Multnomah College to learn auto body repair. He was admonished several times for reports from his landlord and school that he had "gone on drunks" and missed class over the first few months. The PAO wrote the national office in July to explain that Begay had received that month's subsistence check for $120 and left Portland for the Navajo Reservation in Arizona. The letter stated that "this [action] confirmed a rumor which we now know to be well-founded which was that George contemplated leaving for several weeks; however, at every interview with him, he denied he was leaving."[71] There were many other cases of Indians "living off" the program and using federal money in ways that they determined would suit them best. Raymond Watchman ran up a large hotel bill on the BIA's account in Los Angeles and then returned to the reservation before being placed in employment in 1959.[72] A Portland relocation officer commented on the case of a young Colville woman named Merla Jenkins who was taking courses in stenography from Pacific Business College in 1960. Her grades in school were good, but she often missed classes to visit relatives back home or to take day trips to the Oregon coast. Portland officials were never able to convince her that there was anything wrong with her behavior and were constantly aggravated by her savvy in perceiving just how far she could bend the rules without her actions being serious enough to warrant dismissal. A relocation officer noted her strong will and characterized her as "cooperative only so far as it does not interfere with her other plans."[73]

These were "failures" who threatened the "success" of the program, according to relocation officials. Indian people, however, often understand these experiences as valuable and a contribution to their long-term development as active agents in a complex world. One Colville woman frustrated Portland officials by "partying around" and missing her secretarial classes at Behnke-Walker Business College until she was dropped from the program. The training she received nonetheless qualified her for a job as a secretary back at the agency.[74] Nineteen-year-old Edward Spelman left the Makah Reservation in 1958 for relocation to Portland, where he enrolled at Pacific Business College. Spelman went on a series of "drinking binges," missing a number of classes for a few months, and then left Portland with a BIA check meant to cover the next term's tuition. A few years later Spelman enrolled in a forestry program at Everett Junior College in Everett, Wash.; he earned a degree and found work managing tribal resources on the Warm Springs Reservation. Spelman indicated that he "got a lot out of the program" and thanked the BIA for its help.[75] Ernie Peters went back to the reservation for two years but then returned to the city again because, "I couldn't take it. It was worse back there, after living [in Los Angeles], so I came back again. . . I got tired of holding the lamp for my wife to chop wood." Peters reported that on his second time around "I was more adjusted to this environment and I was able to get around and apply myself. And I had contacts here the city." He still found urban life challenging, but by 1960 he had settled into a regular routine that included a steady job, a new home, and activities with local Indian organizations that led him to state that he was finally "in his glory."[76]

Another way in which relocation participants were able to define their own experience despite the efforts of relocation officials was to join with other Indian people in creating urban American Indian communities. This practice rejected Americanization policies by strengthening rather than weakening Indian identity and reimagining rather than forsaking the notion of Indian Country. Floria Forcia, a Chippewa Indian, remembered that, "she heard a lot of stories about [relocation] from people that were here, and came back [to the reservation]. They made it sound really scary." Forcia was able to spend time with her sister and several friends who were also in the city when she relocated to Chicago, however.[77] Yvonne Lamore-Choate eased into life in the San Francisco Bay area with the help of the other single women she met while attending orientation at the BIA field office and later saw at various Indian bars.[78] Glen Yellow Eagle's family went on relocation to Cleveland, where his mother Irmlee became one of the founding members of a community self-help organization called the Cleveland American Indian Center.[79] John and Lois Knifechief first came to Los Angeles on relocation from Oklahoma in the mid-1950s. They formed an Indian dance group named the Road Runners and later helped charter the Orange County Indian Center to provide social services and recreational opportunities for Indians in the Los Angeles metropolitan area.[80] Joe Tafoya and his family also became part of a growing Indian community. Joe and Trudy volunteered their time with several social service groups, such as the Los Angeles Indian Center and the American Indian Free Clinic. They were so busy their son Dennis recalled that "during the week, I never saw them half the time, they'd be attending board meetings for this and that." The Tafoyas were also particularly active Indian dancers. The family became active in two powwow groups called the Drum and Feather Club and the Many Trails Indian Club in addition to working at Disneyland and touring as part of an Indian dance group. Dennis later described how important it was for his family to meet with other Indians in this way:

What was here in Los Angeles was an intertribal community, many different tribes, other folks who came out here on relocation, a lot of Indian families that were here because of military experience. It was kind of a melting pot of tribal people here, more tribes of people from outside California than native indigenous Californian tribes. . . .

I remember very early on, being five maybe six and going to pow-wows here. For my dad it was a re-edification of who he was. Not the Pueblo side, but the Indian side—it was a little different, little different experience. A contemporary Indian powwow here is, as I mentioned, intertribal, Pawnees, Otoes, Navajos, Hopi, Pueblo, Ute, Cherokee, Choctaw, it doesn't matter. . . . We would go to school and I have my non-Indian friends, then on the weekends we seek out our intertribal brothers and sisters and partake in powwow activities. It really was kind of a lifeline. It allowed my dad to continue to appreciate his consciousness and world vision, but at the same time it allowed us to continue to appreciate—because I'm only five years old—to continue to value my Indian heritage.[81]

Dozens of other Indian groups were organized in urban areas as the Indian population of Los Angeles and other cities increased throughout the 1960s, and they relied on the enthusiastic participation of Indians on relocation.[82]

Most perturbing for relocation officials was that many relocation participants and their Indian allies formulated vigorous critiques of the program offered in an attempt to reshape it. The newly organized American Indian Center in Chicago clashed with the BIA's local relocation office in the 1950s over the BIA's refusal to provide the Indian Center with the names and addresses of new arrivals in the city.[83] Members of the Los Angeles Indian Center became especially vocal critics of relocation. Indian Center members believed that the government should help willing Indians move to the city so they could find new opportunities but argued that relocation policy was "dumping" Indians in the city without adequately providing for their needs or enabling Indians to achieve their own visions of social and economic mobility. On the basis of experience working with relocation participants, the Indian Center passed a resolution in 1956 recommending that the BIA make a number of adjustments and changes in relocation policy, including more pre-relocation and relocation counseling on matters such as housing, public transportation, employment, the use of credit, the educational system, laws of city life, and how to pay taxes. The resolution also stated that participants needed to be given long-term health insurance, opportunities to pursue educational goals, better housing, and free burial and transportation of bodies back to the reservation. Finally, the Indian Center stressed the need for relocation participants and their children to retain their rights as tribal peoples regardless of how long they remained in urban areas.[84] Indian Center members and other Indians echoed these critiques and recommendations in community newsletters, newspaper articles, and public forums throughout the 1960s.[85]

In time these critiques came to have a significant impact on the formulation and implementation of relocation policy. The first stirrings of change came in the late 1960s when officials and policymakers considering relocation began to place more value on the perspectives of Indian people. Los Angeles City Supervisor Ernest E. Debs hosted an informal conference on the Indian Relocation Program in 1968 with members of the BIA, state agencies, and local Indian leaders. Debs had developed a relationship with the Los Angeles Indian Center and called the conference to discuss the problems that relocation participants and other urban Indians had in Los Angeles, the scope of BIA services, and the different solutions available.[86] A federal commission appointed to study Indian issues and to recommend policy called the National Council on Indian Opportunity came to Los Angeles that same year to hold public hearings. Dozens of speakers gave testimony. The testimony of LAFRO director D. L. Mahoney was particularly striking. Mahoney showed considerable deference to Indian opinion despite having rebuffed critiques of the program and vigorously defended relocation in the past. Mahoney began by saying that he did not want to appear offensive so he would just answer questions and not give a speech. He then noted that it was good to have so many Indian speakers in attendance.[87] These public forums did not produce immediate results, but they were a sign that policymakers were moved by Indians' critiques of the program and interested in hearing their recommendations.

These shifting attitudes led to changes in the policy and practices of LAFRO officials by the 1970s. Officials began providing new arrivals with the addresses of Indian groups such as the Los Angeles Indian Center and recommending that participants take advantage of their services, after having refused to do so for almost two decades. LAFRO also began referring those seeking to perform charity or social work to these secular Indian organizations in addition to the church groups that had long enjoyed favor. The very tone of correspondence between LAFRO officials and the general public changed to incorporate the perspectives of Indian people. A sociology student wrote to LAFRO in 1971 asking for statistics on relocation. A staff member wrote back suggesting that the student read Indian activist Vine Deloria's recent best-seller, *Custer Died for Your Sins*, and drew attention to its scathing indictment of the motives, methods, and intellectual orientation of non-Indian scholars working on Indian topics. Such exchanges can be partially explained by the fact that the staff of LAFRO included more Indian people to work in the office, counsel newcomers, and make visits to homes of relocation participants.[88]

Some of the most important changes came in the subcontracting of relocation services to local Indian groups. The BIA earmarked $3 million to be used by Indian organizations in cities to take over and run different aspects of the program in 1971. The first grant of $126,000 went to a group of Indian businesspersons formed to promote Indian-owned businesses in Los Angeles called the Urban Indian Development Association (UIDA). UIDA became responsible for the orientation and housing of all new relocation arrivals. Participants arriving in the city were met by a UIDA employee who took them to LAFRO and guided them through the mountains of red tape required by federal officials. The employee took the new arrival to UIDA offices on Wilshire Boulevard the next day to have lunch, sit and talk with other Indians, and discuss various aspects of living in the city. UIDA chartered a bus every weekend for new arrivals to take field trips to see the ocean, visit Indian organizations, attend Indian sporting events, and go to powwows. UIDA Executive Director David Lester explained that this was so "they know there are other Indians in town, that they're not the only ones." Glenna Amos remembered: "[UIDA] picked us up on Saturdays and took us to different amusement parks. They took us to Disneyland, Sea World, places like that. It was nice. We were a young family, we had two small children and we couldn't afford to go to any of those places, so it was nice, to be introduced to different people, and to go as a group." UIDA also assisted new arrivals in finding permanent housing after they settled into school or a job. UIDA sought to consider the needs and desires of program participants and severed relationships with landlords thought to be exploiting relocation participants. Lester stressed that UIDA was not simply taking over the services of the BIA but providing new services in orientation and recreation and offering a fundamentally different viewpoint. Lester argued that the BIA sought to train Indians, find employment, and raise the standard of living. UIDA was also concerned with encouraging relocation participants to become part of an urban Indian community so they would feel like they belonged in the city. Lester felt that UIDA was uniquely qualified to provide services to relocation participants since its members were all Indians who had also struggled with adjusting to life in Los Angeles. UIDA served about 1,000 new arrivals in the first two months of its contract.[89]

These changes in attitudes to favor Indian perspectives and the contracting of services to Indian people were remarkable turnarounds from the practices that had long characterized the relocation program. This shift away from Americanization was not an isolated incident but was indicative of a larger transition in federal Indian policy that occurred in fits and starts during the 1960s and 1970s. An activist movement was building among reservation and urban Indian communities in this period. Indians across the country worked to focus attention on the problems of Indians and to demand fundamental changes in government programs and federal Indian policy. Central to their demands for reform were calls for "self-determination." This meant abandoning BIA policy based on paternalism and increasing the control Indians had over their own communities, while continuing to hold the federal government to its historical obligations to Indian people. This idea of self-determination took root with policymakers and gained momentum to become a force in U.S.-Indian relations beginning with the Kennedy administration. The federal Office of Economic Opportunity and other government agencies began to funnel unprecedented amounts of money to reservation communities under President Lyndon Johnson's antipoverty programs, so that the principles of self-determination were implemented for the first time. Indians acquired funds outside the structure of the BIA and had relative autonomy in applying them as they saw fit. President Richard Nixon was committed to extending the Indian policies of the Johnson administration. Nixon campaigned in 1968 on a platform of self-determination for Indian peoples, and in his 1970 "Message to Congress on Indian Affairs" he called for appropriate legislation that included helping urban Indians. The Office of Economic Opportunity led an effort to establish local, state, and federal programs for Indians in cities based on the principles of self-determination throughout Nixon's presidency.[90]

What happened in Los Angeles illustrates how dramatic was the shift from Americanization to self-determination and how much of a difference it could make in the lives of Indian people. An Indian individual or family would come to the city by car, bus, or train during the first decade and a half of the program. The often disoriented new arrivals followed a series of complicated instructions that led them to the local relocation office. Program participants were then subject to a sustained and multitiered effort to shape them according to middle-class notions of gender, appropriate behavior, and good citizenship. This was all to serve the goal of cutting off their connections to Indian culture and identity and assimilating them into urban society at the lower rungs of the social and economic hierarchy. Indians did not passively accept these policies, but they did face considerable challenges in negotiating them. Their experiences were similar to those of

Indians on reservations and other migrant groups who had faced Americanization policies beginning in the nineteenth century. Relocation ought to be understood as part of this longer historical trajectory

Indians on relocation in Los Angeles by the early 1970s could expect to be met at the bus or train station by Indian employees of UIDA, placed in housing chosen by Indian people, and eased into urban life with the help of a partly Indian-staffed LAFRO and an empowered Indian community. Randy Edmonds ran UIDA's relocation component and commented, "We were a lot more knowledgeable about our own people. It was American Indians running the program for American Indians. Whereas the BIA was more bureaucratic and their approach to individuals that were coming off the reservation was that they were just numbers to them."[91]

Relocation's shift to self-determination makes a strong case for social programs that empower impoverished communities to define and address their own needs. It also enabled Indians to further reimagine Indian Country. The shock and alienation that many Indians experienced in the city during the first years of the program indicates that the reimagining of Indian Country to include cities was limited in the early postwar period. More Indians came to see the city as Native space through the 1960s and 1970s, and they were increasingly insistent on translating that reimagining into policy. The next two chapters will further explore these developments, beginning with a consideration of the growth and diversification of the American Indian population in postwar U.S. cities and the particular ways in which that population worked to define a reimagined Indian Country.

CHAPTER 4

POSTINDUSTRIAL URBAN INDIANS

Life and Work in the Postwar City

G lover Young, a Sioux Indian, traveled to Los Angeles from the Pine Ridge Reservation in 1956 and almost immediately found work at the Chrysler Corporation. While growing up, he went to reservation schools, spent a year at the Haskell Institute, and left before graduating to go home and raise cattle. He was drafted into the military in 1945 and served in Guam, where he worked as a photo lab technician. He went back to Pine Ridge after his discharge to marry and make a living by farming, raising cattle, and breaking horses. In 1950 the family moved to Igloo, S.D., where Young got a job with the Black Hills Ordnance Depot, which paid better and was less dangerous. He liked the work and spent six years there, before a call from his brother convinced him to take his family out to Los Angeles. He got the job at Chrysler, but soon afterward the workers went on strike, so Young signed on with a plumbing firm. He later went back to Chrysler, because he could not get into the plumbers union. Beginning in 1958, Young worked for six years operating and servicing equipment at Western Rolling Mills Company in Commerce, Calif. The company went out of business in 1965, and he found work with another mill as a machine technician and the lead for a five-worker crew on the graveyard shift. He was still with the company in 1970 and lived comfortably in La Mirada, Calif., with his wife and two daughters in a house he purchased with the help of the GI Bill.

Young looked back on it all and reflected that "it was hard to make it out here, I had to fight and have a lot of determination . . . the pressures here are great." He was not surprised that many Indian people returned to the reservation after trying out life in the city. But he had gotten used to Los Angeles, his wife was happy there, and it was all his daughters had ever known. Young supposed that someday they might move to Colorado, where

75

his wife had grown up. He took pains to say, however, that "it would not be because California got the best of us. It would be because that's what we decided. I think we have adapted; I really do."[1]

Young's experiences are similar in many ways to those of other American Indians who came to cities in the first half of the twentieth century to take jobs in industry and agriculture and then settled into the multiethnic, working-class neighborhoods forming throughout urban America. Indians like Young continued to travel to cities in increasing numbers through the three decades after World War II. Postwar Indian migrants also found American cities to be at once exciting and overwhelming and full of both challenges and opportunities that they negotiated in various ways and with differing results. They built on the efforts of Indian migrants from previous generations to further the reimagining of Indian Country to include the urban areas of the United States.

Postwar migrants to American cities arrived in an environment that also was very different in crucial ways from what it had been before the war. Experiences like those of Glover Young and hundreds of thousands of other American Indians who traveled to U.S. cities after World War II must be understood in the context of America's deindustrialization, or a social and economic shift away from traditional heavy industry more toward service, technical, and white-collar work. Steady jobs for unskilled and semi-skilled workers became difficult to find, and American Indians were often among the last hired and the first laid off when industrial production waned. Many American Indians had to persevere through strikes, layoffs, plant closings, and an ever-tightening labor market. All of this was exacerbated by institutional racism that favored white workers and took jobs in expanding economic sectors to areas outside the central city, where people of color had difficulty following them.

Deindustrialization stands as a primary way of understanding postwar America for U.S. and urban historians. Work by historians Thomas J. Sugrue and Robert O. Self has shown how deindustrialization contributed to changing the very nature of American cities, so that they were increasingly marked by a contrast between prosperous, middle-class suburbs and crumbling, inner cities inhabited by the nation's underclass. Both authors emphasize that this economic restructuring disproportionately impacted racialized minorities, especially African Americans.[2] Closer attention might be paid to the wider range of ways that certain groups experienced and adapted to both the losses of industrial jobs and the changes in urban life to which these losses contributed, as historians continue to examine deindustrialization and its impact on American society. Historian Gretchen Lemke-Santangelo has noted that deindustrialization led some African Americans "to fall back on their own institutional and familial resources" to help them weather the changes of the postwar period and even achieve middle-class status, whereas others did not fare as well but instead sank into poverty.[3] Historian Josh Sides similarly has seen the decline in blue-collar manufacturing resulting in "sharply narrowed opportunities for America's industrial workers" and especially African Americans. Sides argues that this loss was partially offset by a corresponding rise in black-owned small business and the growth of a moderately sized black middle class that found employment through office work and in the expanding retail and financial sectors.[4] Looking at the range of ways that American Indians negotiated life in the postindustrial city helps to better account for the varieties of American Indian experiences, while enriching our understanding of how racialized groups as a whole dealt with deindustrialization. Without downplaying the poverty, joblessness, and spatial isolation that came with industrial flight, this dynamic understanding of deindustrialization from the bottom up shows that some people of color managed to nonetheless establish a more secure niche in urban America, contributing to the growth of a small but important middle class that persevered through the second half of the twentieth century. It also continues the important project of putting American Indians at the center of major trends distinguishing twentieth-century U.S. history and society.[5]

Declining opportunities for unskilled and semi-skilled industrial work for American Indians in American cities was a contributing factor, as Indian poverty and its related social problems sharply increased during the postwar period. Native people conversely also were finding inroads into urban middle-class populations. More Indian people received higher education and obtained training that qualified them for work in skilled industries and the professions or to own their own businesses, especially in the 1960s and 1970s. Indian people were able increasingly to establish relatively prosperous and comfortable lives marked by steady paying jobs, homes they owned, and participation in urban Indian communities. During the postwar period it became clearer than ever that Indians were settling into the diverse milieu of urban America, regardless of whether they struggled or prospered in the city. In other words, Native people were increasingly recognizing and defining in complex ways the terms of a reimagined Indian Country in postindustrial America.

TABLE 1 Percentage of Select U.S. Census–Defined Racial Groups Residing in Urban Areas, 1950–1980

Census-Defined Racial Group	1950	1960	1970	1980
American Indian and Alaska Native	16% (56,108)	28% (145,593)	45% (355,738)	53% (827,075)
Black	62%	73%	81%	85%
Japanese	71%	82%	89%	92%
Chinese	93%	96%	96%	97%
White	64%	70%	73%	71%
All Races	64%	70%	74%	74%

Source: U.S. Bureau of the Census, *1950 Census of Population: Volume II, Characteristics of the Population; Part I: U.S. Summary* (Washington, D.C.: GPO, 1953), 88; U.S. Bureau of the Census, *1960 Census of Population: Volume I, Characteristics of the Population; Part I: U.S. Summary* (Washington, D.C.: GPO, 1961), 144; U.S. Bureau of the Census, *1970 Census of Population: Volume I, Characteristics of the Population; Part I: U.S. Summary* (Washington, D.C.: GPO, 1973), 262; U.S. Bureau of the Census, *1980 Census of Population: Volume I, Characteristics of the Population; Chapter C: General Social and Economic Characteristics; Part I: U.S. Summary* (Washington, D.C.: GPO, 1982), 12.

◆ ◆ ◆

American Indian life in postwar cities should be understood in the context of the general urbanization of American society. The number of American Indians and Alaska Natives residing in U.S. cities rose from 16 percent to 53 percent of their total population between 1950 and 1980. Meanwhile, every other major ethnic group (as defined under the category of race by the U.S. census) continued to urbanize. Urban dwellers constituted 74 percent of the U.S. population by 1980, up from 64 percent in 1950. American Indians continued to lag behind other groups in both the number and percentage of their population in urban areas. The rapid pace or urbanization was more dramatic for American Indians than for any other group during this period, however, and the 1980 census recorded a majority of American Indians in cities for the first time (see Table 1). Los Angeles also continued to far outpace other cities with regard to American Indian populations, and during this period the city came to be known as the urban Indian capital of the United States. Los Angeles had the second highest geographic concentration of American Indians after the Navajo Reservation, and it easily surpassed the next largest Native population in an urban region with a census count that approached 60,000 in 1980 (see Table 2).

Migrants to urban centers included those Indians who came to the city on the federal relocation program and Native Americans who chose

TABLE 2 American Indian and Alaska Native Population of Select U.S. Urbanized Areas, 1960–1980

Urbanized Area	1960	1970	1980
Los Angeles–Long Beach	8,839	27,958	60,893
San Francisco–Oakland	3,469	11,582	16,959
Seattle	3,817	7,753	13,868
New York–Northeast New Jersey	4,654	14,669	19,745
Chicago–Northwest Indiana	4,048	8,672	9,216
Minneapolis–St. Paul	3,085	9,578	14,895
Denver	1,365	1,984	7,864
Oklahoma City	3,046	10,871	17,035
Albuquerque	3,416	3,712	8,436

Source: U.S. Bureau of the Census, *1960 Census of Population: Volume I, Characteristics of the Population; Part 6: California* (Washington, D.C.: GPO, 1961), 128; U.S. Bureau of the Census, *1960 Census of Population: Volume I, Characteristics of the Population; Part 7: Colorado* (Washington, D.C.: GPO, 1961), 39; U.S. Bureau of the Census, *1960 Census of Population: Volume I, Characteristics of the Population; Part 15: Illinois* (Washington, D.C.: GPO, 1961), 104; U.S. Bureau of the Census, *1960 Census of Population: Volume I, Characteristics of the Population; Part 25: Minnesota* (Washington, D.C.: GPO, 1961), 66; U.S. Bureau of the Census, *1960 Census of Population: Volume I, Characteristics of the Population; Part 33: New Mexico* (Washington, D.C.: GPO, 1961), 31; U.S. Bureau of the Census, *1960 Census of Population: Volume I, Characteristics of the Population; Part 34: New York* (Washington, D.C.: GPO, 1961), 101; U.S. Bureau of the Census, *1960 Census of Population: Volume I, Characteristics of the Population; Part 38: Oklahoma* (Washington, D.C.: GPO, 1961), 49; U.S. Bureau of the Census, *1960 Census of Population: Volume I, Characteristics of the Population; Part 49: Washington* (Washington, D.C.: GPO, 1961), 44; U.S. Bureau of the Census, *1970 Census of the Population: Volume 1, Characteristics of the Population; Part 6: California* (Washington, D.C.: GPO, 1973), 103; U.S. Bureau of the Census, *1970 Census of the Population: Volume 1, Characteristics of the Population; Part 7: Colorado* (Washington, D.C.: GPO, 1973), 55; U.S. Bureau of the Census, *1970 Census of the Population: Volume 1, Characteristics of the Population; Part 15: Illinois* (Washington, D.C.: GPO, 1973), 105; U.S. Bureau of the Census, *1970 Census of the Population: Volume 1, Characteristics of the Population; Part 25: Minnesota* (Washington, D.C.: GPO, 1973), 81; U.S. Bureau of the Census, *1970 Census of the Population: Volume 1, Characteristics of the Population; Part 33: New Mexico* (Washington, D.C.: GPO, 1973), 46; U.S. Bureau of the Census, *1970 Census of the Population: Volume 1, Characteristics of the Population; Part 34: New York* (Washington, D.C.: GPO, 1973), 88; U.S. Bureau of the Census, *1970 Census of the Population: Volume 1, Characteristics of the Population; Part 38: Oklahoma* (Washington, D.C.: GPO, 1973), 61; U.S. Bureau of the Census, *1970 Census of the Population: Volume 1, Characteristics of the Population; Part 49: Washington* (Washington, D.C.: GPO, 1973), 61; U.S. Bureau of the Census, *1980 Census of Population: Volume I, Characteristics of the Population; Chapter B: General Population Characteristics; Part 6: California* (Washington, D.C.: GPO, 1983), 172, 177; U.S. Bureau of the Census, *1980 Census of Population: Volume I, Characteristics of the Population; Chapter B: General Population Characteristics; Part 7: Colorado* (Washington, D.C.: GPO, 1983), 50; U.S. Bureau of the Census, *1980 Census of Population: Volume I, Characteristics of the Population; Chapter B: General Population Characteristics; Part 15: Illinois* (Washington, D.C.: GPO, 1983), 122; U.S. Bureau of the Census, *1980 Census of Population: Volume I, Characteristics of the Population; Chapter B: General Population Characteristics; Part 25: Minneapolis* (Washington, D.C.: GPO, 1983), 71; U.S. Bureau of the Census, *1980 Census of Population: Volume I, Characteristics of the Population; Chapter B: General Population Characteristics; Part 33: Albuquerque* (Washington, D.C.: GPO, 1983), 36; U.S. Bureau of the Census, *1980 Census of Population: Volume I, Characteristics of the Population; Chapter B: General Population Characteristics; Part 34: New York* (Washington, D.C.: GPO, 1983), 159; U.S. Bureau of the Census, *1980 Census of Population: Volume I, Characteristics of the Population; Chapter B: General Population Characteristics; Part 38: Oklahoma* (Washington, D.C.: GPO, 1983), 56; U.S. Bureau of the Census, *1980 Census of Population: Volume I, Characteristics of the Population; Chapter B: General Population Characteristics; Part 49: Washington* (Washington, D.C.: GPO, 1983), 55.

to come to the city on their own for a myriad of reasons. The experience of World War II had a profound effect in orienting Indian people to the larger world, whether they had served in the military, worked in the wartime economy, or followed the war on the radio at home. The reservation seemed a much smaller and more limiting place after the war for those who had traveled, earned wartime wages, and gained confidence in their abilities to negotiate non-Indian society. Hannah Fixico grew up on the Rosebud Reservation in South Dakota, joined the WAVES after high school, received training at Hunter College in New York City, and served in Hawaii. Fixico worked for several years as a typist for the tribal agency after returning to the reservation, and she made frequent trips to Chicago and Denver to visit friends from the service. She decided to quit her job in 1954 and move to Los Angeles, explaining that "things weren't right to her" on the reservation anymore. "After what I'd been through [in the service]," she went on, "I knew I could make it [in the city]." The Korean and Vietnam wars intensified these migrations. Indian veterans took advantage of the GI Bill to attend urban colleges and universities, and by the late 1960s they were joined by Indians who responded to minority recruitment efforts and the rise of ethnic studies programs. Government termination policies that eliminated federal recognition and trust status also played a role in the decision to migrate to cities for tribes such as the Menominee and the Klamath or California Indians living on *rancherias*. A second and even third generation of urban Indians became a sizable presence in American cities by the 1960s and 1970s, as the children of urban migrants grew up and came of age in the city.[6]

The desires for new experiences, economic security, and expanded opportunities were the main factors that drove Indian migration in the postwar years against the backdrop of these larger social trends. This phenomenon is illustrated by several examples. Andrew Begay, a Navajo Indian who served three years in the air force during World War II and was stationed in the South Pacific, moved to Los Angeles in the 1950s to settle with his wife and five children in Bell Gardens. Begay explained, "I wanted my children to have a better opportunity for education than I did."[7] Richard and Bessie Becenti, another Navajo family, migrated to Los Angeles at about the same time with their three children. Both did farm work and found temporary jobs at an army supply depot back in New Mexico. They decided to leave for the city so that Richard could learn a trade.[8] Amy Skenandore, a Stockbridge Mohican Indian, grew up in Wisconsin but left in 1951 with her husband, because there "was no work up on the reservation." They spent three years in St. Agnus, Mich., where her husband worked on the Mackinaw Bridge and then moved on to Chicago to find steady employment.[9] Marlene Strouse's father similarly left the Tohono O'Odham Reservation in Arizona for Chicago in 1952, because he wanted to find "a better job . . . so he could take care of his family." Her father had been spending half the year away from home following the wheat harvest through the Midwestern states and still "could not support his family . . . very well on what he made." Strouse's father felt confident enough about his employment opportunities to send for her, her three siblings, and her mother after three months in Chicago.[10] Bob Smith, an Oneida from Wisconsin, first came to Southern California in 1959 when he was in the air force. He stayed in the city after his discharge and got a job in aerospace but was soon laid off. Smith returned to his reservation near Green Bay but became frustrated trying to find work. "There seemed to be a lot of prejudice against the Indians in Green Bay," Smith explained. "I couldn't even find menial work." Smith's wife also had trouble adjusting as a non-Indian. "It's very primitive on our reservation," Smith went on. "Of 300 families, only about 5 percent have hot, running water in their homes." The Smiths returned to Los Angeles and settled in Gardena.[11] Fern Charley was born in 1951, one of eleven children in a Navajo family. While growing up, she often had to skip school to work in the fields or to take care of her younger siblings. The family moved regularly between a large farm outside Phoenix, Ariz., where they lived in housing with no plumbing, and Shiprock, N.Mex., where her father sometimes found part-time jobs in construction. Charley left home for the Sherman Institute at age fourteen, and after graduation in 1968 she enrolled at California State University, Fullerton. Charley's father wanted her to return home, but she was determined to stay and finish her degree so that she could obtain a good job. She was joined by her sister Priscilla, who enrolled at Orange Coast College in 1970 in a special program that enabled her to earn a high school diploma.[12]

Unskilled and semi-skilled jobs in the industrial sector constituted the type of work most readily available to Indian migrants, especially in the 1950s and 1960s. The Sherman Institute (the BIA boarding school in Riverside, just outside Los Angeles) reported that, during the winter of 1954, thirty-six members of its most recent graduating class were working in Greater Los Angeles, and all had taken either industrial or domestic service jobs.[13] The BIA estimated a year later that 500 companies in Los Angeles were employing 6,500 Indians as unskilled laborers.[14] Examples are Edmund and Jeanette White, a Navajo couple who graduated from Sherman in 1954 and moved into an apartment in Los Angeles. Edmund worked on the assembly line at the Chrysler automobile plant, and Jeanette was a sewing machine operator at Blumenthal Manufacturing Company. Other occupations held by Sherman graduates and likely common to other Indian migrants to the city during this period included engine installer, laborer, mill helper, mechanic, painter, saw operator, baker's helper, assembly line worker, and hospital attendant.[15]

One Los Angeles firm seized upon the migration of Indians to the city as a particular opportunity to secure an unskilled industrial workforce. North American Aviation, Inc. (NAA) employed 120 Indians for its factory in Downey, Calif., by 1952. Indians at NAA were almost all doing unskilled work, and just a few had semi-skilled jobs. The number of Indian employees rose to approximately 500 by 1955, and the head of employment at NAA noted that "we look on Indians as a great untapped source of workers in a tight labor market."[16] One of these employees was Dale Beck, a twenty-seven-year-old Kiowa Indian, who lived in Redondo Beach, Calif., with his wife and two children and worked at NAA as an aircraft assembler. Beck had inherited an allotment of 320 acres of land back in Oklahoma, but his family preferred to stay in Los Angeles, where they hoped to be able to buy a home.[17]

Temporary labor services were another option for Indians with limited job skills moving to cities in the postwar period. Ed Goodvoice, a Sioux Indian from the Rosebud Reservation, moved to Chicago in 1957 after some time with the military. The federal relocation office helped Goodvoice find a job at the Continental Can Company, but he was laid off a few weeks later at the end of the Christmas rush. He was referred to the Readymen Labor Service, which employed dozens of Native Americans. Goodvoice and other Indians worked in and around Chicago through Readymen as lumber handlers, teamsters, and gandy dancers (railroad repair workers). Temporary labor contractors provided jobs on demand that required little training and no commitment beyond a day's work. They also paid immediate wages that could support a life at the lower end of the city's economy.[18]

Indians embraced the chance to take these types of unskilled and semi-skilled jobs, especially because they paid so much better than the work they had access to back on and around the reservation. Indian workers nonetheless faced challenges that were both common to industrial work in the postwar era and particular to Indians and other workers of color. The country's industrial economy was on a downturn by the late 1950s and early 1960s. This downturn was the beginning of a larger economic shift that would become known as deindustrialization. George Felshaw, the head of the BIA's Los Angeles Field Relocation Office, was unusually frank in his bleak assessment of work opportunities during an address to the Sherman Institute in 1960. Felshaw noted that California's unemployment rates were the highest since before World War II, and he went on to state: "There are no bright spots in the employment field. The outlook for the next six months is dark. This year's graduating class will not have an easy time finding jobs. They will have to take the first job offered and be good, dependable workers to hold them. They must remember that they can be replaced by other men wanting jobs."[19] Indian workers were heavily burdened by their dependence on unskilled and semi-skilled labor in this declining industrial economy. Indian people were among those who were the last hired and the first fired—which subjected them to long periods of unemployment or forced them into the lower-paying service sector of the economy.[20] Sam Pinto (Navajo) moved to Los Angeles in 1963 and found a job delivering furniture for a Santa Ana company. He earned so little that he decided to take a second position at a fast-food restaurant. Pinto's hard work eventually earned him a promotion to night manager, but he quit after twice being robbed for the store's receipts. Pinto found another job as a window cleaner in 1965.[21]

Dennis Tafoya (Santa Clara Pueblo) remembered how the fluctuations of the postwar economy and the ways that racism was institutionalized in the industrial workplace affected his father, Joe Tafoya: "[My father] had experience working on aircraft during the war. Of course, [in 1955], the aerospace industry was expanding here in Los Angeles, so he thought being an aircraft mechanic and understanding aircraft, he would have an opportunity here. Well that wasn't really the case, at the time the unions had closed shops and he couldn't get in the union, because he was a minority . . . so he was basically pretty much shut out of working in the aerospace industry for a couple more years before he was able to break in and get a job at AiResearch Company." Joe Tafoya continued to face discriminatory practices in the workplace for the next ten years. Dennis recalled: "Every time there was a layoff, because of an economic downswing, he was the first to get laid off . . . and that's just the way it was . . . my dad was probably laid off three or four times, as recently as 1968."[22] Noel Campbell, an Indian from Idaho, testified before the federally appointed National Council on Indian Opportunity (NCIO) during hearings held in Los Angeles in 1969: "I don't think that our problem here is one of being turned away because you are Indian. I believe it is one of under-employment rather than unemployment. You are usually put into a job that is probably below what you are trained to do. For instance, myself. . . . I was lucky enough to go through an engineering course. I went through calculus and physics and the whole bit. After I graduated, the job I was placed on as an expediter, which is, as you know, a shipping clerk actually."[23] Other major sectors of the Los Angeles postwar economy, such as the petroleum industry, were known to resist the hiring of Indians and people of color altogether.[24]

These types of racial discrimination in the workplace mark American Indian experience as similar to that of other workers of color in America's postwar economy. Native people had a unique experience with racism in other ways. Many working- and middle-class Indian migrants found that they experienced *less* discrimination in postwar American cities than back on and around their reservations. This was one factor that attracted them to cities in the first place. Phyllis Fastwolf, an Oglala Sioux Indian, moved from South Dakota to Chicago in 1955 after becoming fed up with the prejudice that her children experienced in the public school system.[25] Hannah Fixico (Sioux) similarly remembered going to Rapid City, S.D., and seeing signs proclaiming "No Indians or Dogs Allowed" and experiencing racial prejudice, even when she was dressed in a military uniform. Life in Los Angeles was relatively free of discrimination for her, in comparison.[26] As a child in Oklahoma, Lena Haberman (Kiowa-Sioux-Creek) used to run home crying from school when her classmates used racial epithets. She did not experience any discrimination once she moved to Los Angeles and found that most people were interested in her Indian heritage.[27] Cornelia Penn (Sioux) remembered that she "was used to" discrimination in Omaha, Nebr., near the Winnebago Reservation, saying that "in Omaha they're really prejudiced." She did not "think [she] ran into very much of that" after moving to Chicago, however.[28] Mrs. Calvin Brown felt that there was less discrimination in the city than on the Pomo Reservation in California. She noted, "Here you are just as good as the next person and that makes you feel good."[29] M. M., a Winnebago Indian, pointed out that in his neighborhood in the 1960s there simply were not enough Indians around for racial prejudice to rear its head:

> It was like the neighborhood kids, they knew my uncle was Indian, because he was very obviously Indian, but that really never seemed to be an issue. And when I went to school I don't think it ever became an issue really. It was back in Iowa and Nebraska, but once we got out here, no, it wasn't. . . . [I]n Glendale white people didn't re-

ally see Indians as part of the equation. I remember when one of my classmates saw my mother and me and he said, "what is she, is she Italian or something?" And I just said, "no," and I sort of ignored the question, but it was like it wasn't even part of the consciousness that there would be any Indians around.[30]

Carole Bowen (Wintu) similarly thought that being Indian was never a problem for her children, because there were few Indians in the Los Angeles public schools they attended while growing up. She added that her sons "were very big football players," and that could have minimized any problem.[31]

Racial discrimination, however, was clearly a factor in the industrial workplace. For other Indians racism was in fact a daily reality of postwar urban life. Indians who frequented skid-row areas often found themselves targeted by city police departments that harbored stereotypes about Indians and drunkenness. Fred Gabourie, a Seneca Indian and a defense attorney in Los Angeles, testified to the NCIO in 1969 that "police officers, if they see an Indian [downtown] they might figure he is drunk and just haul him in."[32] Edward Olivas, a Chumash Indian living in Los Angeles, elaborated in an interview conducted in 1972: "Well, I've had these experiences with policemen. They'll kick you in the ass when you're down in the gutter, pick you up to take you to jail, and if you utter the least resistance, they'll beat you up."[33] H. Brown, a Winnebago Indian, remembered being arrested repeatedly in the 1950s and 1960s around downtown Los Angeles and charged with being drunk: "I'd be walking down the street, here come detectives. 'Come on. You know, you didn't do nothing, but we got to take you with us, I got to fill my quota. We got to make so many arrests this week.' And they would take me to jail. And it used to be like that downtown. They had to have so many arrests . . . it didn't matter if you were sober or not." Brown also recalled that these arrests often led to jail time: "The most you would get was 90 days. They would give you 10, 15, 20 [days]. But if the [judge] seen you twice, in a couple of months, he'd give you 90 days or 60 days. They'd send you out to [a county work farm to serve your sentence]."[34] The rise of the Red Power movement in the early 1970s and high-profile events such as the occupation of Wounded Knee also had a backlash for Indian residents in their dealing with police. The Los Angeles Indian Center listed dozens of complaints of police harassment in 1973. One individual reported that he was stopped by police officers and searched after he had witnessed a fight. The officers found an American Indian Movement membership card in his pocket and responded, "Oh, you're one of the bad guys," then beat him up, threw him in the police car, and charged him with being drunk.[35] These kinds of police and Indian interactions continued, but some efforts to address them began. In 1975 police officers arrested several Indians who were sitting on couches in front of a house run by a Los Angeles alcohol treatment center after supposedly identifying them as suspects in a robbery. Officers also "unduly harassed and threatened" the center's staff. A complaint based on the incident was sent to the mayor's Los Angeles Human Relations Commission and led Mayor Tom Bradley to request an investigation by the police commission.[36]

Alcohol abuse also was a very real problem among American Indians living in postwar cities. Alcoholism has at times come to be understood as synonymous with urban Indian life and personified by homeless or struggling Indian individuals frequenting the streets, Indian bars, single-resident-occupancy hotels, and apartment houses in the seamiest and most run-down areas of America's cities. These interpretations were advanced by some anthropologists in the 1960s and 1970s and should be tempered with a better understanding of urban American Indian populations and the wide range of experiences Indians have had in the city.[37] Scholars also have often overlooked the communities that developed around Indian bars and other areas where Indians gathered to drink. A handful of accounts from Indian people portray an alternative to a life of work and mainstream respectability that could offer companionship, fun, and the opportunities to build important social networks, even if these qualities ultimately were fleeting or came with consequences. H. Brown remembered going to Indian bars and drinking on the streets of downtown Los Angeles in the 1950s: "All I did was hang around Skid Row downtown. But there was a group of Indians down there too. So we'd just, you know, drink all day. . . . We'd just, you know, hang around out here because it was so nice and warm in the wintertime. . . . There used to be a bar down on Main Street called The Ritz. Everybody hung out there. There was The Columbine. Everybody hung out there. There were two [Indian] bars." Brown also fondly recalled that "you could sleep outside and nobody would, you know, come up and rob you or beat you up or anything. You could just lay there and nobody would bother you, it was nice."[38] Bernie Whitebear (Sin-Aikst) moved in the late 1950s to Tacoma, Wash., where he came to earn a living by driftnet fishing in the Puyallup River with Indians from the region. He and his friends called themselves the "Skins" and likened their group to fraternal organizations such as the Elks, Moose, and Shriners. The three Indian taverns located between 13th and 14th streets served as their "lodges." Whitebear and his friends also looked out for one another in a city that harbored a great deal of discrimination against Indian people.[39] Historian Edmund Danziger has described the social network in a downtown Detroit neighborhood around the corner of Michigan and Third avenues. Indian newcomers arrived in the postwar years, and "taxi drivers and bus station attendants invariably directed them" to this part of the city where Indians congregated in "the bars, on street corners, in second-floor apartments above the shops—just to socialize or to get useful leads on jobs and housing."[40]

Ed Goodvoice has similarly offered a remarkably positive narrative recounting his seventeen years on the streets of Chicago, beginning with his move to the city from the Rosebud Reservation in 1957 at the age of 27. He came to depend on work that he got through temporary labor services to support his life on skid row. Goodvoice and other Indians would head to bars like the Barrel House on North Avenue and Halstead Street after a day's work to cash their checks. They would move on to another bar or buy jugs of wine to take out on the streets or to a flophouse. One Indian bar called the Jack Pot was "known as a place where you could get hustled, jack-rolled, beaten, and thrown bodily out in the street. However, the Jack Pot also had its good points." The Jack Pot was safe and comfortable for regular customers. The management allowed many Indian customers to buy jugs of wine and hang around until closing time. It provided free hot dogs and ham sandwiches most nights and a complete dinner on Sunday. Raffle tickets also were issued for each drink purchased. Twice a night drawings were held for a $4 prize, and at 2 A.M. a winner was chosen for a take-home half-pint. The Indian railroad workers had their own drinking place that was a flophouse where they put jugs on the floor and told tales of their work. Anyone could come in and take one drink from each jug. Other Indians worked less regularly but took part in the life on the streets by frequenting the missions, soup lines, Catholic charities, Salvation Army, and other social service organizations around skid row; "putting the hammer to" (panhandling) non-Indians; and hustling the customers at places like Vogt's Liquor store. Goodvoice noted that Indians living on skid row in Chicago were close and helped each other by cooperating to find and share food, alcohol, and shelter. He stated, "After the many years of living and interacting with Native Americans on Skid Row, I have found that most were comfortable with the environment and lifestyle. Prices on Skid Row were within the reach of a Readymen paycheck. Despite what seemed to be a life of hardship, the tragic deaths of drinking companions, 'carrying the stick' (staying on the street all night) and standing in souplines, Skid Row was a sort of home to many Indians".[41]

Another depiction of Indian community on the streets and in the bars of American postwar cities can be found in a low-budget "semidocumentary" made in 1961 titled *The Exiles*. The film starred amateur Indian actors and followed a group of young Indian women and men for a night as they went carousing around downtown Los Angeles. The characters were not the down-and-out stereotypes portrayed in anthropological literature. Instead they embodied the rebellious characters featured in movies of the period, such as *The Wild One* (1953) and *Rebel Without a Cause* (1955). One of the main characters was an Indian from Arizona named Homer, who claimed that he came to Los Angeles for the same reasons that a lot of other Indians did: to "drink and raise hell." His friend Tommy, "just like[d] to have kicks, to drink, to get high, and to have fun" and pitied "those who work everyday, regular routines." The characters spent the evening going to bars, dancing to rock and roll, trying to pick up members of the opposite sex, riding around in fast cars, and getting into fights. They eventually made their way a half-mile from downtown to Hill X, where they met other young Indians who had gathered to beat drums, sing tribal songs, drink, pair off, and otherwise have a good time, with the lit buildings of downtown in the background. Homer explained that "Indians like to get together and turn loose, be free" and to go where "nobody will watch your every move you make." Of Hill X, he said: "It's pretty good, you know. It's cool up there, you sing your own tribal songs, you know, anything you want to do, you know, kind of reminds me of home, too, you know. You wonder how's everybody back home you haven't seen for a long time, especially [when] a guy from your home, you know, comes around there, you know, and then you sit there and talk about old times, man, it's good." Homer, Tommy, and two Indian women drove back to Bunker Hill, where they lived in an apartment, after waking up on the hill the next morning. Stumbling down an alley together, clowning around and laughing, Tommy declared, "Tonight we'll start all over, I've got a couple of dollars left."[42] Martin Seneca, an Indian and a graduate student in sociology at California State University, Los Angeles, described a similar social scene a decade and a half later: "We go [to the Irish Pup, an Indian bar on Pico Boulevard] to dance to a bit of rock on holidays and every Friday and Saturday night. After it closes at 2, we head for Johnny's Shrimp Boat on Main between 3rd and 4th. It's open all night. And I've seen 50 carloads of us drive up to the Shrimp Boat parking lot. Everybody has a six-pack. . . . Somebody will take out a drum and begin to play it. Or maybe somebody will begin to tap like a drum on a car—anything to get a beat going. And we'll sing and dance and drink all night until dawn, by ourselves."[43] The Indian bars, streets, and other places where Indians gathered to drink and socialize were important to Indian people and created a kind of Indian community that both drew on and distanced itself from the conventions of urban life.

Alcohol also was a very real problem, with destructive consequences for Indian people living in postwar American cities. Bernie Whitebear emphasized the support network that was nurtured in the Indian bars of Tacoma, Wash., but he also recognized that Indian drinking stemmed from the anger and frustration he and his friends felt over the difficult job of finding steady work in an economy going through deindustrialization, the prejudice from white urban residents, and the lack of recognition by the government.[44] The places where Indians gathered to drink also could become scenes of violence that included personal injuries and sexual assaults. Homer in *The Exiles* got into a bar fight simply because he was drunk and looking for something to do. Another fight ensued on Hill X after Tommy struck a young Indian woman who rejected his sexual advances. M. M. remembered that when he was growing up in Glendale, Calif., during the 1960s his grandmother discouraged associating with other Indians in the city: "[In her experience when Indians got together] there was violence, there'd be the fights or the drunkenness. . . . So there were certain people that she would write to or associate with, but . . . she didn't see most Indians as somebody she wanted either me or her daughter or other people to associate with. I can remember there was a lot of drunkenness and there was a lot of violence."[45] Indians began meeting and sleeping at "The Tombs," an underpass at the conjunction of Interstate 5 and Interstate 110, after the construction of Dodger Stadium razed Hill X in the 1970s. This area too gained a reputation as one marked by alcohol, drugs, and violence.[46]

Drinking among Indians in postwar cities also led to problems with the law. Attorney Fred Gabourie handled hundreds of cases for Indian clients in Los Angeles during the 1960s and 1970s that involved murder, rape, car theft, and burglary, among other crimes. Gabourie estimated that alcohol was involved 75 to 80 percent of the time, or 95 percent of the time when the charge was a violent crime. The most common violation Gabourie saw was "drunk and disorderly." Some of his Indian clients were arrested up to forty times on "drunk" charges over the course of a year. One particular Indian client racked up sixty-five "drunk" arrests.[47] The alcohol program coordinator for Los Angeles County reported in 1970 that approximately 200

American Indians arrived in county court per month on "drunk" charges.[48] Ed Goodvoice also noted that trouble with the law was not unusual for Indians living on the streets of Chicago and that "Over time, many of us have lost count of the number of times we have been arrested for being intoxicated." Being arrested for public drunkenness in Chicago often meant being beaten by police wielding nightclubs, riding to jail in a paddy wagon, and trying to find a place to sleep on a cold, crowded, vomit-covered jail cell floor.[49]

Individual stories are especially poignant and illustrate how urban poverty could be a vicious cycle in which alcohol use intensified when combined with other urban stressors, making it extremely difficult to break free. Edward Olivas (Chumash) drank steadily through the 1940s and 1950s, beginning at the age of sixteen while living in Los Angeles. He later said, "I drank and it did something to me. I liked it. . . . I always used alcohol to face life, to face hard times, to face discrimination, to face stern judges, and bosses, and all these hardships of life. I always had to have alcohol. It just became a part of me. When I moved away from the reservation, we came to the city, and my parents drank and the people we associated with drank, and I naturally drank right along with them whenever I could."[50] A Los Angeles newspaper reported in 1971 on the tragic story of a twenty-two-year-old Navajo Indian from Arizona named Joe. Joe was discharged from the marines for being an alcoholic after serving a thirteen-month tour in Vietnam. Joe moved to Los Angeles but could not find work. He explained that he "went to a lot of places and they asked me what kind of experience I had in the service. I found out that there just aren't too many jobs for mortar crewman in the Los Angeles area." Joe pawned his turquoise belt buckle, boots, jacket, and watch to get money for drinking. He spent most of his time wandering from bar to bar and slept periodically under the 110 freeway. Joe did visit the BIA office in Los Angeles seeking help, but he was told that he would have to return to his reservation before the BIA could do anything for him.[51]

All in all, the challenges of securing good-paying and steady jobs, various forms of racial discrimination, the lure of escapism through alcohol, and the rapid transition from reservations to cities were all factors for many American Indians that contributed to a slide into poverty after moving to the postwar, postindustrial American city. Only when the issue began to get some public attention in the late 1960s and 1970s did a handful of studies emerge to document and quantify these trends.[52] Researchers working in Portland found that Indians experienced high rates of unemployment;

suffered disproportionately from malnutrition, mental disorders, drug addiction, alcoholism, and tuberculosis; and became regular targets of police harassment.[53] A 1970 study by the Los Angeles County Health Department revealed that Indian people experienced infectious respiratory diseases at rates five times higher than any other ethnic group, while also suffering disproportionately from strep throat, dysentery, and infant mortality. Life expectancy for Indians in Los Angeles was just forty-five years.[54] A. David Lester, a Creek Indian and executive director of the Los Angeles-based Urban Indian Development Association, cited a list of the problems that Indians in Los Angeles faced a few years later: unemployment rates of approximately 25 percent, vast underemployment, low income, health care below the national standard, high birth rates, and some of the worst housing in the city.[55] The Greater Los Angeles Community Action Agency estimated in 1976 that 60 percent of Indians in Los Angeles qualified for some type of public assistance.[56]

Not all Indian migrants found the pressures of the postwar city quite so overwhelming. Industrial work in particular could serve as the foothold that Native people needed to eventually move into the ranks of the city's more prosperous working- and middle-class residents. This was especially true for Native migrants who were tenacious in trying to make their way through workplace hierarchies. Randy Edmonds (Kiowa-Caddo) came out to Los Angeles in 1954 from Oklahoma when he was just twenty years old. Edmonds began as a general helper at Northern Aircraft in Hawthorne. He mostly cleaned up around the plant and then moved up to the position of fabricator. Edmonds got another job with U.S. Gypsum Company after a layoff. He remembered: "I put in a lot of hours, working overtime, trying to learn the business, and within a couple of years, I was made assistant foreman, in the paint department. And then, oh, three years ago [in 1968], I was made general foreman. I had 49 employees, [including] three shift foremen that I was in charge of." Edmonds stayed at U.S. Gypsum for twelve years, before quitting to work with relocation participants as the project manager for the Urban Indian Development Association.[57] Art and Betty Ketcheshawno also migrated from Oklahoma to Los Angeles in the mid-1950s. Art worked for twelve years in paper mills and furniture factories. He then began taking classes at a technical school and got a job working with computers at North American Rockwell. Betty worked for another aerospace company, and the couple had two sons born in Los Angeles. The family lived on a quiet street in Bell Gardens and was active in local sports leagues and Los Angeles area Indian organizations.[58] Peggy Berryhill remembered her family moving to Oakland in 1952 when she was just eight years old to live in the Alameda High Street Housing Project among several other families of Oklahoma Indians. Berryhill's memories were of a comfortable and happy life. Her father worked at the Crown Zellerbach Paper Company in San Leandro, Calif., and her mother worked at a nearby dry cleaners. Their weekends were spent visiting family around the San Francisco Bay area.[59] Aletha and Bernard White began building a life together in Portland, Ore., when they got engaged during World War II. Aletha's position as a secretary and Bernard's work as a welder supported their family of three children and allowed them to purchase two cars and a home.[60] Phyllis Fastwolf's husband found steady work immediately on moving to Chicago in 1955, because he had learned to be a boilermaker back on the Pine Ridge Reservation. Fastwolf had a Bachelor of Science degree from Black Hills State College in South Dakota, and that helped her get a job and work her way up to senior bill adjuster at Carson Pirie Scott (a Midwestern department store chain). The couple soon bought a home on the South Side, then later sold it to buy into a higher-priced neighborhood. They sent all seven of their children to college, to places such as the University of Wisconsin at Green Bay, the Art Institute of New Mexico, and the University of New Mexico. Fastwolf believed that they were part of a segment of the Indian population for whom the move to the city was a positive experience, stating: "Right here in Chicago, I could tell you [about] a lot of [Indian] people who own their own homes, kept their jobs and retired."[61]

Some Indian migrants took advantage of the continuing fascination that non-Indians had with Indian culture to support their lives in the postwar city. They found that performing Indianness enabled them to earn a living, much like the Indian actors who worked in Hollywood before World War II. John Knifechief, whose story began the Introduction, worked for several years at Disneyland in Anaheim, Calif., during the 1960s. He started at the park as a ride operator, paddled "Indian" canoes for visitors to the "Frontierland" section of the park, and then began singing and dancing for the park's Indian Village. The dancers were paid $35 a day and were relatively well treated as park employees. This was in large part because the Indian Village was a pet project of the park's founder, Walt Disney. John was joined at the Indian Village by his fifteen-year-old son Tom in 1963. Tom was fond of his experience at the Indian Village, because he felt that it gave him an opportunity to show non-Indians, tourists, and movie stars what "Indians are really like." The dancers at the Indian Village wore well-made, authentic Indian dress and did "real Indian dances," according to Tom.[62]

Joseph F. Tafoya Jr. at work on aircraft parts, AiResearch Manufacturing Co., Torrance, Calif., 1958. Courtesy of Dennis Tafoya.

Perhaps no single family took advantage of the opportunities for Indian dancing more than the Tafoyas. The family's work as entertainers helped them to achieve a higher standard of living and provided an economic safety net in the midst of a deindustrializing economy. Joseph Filario Tafoya was born at Santa Clara Pueblo in New Mexico in 1891. He began traveling to Manitou Springs, Colo., where along with other Pueblos he spent the summers dancing to entertain tourists in the years following World War I. Tafoya's son Joe followed suit as he grew up. Dennis, who was born in 1950, became part of the third generation in his family to work as an Indian dancer. He joined his grandfather, father, and older brothers to tour the western United States and perform at primary and secondary schools under the auspices of the National School Assemblies. Joe heard about the opportunities at Disneyland soon after moving to Los Angeles in 1955. Eventually the whole family worked there, as Dennis recalled:

> My dad in '56 or '57, looking for other ways of making money, he
> ventured out to Disneyland and got a job in the Indian Village, right
> around the time it opened. It opened in '55, so, about '56 or early
> '57, my dad gets a job there. It's one place, if you can Indian dance,

if you're any good, and if you can do a variety of different types of dances—you have to be very versatile, it's not just doing just one kind of fancy dance, you have to be knowledgeable about a variety of different types of dances—you'll probably get a job there. It was a way of making money on the weekends, during the summer, and holidays. So that became one of our legacies as a family, we were one of the first families to dance at the Indian Village in Disneyland. So my dad started there in '57. We had a lot of friends over the years that worked with us. My older brother started there in probably '58, my next older brother went there in the early sixties, I began dancing out there in '65. I worked out there dancing on weekends from 1965 to 1970, until they closed it down.

The Tafoyas also danced for civic groups, events, and private parties: "We danced for Boy Scouts, Cub Scouts, Indian Guides, birthday parties, Bozo the Clown on TV. We were in parades, Miss Universe Parade, Rose Parade, always doing something. . . . [It became] a means for us to supplement our income, whether we were dancing at Disneyland, or getting shows, as I said we danced for Knights of Columbus, anybody, anybody that wanted a demonstration of American Indian dancing, we'd do it, if the money was good enough." The Tafoyas broke into television and were able to take their dancing overseas during the 1960s. The family appeared on *Stoney Burke* and *The Brady Bunch* and traveled with various Western shows to Spain, Sweden, New Zealand, Australia, Indonesia, and Japan. Dennis recalled how meaningful it was for him and his family members to be able to spend so much time immersed within a community of Indian dancers and entertainers. They shared and learned Indian culture with Indian people of many different tribes, while also serving as "cultural ambassadors" to non-Indians. Indian dancing was crucial to the family's economic stability:

[After getting laid off] my dad would say okay, he'd go out and find odd jobs, we'd try and ratchet up the Indian dancing a little more, thank goodness for Disneyland. In fact, my older brothers and myself, we danced at the Indian Village and we got paid, all that money went back into the family bank, that was our contribution to getting us through those hard times. I think that was true of most Indian families. When I made money Indian dancing, it didn't go into my pocket, it went into the family's pocket. There's no two ways about it, that's just one of the things we valued.

Indian dancing allowed the Tafoyas to live a comfortable, middle-class life in postwar Hermosa Beach, Calif., by supplementing Joe's work at AiResearch Company. Dennis remembered that his family's life was otherwise much like that of their non-Indian friends, neighbors, and classmates, even as they were active in the Los Angeles Indian community through dancing and other activities.[63]

Another route for Indians to a middle-class life in postwar and postindustrial urban America was a college education. Indians in this category tended to be veterans taking advantage of the GI Bill or those who migrated to the city at a younger age and attended public schools in the 1950s and 1960s. Peter MacDonald left home on the Navajo Reservation at age fifteen with just a sixth-grade education, and he joined the marines. MacDonald used the GI Bill and tribal and university scholarships to go to Bacone College in Oklahoma after his discharge, and he graduated with a degree in engineering in 1952. MacDonald became a senior engineer in electrical test equipment at Hughes Aircraft. By 1960 he lived in Inglewood, Calif., with his wife, a Comanche Indian, and their two children.[64] Alvin Deer came with his parents to Los Angeles from Anadarko, Okla., and graduated from high school in the city. Deer returned after a year at Brigham Young University and began working for California Savings and Loan in 1963. He earned a degree in financing five years later by going to night school and became a supervisor for the company.[65] Fred W. Gabourie, a Seneca Indian, was born in Los Angeles, where his father worked as a construction superintendent for MGM studios, but he grew up on the Six Nations Reserve in Canada. He returned to Los Angeles in 1947 after serving in the U.S. Army and found work as a stunt man and a professional race-car driver. He received his Bachelor of Science degree from Loyola University, took classes at the University of Southern California, and earned a law degree from Southwestern University School of Law in 1963. Gabourie was a partner for a successful law practice in Sherman Oaks, Calif. The firm served Indian tribes and Indian individuals in the city through the 1960s and the first half of the 1970s. He then became the first Indian to gain a California judgeship, when Governor Jerry Brown appointed him to the Los Angeles Municipal Court in 1976.[66]

By the 1970s Indians with college educations also were increasingly finding work with organizations and programs serving the city's Indian populations. Federal funds expanded the number, size, and scope of Indian service organizations in American cities under the Lyndon B. Johnson ad-

The Tafoya family in tribal regalia, ca. 1961. Pictured with parents Joseph Tafoya Jr. and Trudy Tafoya are (left to right): Linda, Robert, Michael, Leonard, and Dennis. Courtesy of Dennis Tafoya.

The Tafoya family having dinner at Clifton's Cafeteria in downtown Los Angeles, ca. 1956. Left to right: Joseph Sr., Petra, Trudy, Michael, Leonard, Dennis, and Joseph Jr. Grandparents Joseph Sr. and Petra had recently arrived in Los Angeles on a visit from New Mexico. Courtesy of Dennis Tafoya.

ministration's War on Poverty and the subsequent initiatives of the Richard M. Nixon administration.[67] Thousands of new positions were created for clerks, counselors, social service workers, managers, and other office workers and professionals. The vast majority of these jobs were filled by Indian people. Indian Centers, Inc. (more commonly referred to as the Los Angeles Indian Center, or simply, the Indian Center) received $356,327 in federal grants for the 1972–73 fiscal year. A total of $106,200 went to pay the salaries of its twelve administrators; $75,000 funded nine positions in employment, education, and community services; $41,160 paid the staff at its two satellite centers; $33,420 went for fringe benefits such as workers' compensation and health insurance; and the remainder paid for operating expenses, advertising, and welfare services. The Indian Center was hiring to fill several of these positions over the summer, including community service coordinator, public information assistant, education coordinator, transportation coordinator, secretaries, employment interviewer, community aides, client support specialist, and bookkeeper.[68] New initiatives to diversify city government also benefited Native people. Indians were hired to fill eighteen different jobs in Los Angeles city health care programs in 1974.[69]

Indian people often moved between jobs on reservations and in cities and gained a wide range of professional skills in the process. Jim Looking Glass's experiences are illustrative. Looking Glass (Apache-Comanche) was born in 1944 and grew up working on farms in Oklahoma. He joined the marines at age seventeen, and his travels around the world included a tour in Vietnam, where he was seriously wounded. Looking Glass later settled in Los Angeles and began working for McDonnell-Douglas. In the 1970s he met a recruiter from California State University, Long Beach, who encouraged him to enroll. Looking Glass took courses for two years in manpower services. He also spent the summers working for the Los Angeles–based Urban Indian Development Association and in the establishment of a health clinic for American Indians in Huntington Park, called the Indian Free Clinic. Looking Glass then returned to Oklahoma to help the Apache Housing Authority set up a housing program. He also worked as both a manpower counselor for the Kiowa Tribe and as a business development specialist with Oklahomans for Indian Opportunity. Looking Glass came back to Los Angeles again to take took the position of job developer at the Orange County Indian Center. He switched to the Los Angeles Indian Center in 1975 and became the manpower services coordinator.[70] Sandra Osawa, a Makah Indian from Washington State, is another example. Osawa grew up on the Makah Reservation in a family of eight as the daughter of a commercial fisherman. She worked with her tribe developing and directing its first Head Start program and Community Action Program after earning a B.A. degree in the mid-1960s. Osawa then began advising the Makah Housing Authority and working on a Housing and Urban Development program for low-rent housing. She moved to Los Angeles in 1972 to take a job with the Los Angeles Indian Center in the public information department and served as editor of the organization's newsletter, *Talking Leaf.*[71] John Spence grew up on the Blackfeet reservation in Montana. He attended the University of Washington and Rutgers University to earn a master's degree in social work. In 1969 Spence moved to Portland, Ore., where he spent several years working as the director of the Alcoholism Counseling and Recovery Program and as assistant professor and director of the Indian Education Program at Portland State University.[72] Yvonne Lamore-Choate, a Quechan Indian, moved to the San Francisco Bay area in 1969 and immediately got a job in the University of California, Berkeley, Native American Studies Office. She remembered, "It was like a dream; one day I'm in [business] school and the next I'm working at one of the most prestigious universities in the country, in one of the first Native American studies programs in the nation. . . . My years at the Native American studies office were very exciting and rewarding—I couldn't have dreamed up a more exciting job!" Lamore-Choate later worked at the American Indian Higher Education Consortium and the American Indian Education Program of the Oakland Public Schools.[73] Thousands of other Indians also took college classes and found work with Indian organizations in the 1970s, helping to create a generation of professional Indians attuned to the pragmatics of working for their communities in conjunction with local, state, and federal agencies.

Another indication of a growing Indian middle class in American cities was the increasing number of Indian-owned businesses, especially in the late 1960s and early 1970s. Seven Los Angeles-based Indian businessmen formed the Urban Indian Development Association (UIDA) in 1969 to help Indian entrepreneurs in the city. Established, fledging, or soon-to-be Indian businesspeople could drop by UIDA offices in West Los Angeles to browse through the resource files, consult with the staff of counselors, and attend a series of workshops titled "How to Succeed in Business by Really Trying." UIDA also attempted to build a community of Indian businessmen throughout the city. It produced a monthly newsletter that promoted UIDA activities and reported on Indian business, published a yearly Christmas shopping guide and directories of Indian businesses in Los Angeles, and annually honored an "Indian businessman" of the year. UIDA's *Indian Business Directory* listed fifty-eight Indian-owned businesses in the city in 1972. They employed more than 600 workers and achieved annual sales of $8.5 million by the following year.[74]

These Indian-owned businesses provided a wide range of goods and services. Indian arts and crafts were available from six different shops and several Indian individuals living in the city in 1972. Other Indian-owned stores specialized in antiques, automotive parts, books, electronics equipment, flowers, office machines, radios, televisions, and tools. Several Indian-owned manufacturing companies made auto accessories, boats, electronics, fiberglass parts, furniture, leather goods, plastics, and toys. Among the many Indian businesses providing various services were three accounting and tax service offices, two advertising and public relations firms, an appliance repair shop, an auto repair garage, two beauty salons, a catering company, two carpet services, a trucking company, two dry cleaners, two electronic equipment repair firms, a television repair shop, and two window washing services. Specific examples included College Florist, which was established in 1949 by Joe and Nunny Noonan. The shop featured flowers and Indian pottery, baskets, and paintings by Joe, who worked under the name Joe Waano Gano. Everett Houston began Houston's Barbecue in Carson, Calif., in 1968 and offered catering for parties, groups, and organizations. Kenneth Clifford founded Mile Hi Construction Maintenance in 1969 and by 1972 employed eight workers to provide construction maintenance and cleanup, grading, hauling, and window cleaning. Owen Enterprises, Inc., was established by Charles Owen in 1970. Its seventeen employees operated out of its plant in Wilmington, Calif., and manufactured aircraft and missile replacement parts out of reinforced plastic for the aerospace industry. Rick Romero ran RJ's Saloon, a bar in downtown Los Angeles that in 1968 began offering beer and wine, food, and pool tables. In 1970 Reynold Howe opened a barber shop he named Reynold's Scalpin' Teepee. Luckie Drapeaux founded Sioux Electronics in Lancaster that same year to specialize in the sale and repair of citizens band radio accessories and equipment. Len Fairchunk established the White Buffalo American Indian Workshop in Burbank to make educational toys. It counted among its major customers Montgomery Ward, Sears, and Toys-R-Us. One of the most established Indian-owned businesses in Los Angeles was Sloan's Drycleaners and Laundry. Sloan's grew to thirty-eight locations with more than 100 employees after opening its first store in 1935. It offered dry cleaning, laundry, drapery cleaning, and commercial and linen rental service.[75] Edna and Charles Ron Cooke opened multiple businesses in the Los Angeles area. Ron, who was born on the St. Regis Mohawk Indian Reservation, spent eight years working for a fire sprinkler system business in Syracuse, N.Y. Edna, who also was from St. Regis, attended cosmetology school and took business management courses. The couple opened three businesses in Glendora, Calif., between 1974 and 1979: Lazar's Beauty Shop, Eagle Fire Protection, and Jacques' Restaurant, which served French, Italian, and American cuisine, with Ron as the chef.[76]

The Cookes' lives in Glendora and those of their fellow Indian businesspeople seemed a world apart from the experiences of Joe, the Navajo from Arizona, and other homeless Indians who frequented city bars and streets. But if class differences are important markers that suggest the diversity of Indian experience, a significant portion of the Indian population in America's postwar, postindustrial cities nevertheless continued to draw on and strengthen the similarities that connected them. America's shifting economy, the increasing migrations of Native people to cities, and the development of urban American Indian communities gave rise to a broad reimagining of Indian country throughout the decades after World War II. Indians developed a presence in urban neighborhoods and on the streets, in factories and storefronts and office buildings. They struggled with many obstacles along the way. By doing so, they claimed the city as their own.

Indians also came together through the work of city-based Indian organizations. These groups were diverse and had varying goals that changed over time, depending on the needs and interests of their members. The next chapter will trace the development of urban Indian organizations and show how they connected Indian populations, ultimately fostering new ways of being Indian that furthered the reimagining of Indian Country.

CHAPTER 5

BEING INDIAN IN THE CITY

American Indian Urban Organizations

On a balmy autumn day in September 1964 the Los Angeles Indian Center sponsored the annual Indian Day festivities in Sycamore Grove Park, just north of downtown Los Angeles. The event honored the founder of the Indian Center and other former council members who, over the years, had passed away. A crowd numbering in the thousands turned out and was entertained by a number of Indian performances that included dancing by Joe Whitecloud Tafoya and his family, the knife and tomahawk throwing of Skeeter Vaughn and Little Fawn, and Western rock and roll music performed by Peter McDonald and Irish Pup. Indian Day reflected the vibrancy and enthusiasm of the ever-growing American Indian population of the Greater Los Angeles area. It had done so since the first celebration of Indian Day at Sycamore Grove in 1928.[1]

The annual Indian Day festivities are just one example of the enduring work undertaken by urban American Indian organizations throughout the twentieth century. American Indian migrants came together to address concerns relating to both national issues and life in the city in the decades before World War II. These clubs were some of the first American Indian–controlled organizations in the country. They provided Progressive Era reform-minded American Indians with ways to "be Indian" in places that were dominated by non-Indians and often far away from tribal lands and communities. Members also were able to maintain the "respectable" norms of American society learned during their years in federal boarding schools. Club members in this way became part of what historian Frederick E. Hoxie has described as a generation of Indians grappling for the first time with the meanings of "being Indian" in modern society and attempting to "define ways in which their communities and their traditions might be valued in a new setting."[2] Members of early-twentieth-century urban Indian organizations complicated notions of American progress and rejected demands to abandon Indian culture even as they sought acceptance by non-Indians, much as their contemporaries working on reservations did.

American Indian organizations in cities quickly grew in number after World War II to match the rapid increase in Indian urbanization. Native people built on prewar precedents and organized clubs and groups where they could socialize, plan group activities, address national issues of concern to Native people, and provide welfare services to poor Indians. These groups primarily were organized and patronized by working- and middle-class Indians living relatively comfortable lives. In their charitable efforts and some of their social activities they also drew in Indians who were struggling with life in the city. These organizations helped to foster new ways of being Indian in the city that combined tribal and intertribal identities with their specific experiences and the circumstances of urban life.[3] Together, both prewar and postwar urban Indian organizations worked to define a reimagined Indian Country.

❖ ❖ ❖

American Indians who traveled to cities from Indian reservations in the first half of the twentieth century often left harsh conditions that included crippling deficiencies in health, housing, education, and economic development (as discussed in Chapter 1). Federal Indian policy worked to steadily erode the tribal land base, develop natural resources for the benefit of non-Indians, and attack Indian cultures.[4] The city offered some respite from federal policy, but in turn Native people found a world in which non-Indians dominated social, cultural, and political life and where the presence of living Indian people garnered little consideration or respect.

The anxieties brought on by industrialization, immigration, and the end of the "frontier" encouraged some Americans to look inward and to reevaluate American national identity in ways that had implications for Native people. Progressive Era reformers saw Indian experiences as an essential precursor to contemporary society and sought to cultivate the "purity" of that earlier era in all persons to teach them the values of America. New organizations such as the Boy Scouts and the Camp Fire Girls took up this project by emphasizing the natural environment and developing activities based on Indian stereotypes. This fascination was mostly limited to imagined Indians of old, however. Some Americans saw contemporary Indians as "exotic" and "noble," but only if they provided tourists and scholars with the sense of the past that was expected and unencumbered by the trappings of modern society.[5]

The idea of American Indians living in the midst of urban society was so alien to most Americans that Native people in the early-twentieth-century city were hardly recognized as such. Native migrants were often lumped together with ethnic Mexicans and other peoples of color, or they learned to avoid racial prejudice by passing as white. Some who continued to identify as Indians lived with extended families, informally socialized with other Indians, or frequently traveled back to visit their reservations. Still others formed clubs and organizations where Indian people could come together to associate and work toward common goals. These groups formally established the presence of Indians in early-twentieth-century American cities and provided Indian migrants with ways of "being Indian" in what on a day-to-day basis was an overwhelmingly non-Indian and sometimes racially hostile environment. In other words, early-twentieth-century urban Indian organizations contributed to the earliest efforts at reimagining Indian Country.

The first urban Indian organizations reflected the interests and experiences of their members, who tended to be educated and financially stable. They were most often graduates of federal boarding schools for Indians, and they had moved to the city after graduation to find steady work. These groups focused on Indian people living in the city but also addressed national issues of Indian welfare and the complex question of what it meant to live as an Indian in modern American society. Urban Indian organizations in this sense resembled the Society of American Indians (SAI), the first national Indian advocacy group run by Native people, which was founded in 1915 by federal boarding school alumni. Members of both the SAI and local urban groups struggled to reconcile the educations they had received and their attractions to modern American society with a desire to identify as American Indians and to work toward reform in the conditions and treatment of Native peoples.[6]

The American Indian Progressive Association (AIPA) is a good reflection of the movement in early-twentieth-century urban America to be both Indian and American. The group incorporated in Los Angeles in 1924 and combined elements of American patriotism and Indian welfare into a program for the betterment of Indian people.[7] In some ways the AIPA absorbed the ideology of American assimilation that its members received through their experiences with federal officials back on reservations and years of government education by stressing that Indian people should take their place as citizens of the United States. The AIPA emphasized Indian self-reliance, urged Indians to vote and take part in civil affairs, and identified education as a promising route for Indian economic and social mobility. The Articles of Association stated that the AIPA was formed "to encourage the progressive development and education of the American Indian" and "to cooperate with such constructive movements that have for their purpose the obtaining of the proper social and political status of the American Indian as a citizen of the United States of America."[8] AIPA founder Pablo Narcha, an Indian from Arizona, went on to state in a 1926 editorial that appeared in its newsletter:

> The AIPA offers an opportunity to serve America as well as America's Indians. The Association holds out no inducement to Indians of lands, monies, or other illusory promises. It believes that the Indian's first opportunity to take up the burden of service is that of being able to help himself, to discharge his duties in whatever walk of life he may find himself as man or women with a sense of responsibility and sacredness of citizenship. We want to avoid the great mistake of the majority of movements to help our Indians, i.e. a loud denunciation and practical declaration of war upon the Government.[9]

Such statements supported government investigator Lewis Meriam's 1928 assertion that members of the AIPA were part of a younger generation anxious to "get away from the reservation and take [their] place alongside the white man in his own stronghold."[10]

Yet, AIPA members maintained their identity as Indians even as they sought to participate in modern urban society. "Being Indian" in Los Angeles to them meant using their skills and experiences to work toward "uplifting" other Indians to social and economic parity with non-Indians. Part of this effort was insisting on their qualifications to play a role in formulating Indian policy. Membership in the AIPA was restricted to Indians so as to attain "a real Indian viewpoint in regard to his own interests." Narcha wrote:

> In the same breath [that we condemn verbal attacks by Indians on the U.S. government] we wish to invite the attention of those who are administering Indian affairs to the fact, that we . . . have banded ourselves together in an effort to give them whatever aid is necessary to carry on to completion a constructive and successful solution to our so-called Indian problem. We wish to advise you that a large

majority of us are products of the Government Indian educational system, and that if our experiences, our advice, our opinions are not worth consideration in their work, then their work has been a great waste of public monies.[11]

AIPA members clearly continued to identify with the communities from which they came and sought to use their experiences to contribute to legislative reform and Indian welfare, even if they had chosen to live apart in a place such as Los Angeles. Historian Nancy Shoemaker has described similar types of Indian organizations in 1920s Minneapolis, noting how such groups advocated assimilation and self-sufficiency but also came together along ethnic lines to pursue Indian issues. The Twin Cities Chippewa Council met at the home of Frederick W. Peake, who had grown up on the White Earth Reservation, had graduated from Carlisle Indian School, and was a practicing lawyer. The council worked as a lobbying organization for Ojibwa men in the city. It tried to influence both national Indian legislation and reservation policies.[12]

The practices of these groups reveal more about how the complex identities of their members played out. AIPA members met periodically through the 1920s to work on its projects, discuss strategies for Indian improvement, and connect to other individuals and groups interested in their cause. Members were able to make their claims to being both productive American citizens and American Indians by participating in these activities. AIPA members representing "nearly a dozen tribes" gathered at the Hollenbeck Heights Public Library in 1928 to hear addresses from non-Indian welfare workers. A *Los Angeles Times* reporter covering the event noted that "there was no hint of the primitive redskin among those who attended the meeting. Most were well educated and interested in bettering the condition of their race." AIPA members likely would have approved of the assessment, because it encapsulated their desire to show their "progress" without disassociating themselves from their ethnic identities. AIPA members pushed this Indian identity further by showcasing the kinds of talents and lifestyles accepted and valued by middle-class society. Entertainment at the meeting was provided by an "orchestra made up of full blooded Indians, followed by a quartet of four Papago women" and the AIPA glee club. The AIPA took special efforts to present Mrs. Nellie Angelo, a Pauite Indian living in Los Angeles, who was deemed "a splendid example of the modern Indian woman" and presumably what AIPA members sought to encourage among other Indian people.[13] AIPA members were attempting to show that Indians could be upstanding citizens and valuable members of an educated, aspiring middle-class society. They also could continue to be identified as Indians as they worked to improve Indian welfare and "uplift" other Indians.

An Indian-led group that formed in Los Angeles at roughly the same time, called the Wigwam Club, was closely associated with the AIPA. Like the AIPA, the Wigwam Club sought to address national issues, but it also worked to serve the social needs of the city's Indian population. In addition, the Wigwam Club emphasized the adoption of middle-class American standards and values in some ways. The two groups jointly hosted biweekly Saturday night dances for Indian youth that had "more than a strictly recreation purpose," according to a Wigwam Club member: "They are to teach Indians how to behave. The only other public dances open to them are 'tough' and are attended by the lowest class of the 'dark races.' Unless Indians have nice manners they can't progress. If the Indians don't have nice dances of their own in the cities where they live, then their young people will go off to other dances that may be 'tough.'" The club member went on to lament that Indian girls from Sherman Institute who were working as domestics in the city were not allowed to attend their dances, which was unfortunate since the dances were "a good opportunity for school girls to meet and perhaps marry nice young intelligent Indian men."[14] A similar group organized during the 1930s in Oakland for young Pomo Indian women working in the city as domestic servants. The Four Winds Club, met socially at the local YWCA on Thursdays (the day off for domestics). The group also had a dinner and dance once a month to host Indian men attending the University of California, Berkeley.[15]

These social groups, such as the Wigwam Club and the Four Winds Club, also promoted a type of urban Indian identity that made more room for the cultural traditions of Indian people. The Wigwam Club began hosting the annual Indian Day celebration at Sycamore Grove Park in 1928. The club advertised: "Indians of all tribes are specially requested to attend. No admission fee. Monstrous program of speaking and music. Free coffee. Free green corn. Bring your lunch and cup. Picnic starts early in the morning and lasts all day."[16] The event drew approximately 1,000 people and included both political activities and Indian cultural entertainment. Attendees rallied in support of the re-election of President Herbert Hoover and especially of Vice President Charles Curtis, who was of Kaw Indian heritage. More than a dozen tribes were represented, with some attendees "in paint and feathers [and] a few headdresses here and there." Several Indian actors supplied the entertainment that included Indian singing and dancing and a bow-and-arrow exhibition. Leaders also announced that the following weekend a woman's auxiliary to the Wigwam Club, called the Indian Busy Bees, would hold a bazaar. Indian handiwork, basketry, jewelry, handmade embroideries, candles, and other items would be offered for sale, and the proceeds would go to Indian welfare in Los Angeles.[17]

Performances of Indian culture by urban Indian groups also could be linked to activism for Indian people. Some Indian reformers believed that getting Americans to value and appreciate Indian culture could build support for the reform of federal Indian policy and other Indian issues. The best example of how this linkage was made can be found in the celebration of American Indian Day, a holiday first promoted by the Society of American Indians (SAI) in 1912. The SAI recommended that American Indian Day be observed in schools, colleges, churches, and historical and fraternal organizations to highlight "the true history of the Indian, his true character and habits before the coming of the white man and to his present social and economic condition today."[18] Founding SAI member Arthur Parker (Seneca) made the call for an annual weekend of American Indian Day activities in schools, literary and historical societies, and churches in 1916. He recommended that the observance involve a hearty dose of patriotism that would include the playing of the *Star-Spangled Banner*, saluting of the American flag, and an address on "The American Indian as a Patriot." Readings from Indian legends and famous Indian speeches, Indian songs, and lectures on the "The Indians of Our State" and "The American Indian in Literature" were to emphasize Indian culture and contributions.[19]

Urban Indian organizations throughout the United States then took up the celebration of American Indian Day and to varying degrees emphasized the contributions of American Indians, the promotion of Indian culture, and the advancement of Indian causes. The Denver chapter of the Tepee Order, a fraternal organization of Indian and non-Indian members, sponsored a celebration of American Indian Day to coincide with the SAI's annual conference in 1922. The highlight was a program at Denver's Grace Community Church. It began with a procession by the Camp Fire Girls, Boy Scouts, Improved Order of Red Men, Fraternal Order of the Eagles, and Sacagawea Council; a prayer to the Great Spirit; and a lighting of a ceremonial peace pipe. The governor of Colorado and the mayor of Denver offered tributes, and the Camp Fire Girls sang "Indian Mother Song." American Indian reformer and SAI founder Sherman Coolidge closed the proceedings with a keynote address that included a scathing indictment of Indian-U.S. relations and an appeal to Christian ideals in demanding reparation.[20] The Indian Fellowship League (another group composed of Indians and non-Indians) began celebrating American Indian Day annually in 1926 in Chicago with encampments at forest preserves throughout the city. The celebrations featured tens of thousands of visitors, representatives from dozens of tribes, singing, dancing, and other displays of Indian culture.[21] The commemoration of American Indian Day became an annual event for various groups of Indians and non-Indians in New York City by the 1930s. A celebration attended by 2,000 people took place in 1934 at Manhattan's Inwood Hill Park, with speeches, poetry, dancing, and a re-creation of an "Old Indian Encampment."[22] The event catered to 3,000 people the following year and included a lighting of a peace pipe and calls for "better understanding" of Indian matters.[23] Another 3,000 people attended the 1936 celebration that featured fifty performing Indians from twenty-five tribes and included speeches by the commanders of the Inwood Post of the American Legion and the Catholic War Veterans.[24] Members of the United Indian Tribes of America performed dances, gave speeches, and inducted a "paleface" into the "tribe" through a blood-mingling ceremony for 1,000 spectators the same year in Brooklyn's Prospect Park.[25] The annual Indian Day celebration at Sycamore Grove Park in Los Angeles began under the sponsorship of the Wigwam Club in 1928. By the late 1930s the sponsorship shifted to a Los Angeles–based group interested in political rights and land claims called the California Indian Rights Association. This led the celebrations to take on a more overtly political tone, such as in 1942 when the keynote speech was given by State Attorney General Earl Warren, who had represented California Indians in land-claims cases.[26]

There were other groups in cities that sought to serve the local community by offering places for Indians to socialize and welfare to needy Indians. Two World War I veterans, George Peake (Ojibway) and Warren Cash (Dakota), ran a chapter of the Tepee Order in Minneapolis that sponsored dances and other social functions and opened a fraternity house for Indian students in the city's schools. The chapter also worked to get American Indian Day recognized as a national holiday. The Twin Cities Chippewa Council lobbied for welfare relief to reservation residents and had a benefit dance in 1932 to raise money for the cause. The Minnesota Wigwam Indian Welfare Society performed welfare work. Member Amabel Bulin, a Sioux Indian and graduate of New York University, worked to find housing for both children and reservation residents attending city schools or visiting hospitals and to find jobs and housing for Indians migrants. Bulin began an organization called Sah-Kah-Tey ("sunshine" in Ojibway) in the late 1930s to sponsor young Indian women going to school or working in Minneapolis.[27]

Many of these groups in Minneapolis and other cities that began in the first half of the twentieth century were short-lived. They struggled to maintain funding and regular membership, serving a relatively small and often transient urban Indian population. The ephemeral nature of these groups speaks to how the reimagining of Indian Country was a slow, uneven, and halting process in the years before World War II. One group founded in the 1930s in Los Angeles proved, however, to be among the most enduring urban Indian-run organizations in the country. This can be explained by the size of the city's Indian population, its social needs, and a handful of dedicated individuals that kept the organization running. Mira Frye Bartlett, an Oklahoma-born Kickapoo Indian, began the Lowansa Tipi in a building just west of downtown Los Angeles in 1935. She changed its name to the Los Angeles Indian Center soon after.[28] The memory of the Indian Center's founding was still alive among its older members on the occasion of the Indian Center's fortieth anniversary, when they wrote:

> As early as the 1920's, Indians in Los Angeles began meeting — grouping together on a social level — in an attempt to keep intact an Indian spirit of identity in a large and bewildering city. Having left the rural areas and reservations, far from their ancestral lands and family this new existence was to become a great challenge. By 1930, Indians began to emerge as an invisible community throughout the city, and it became necessary to find a regular meeting place. Slowly, an Indian nucleus took shape, headed by a few Indian hopefuls whose vision and determination created the . . . [Los Angeles] American Indian Center.[29]

Members of the Indian Center produced and circulated a mimeographed newsletter that was designed to keep Indians in the city informed of various events and activities, but the Indian Center in its early years was mostly a place where Indians could get together and socialize. Iron Eyes Cody, an actor of Sicilian heritage who passed as Indian, remembered the Indian Center during this period as a place where "we used to go . . . to meet [other Indians] and use the phone."[30]

The number of urban American Indian organizations and the scope of their activities grew when more Indian people made their way to cities after World War II. This signaled an expansion in the reimagining of

Indian Country by Indian people. The San Francisco Bay area was home to approximately 2,500 American Indians in 1955, and the Four Winds Club was the only formal group to serve this population. By 1962 there were more than 10,000 Native people in the region and sixteen Indian-run organizations.[31] The increasing populations of Indian people dramatically raised demand for Indian organizations and allowed for more varied and sustained expressions of urban American Indian identity. Working- and middle-class Indians established or energized existing organizations that focused on socializing with other Indians, planning and engaging in group activities, addressing national issues, and providing welfare services to poor Indians.

New organizations in Portland, Ore., illustrate how some Indian migrants reached a place of relative security and affluence in the postwar city and then began looking for additional ways to express their Native heritage within their new surroundings. Indian-run organizations helped to create communities and encouraged group activities that cultivated a sense of Indianness, or Indian identity, as a complement to more typically American lives. The first of these groups in Portland was established in 1959 by three Blackfeet women as the Voice of the American Indian Association (VAIA).[32] Its members were primarily Indian women who had grown up on a reservation and married before coming to Portland, where their husbands found industrial and professional jobs. They had established comfortable places in the city, and they believed in helping other Indians whom they regarded as less fortunate. This mission first took the form of serving poor Indians on reservations. The group opened a thrift shop in Northeast Portland to receive donations of clothing, toys, and other items that were either sold for operational costs or packaged and shipped to reservations. Sales stagnated at that location, so the store moved to a more frequented area of downtown in 1961. The strategy paid off, and the group sent 4,000 pounds of food and clothing to reservations in Oregon, Washington, Idaho, Montana, and South Dakota by the end of the year.[33] The move also helped shift the focus of the VAIA, so that it began to concentrate its charitable activities on Indians living in the city. The thrift shop soon became a community space where Indian people from various tribes and social levels could gather to talk, share information, volunteer to work, and receive free food and clothing. An Indian woman from eastern Oregon noted that a new sense of ethnic identity was developing, stating that "though we are from different tribes, we have the same goals and the same interests, because we are all Indians."[34] This emergent sense of urban Indian identity also included an interest in Indian culture. The VAIA sponsored a fund-raising program at Portland's Civic Auditorium in 1961 that featured the singing and dancing of "Chief Sitting Calf and his Blackfeet troupe."[35] By 1962 the group had shifted the store's focus from secondhand clothes and household items to Indian arts and crafts. A sign announced "Indian Curios for Sale," and members made elaborately decorated baskets, moccasins, purses, and belts. The group also began to collect arts and crafts from area reservations for sale in Portland.[36]

The community that the VAIA created through charity work and its dealings with Indian culture went a long way toward developing an urban Indian identity for its members. Yet, the VAIA needs to be understood as rooted in middle-class notions of identity and culture. The group's major influences included established civic and religious organizations whose models of charitable work promoted a broad sense of citizenship and of what it meant to be an American. The Portland Council of Churches involved itself with VAIA activities and in 1962 organized an advisory board composed of local members of the Salvation Army, Oregon Labor Bureau, Urban League, and Community Council. The Christian Women's Fellowship of the Mallory Avenue Christian Church also became a sponsor of the Indian Center. The United Church Women offered advice on rummage sales and approached other Oregon churchwomen's groups asking for aid and for inclusion of the Indian Center in charity budgets. Alcoholics Anonymous supported the Indian Center and began weekly meetings in a back room.[37] The VAIA did not simply become a carbon copy of these other groups but established models of charity, and the values that accompanied them formed a substantial influence. The result was an organization based on middle-class Americanism with a strong ethnic identification that worked to expand the boundaries of what it meant to be both American and Indian. VAIA members personified these complexities in their everyday work. Before each meeting they shared a meal of sandwiches and coffee, said a Christian prayer, and recited the Pledge of Allegiance, then set about planning how to help Indian people in the city and across the country.[38]

The VAIA disappeared by the mid-1960s, when another group of established and relatively affluent Indians emerged in Portland. The Portland American Indian Center (PAIC) also was composed of middle-class Indians and included a contingent of workers from the Portland Area Office of the BIA. The group paid less attention to matters of Indian poverty and was more interested in nurturing Indian culture in the city. Members still identified strongly as middle-class Americans and went further than their predecessors in finding ways to be Indian. PAIC members especially cultivated and expressed Indianness with group activities. The group built exhibits featuring Indian arts and crafts and provided dancers and singers to help celebrate local festivities throughout the 1960s. PAIC members participated in Portland's Bureau of Parks Summer Festival and the Family Camping Fair, built floats for the Merry Kana and Fun-O-Rama parades, and staffed an information booth at the Oregon State Fair in Salem. PAIC members also held events or performed by invitation. The PAIC put together a program of Indian dancing at Portland State University, constructed a display at the university's bookstore, and gave presentations for local Cub Scouts, the Portland School District, the Georgia Pacific Corporation's retreat, and the Oregon State Penitentiary in Salem.[39] Popular middle-class activities also provided an opportunity for group members to be Indian in the city. The PAIC held a number of annual events, including a club picnic, a Christmas party for Indian children, and the annual beauty contest to crown Miss Indian Northwest. The group also fielded city league basketball, bowling, and softball teams and sponsored the Portland All-Indian Bowling League and Tournament. More regular club events included potluck dinners and bingo nights. The PAIC made efforts to involve its members in fund-raising by holding bake sales and participating in a radio contest that rewarded groups that turned in "points" found on the packages of popular brand-name groceries.[40] These typical "American" activities helped PAIC members define an ethnic community and cultivate a sense of Indianness for members to incorporate into their lives.

The Los Angeles Indian Center was another postwar urban Indian organization that catered to a growing working- and middle-class Indian population. The Indian Center was mostly a meeting place for Indians in the 1930s and 1940s, as discussed above. It became more of a formalized organization after World War II, with a schedule of recreational activities and a mission to provide welfare services. The American Friends Service Committee (AFSC) began supporting the Indian Center in 1948 with a monthly operating budget of $550 that it continued to renew for the next six years.[41] Non-Indian staff members of the AFSC initially took over key staff positions at the Indian Center and relied on Indian volunteers to serve as cooks, instructors, special event organizers, and hosts. The AFSC also formed an advisory board of twenty-five Indian members to "guide the staff of the Center in thinking through its policies and program activities ... because it was recognized that without the advice and support of Indians, the Center program could not possibly be a really adequate one." The Indian Center moved to the Euclid Heights Methodist Church on Euclid Avenue in 1949 after the building it had occupied since 1935 was slated for demolition. The Indian Center was open "all day, 7 days a week, as a place for Indians to read, write, rest, and meet their friends," and again several nights a week for "classes, meetings, dinners, and services." The classes enrolled about 115 people per month and included Indian arts and crafts, Indian dancing for children, and folk dancing. Other Indian organizations in the city also used the Indian Center for meetings. About 100 people were served dinner and stayed for evening vespers on Sundays. The AFSC staff included a social worker who distributed clothes and tried to direct Indians in need to the appropriate city agencies.[42]

Indian Center members found ways to create an Indian community and cultivate Indian identities even as they engaged in social activities common to other middle-class Americans. By 1951 the Indian Center had relocated to a building on 6th Avenue in downtown Los Angeles that provided it with the space to expand its recreation program. Indians visited the Indian Center through the 1950s for a range of social activities that included canasta and Chinese checkers tournaments, movie nights, arts and crafts, guitar lessons, sewing circles, and Sunday dinners followed by nondenominational vespers. Jack Forbes, of Powhatan and Delaware Indian descent, was attending college and graduate school in Los Angeles, and he went to the Indian Center to meet other Indians and listen to records. The Indian Center's Youth Club also met once a month to plan activities for the coming weeks. The youth held parties, dances, and barbecues at the Indian Center and got together for miniature golf, bowling, basketball games, picnics, swimming, hiking, roller skating, and trips to fairs and amusement parks. Special festivities took place around the year-end holidays. The Indian Center held its annual fund-raising and organizational dinner every October. Attendees were served a turkey dinner and enjoyed the camaraderie of other Indians for a modest fee. In 1951 dinner was followed by the singing of "familiar songs," a performance of "Indian Love Call" on the harp, the election of members to the Indian Center advisory board, and a square dance. It was reported that everyone had a good time despite the small profit that was generated. Christmas also brought regular Indian Center activities that included a children's party with presents and candy bags, Christmas caroling, and an open house and turkey dinner on Christmas Day.[43]

The Indian Center also became known as a friendly place for Indians traveling through the city. In the early 1950s several groups and individuals from outside Los Angeles were noted to have dropped in to visit the Indian Center. The Indian Center welcomed twelve Sioux Indians from the Pine Ridge Reservation who were in town to work on a movie in May 1951. Members took the visitors on a tour of the Los Angeles area that included Beverly Hills, Westwood, Redondo Beach, Long Beach, the Todd Shipyards, and the Signal Hills oil wells. Everyone went back to the Indian Center afterward for dinner and a "hilarious evening" of square dancing. A member proclaimed that the visitors would "always find a welcome home at the Indian Center."[44] Elizabeth Roe Cloud, the field secretary for the National Congress of American Indians, dropped in while on a trip through the Southwest the following November and gave an impromptu talk on her experiences traveling among Indian communities.[45] The Indian Center's Youth Club made special efforts to welcome students from the Sherman Institute. In 1951 the Youth Club hosted forty Sherman students who were spending the summer working in Los Angeles, offering them games, a dinner, and square dancing. Youth Club members explained the Indian Center's program and urged the students to think of the Indian Center as "a second home."[46] A member noted at the end of the summer that the students had continued to visit and "use the Center as a central meeting place."[47] Indian servicemen also found a welcoming community at the Indian Center as they were passing through Los Angeles. J. S. Arquero (Cochiti Pueblo) and J. M. Abeita (Santo Domingo Pueblo) heard about the Indian Center while serving in Korea and stopped in on their way home on furlough.[48] Private Bobby Begay wrote back to the Indian Center from his station in Bridgeport, Calif., to say that he had had a good time on a recent visit, when he had enjoyed a cup of coffee and played Chinese checkers.[49]

The organization also helped foster a working- and middle-class Indian community in Los Angeles through a newsletter that began regular monthly publication in 1951. A contest to name the newsletter resulted in the choice of *Talking Leaf* (an adaptation of "talking leaves," the term used at times by Native people to refer to treaties and other written materials introduced by non-Indians; other entries included Smoke Talk, The Redskin, Blanket Signals, Indian Messenger, Moccasin Tracks, Powwow Doings, Talk of the Tribes, and Tribal Newsletter).[50] *Talking Leaf* served as a community billboard for Indians in Los Angeles by advertising the activities of the Indian Center and reporting engagements, weddings, births, sick persons, deaths, funerals, and free puppies. Some of these announcements resembled the "society" pages of city newspapers by gossiping about the happenings among the Indian population of Los Angeles. They included regular reports of Indian actors working on Hollywood films, Indians taking trips out of the city, and Indian people visiting Los Angeles.[51] A report in the February 1952 issue was typical: "Mr. and Mrs. Walter Simons (Yakama-Flathead) and their daughter, Madelyn, were in town for the New Year. They had a pleasant visit with Mrs. Simmons' sister, Mrs. Tom Mullen. While here they visited many places of interest in Los Angeles and vicinity. Mr. Simmons is the brother of Chief Yowlachie."[52] The following notice ran in the same issue: "Jim and Pierce Kewanytewa (Hopi) are on their annual vacation visiting friends. They stopped at Needles, Las Vegas and Barstow and are now the guests of Mr. and Mrs. Stanley Bahnimtewa. Jim Kewanytewa is curator of the Museum of Northern Arizona in Flagstaff and Pierce Kewanytewa lives in Zia, New Mexico. Jim seems to be taking a Postman's Holiday in Los Angeles visiting the museums in town."[53] Indian servicemen particularly noted their appreciation for *Talking Leaf* while away from home. Corporal F. F. Mannie, a Navajo Indian, wrote from Camp Pendleton near San Diego to say hello to his friends at the Indian Center and to say that he was reading the newsletter.[54] Private Begay hinted at the loneliness he felt while stationed at Bridgeport, Calif., by noting, "I really need Talking Leaf to read." Corporal Clarence N. Gorman stopped at the Indian Center before shipping out and later wrote, "I must say I enjoyed reading [*Talking Leaf*] here in Korea."[55] It is likely that *Talking Leaf* served a similar function for many other Indians both in and out of Los Angeles, who could catch up on community news and find out about the wealth of activities open to them and the opportunities to socialize with Indian people in the city. *Talking Leaf* grew from four to ten pages and reached a circulation of 700 after just one year of regular publication.[56]

One phenomenon that has interested some scholars studying urban American Indian organizations has been the creation of what has been termed a "pan-Indian identity." Anthropologists have argued that, within the context of the city, tribal distinctions fall away in favor of a larger sense of being "Indian."[57] The heterogeneous nature of many postwar urban Indian organizations did foster intertribal identities among the Indians who participated in their activities. People at the Los Angeles Indian Center consciously cultivated a larger sense of Indianness that transcended tribal differences. An Indian Center publication stated that "All American Indians are welcome at these events regardless of tribe, religion, or state of pocketbook."[58] The Indian Center's Youth Club similarly was described as "made up of various tribes in Los Angeles and the outskirts of the city."[59] The Indian Center advertised a 1952 powwow by writing that "tribal regalia, drums, bells, and feather are in order. Anyone who wishes can join in the fun, so let's be Indian!!"[60] Notices in *Talking Leaf* often regarded the mingling of tribes in the city with a sense of both wonder and amusement. A 1951 issue noted, "Anything can happen in Hollywood. We counted thirteen tribes working together on an RKO picture. [Three days later, members of] four more tribes joined them."[61] The same issue continued, "At a night spot in downtown one April night were an Alaskan Indian, Pima, Papago, Navajo, Chemehuevi, Mission, Yuma, and bunch of Indian servicemen."[62] Notices in *Talking Leaf* also regularly used the term "Los Angeles Indian," as in a 1951 notice that stated "a group of Los Angeles Indians went to Palm Springs to give a performance to raise money for a church on the reservation."[63] The very name "Indian Center" and the many suggestions for titling *Talking Leaf* reflected some type of connectedness among tribal peoples that was a common ground for coming together and basing new identities.

Activities by Portland Indian groups also illustrate how a larger sense of being Indian could be created in the city. One popular PAIC event was the preparation and presentation of "authentic Indian feasts." These events offered a chance to learn, practice, and take part in the traditions of others, thereby reinforcing the sense that all tribes were linked together by a common ethnic bond. PAIC members held an Indian dinner in 1972 to raise money for the summer's powwow. They prepared a variety of foods from fifteen tribal traditions and served them together as an "Indian meal." Guests ate salmon lacamean, dried seaweed cooked with smelt, dried corn stewed with deer meat, whole grain cereals cooked with dried whitefish, Indian fry bread, bannock bread, Oneida bread, wild rice, squash, Navajo-style lamb and chili, Indian-style gelatin dessert, bitterroot, camas root, biscuit root, cattail root, beaver meat, and wocus seeds.[64] Just the planning of an "Indian feast" organized by an "Indian Center" supports the idea that intertribal identities were being created in the city.

At the same time, Indian people maintained and continued to develop tribal identities. Intertribal and tribal identities should be understood to have existed and been developed side by side or together in multiple layers. Urban Indian activities brought different tribes together into a common arena, but members were still conscious of tribal differences, even as they shared tribal culture and learned from one another. The fact that activities were consistently described with references to multiple tribal affiliations speaks to this point. *Talking Leaf* reported on an impromptu Los Angeles Indian Center powwow that was held in December 1951: "Corn soup and fried beans were in order when the visiting Sioux, Mr. and Mrs. Jim Hawkins (Chief Big Snake) and Laura Woodlock (Mrs. Standingbear) volunteered to put on their costumes and perform real reservation style dances and songs. This inspired several locals to don their costumes . . . and Indian bells were ringing far into the night. One GI from Pine Ridge, a neighbor, heard the drum and joined the festivities. Several members of the Youth Club wore Navajo costumes and it was a picture to see their full skirts twirling in the square dances that followed."[65] Tribal affiliations were also consciously invoked when describing the Indian Center's membership. A 1953 item noted that among the new faces around the Indian Center were members of the Otoe, Cherokee, Sac-Fox, and Ponca tribes. "In fact," the item went on, if "we keep seeing more Poncas, we will have to have a Ponca reunion."[66] *Talking Leaf* similarly reported in 1954: "Visitors at the Center this month included persons from the following tribes besides all the regulars that come. They were Nootka, Alsea, Ponca, Sac & Fox, Pawnee, Arikara, Chippewa, Miwok, Micmac, Nez Perce, Shoshone, Blackfeet and Caddo. We really get a good representation of tribes as visitors every month and we are always happy to see new faces."[67] Tribal affiliations were clearly still important to Indians in cities, even as they came together around the idea of "being Indian."

Some Indian organizations and activities stand as especially good illustrations of how such complex and multilayered identities could be cultivated by Indians living in America's postwar cities. The All-Indian Sports Leagues was organized in Los Angeles in 1960. Its founding was recounted in *Talking Leaf* a few years later: "Many of the different tribes from all parts of the country were playing in various sports activities throughout the Los Angeles area in municipal, industrial and church leagues. Many of the team members were of the opinion that some of these teams could be formed into one league in their various sports activities, since there were enough Indians in the area. Efforts were made by the coaches and managers to bring this about." The organization began with an All-Indian Softball League and an All-Indian Basketball League. The group changed its name to the American Indian Athletic Association (AIAA) and grew considerably by 1963. The softball league included twelve teams in two divisions, and the best teams went on to play tournaments in cities and on reservations throughout the Southwest. Fifteen teams made up the basketball league. It held an annual Los Angeles Basketball Tourney that increasingly drew teams from Northern California and out of state.[68] Glenna Amos, a Cherokee Indian from Oklahoma, remembered how much she enjoyed these early games:

During the height of relocation, so many different people were here for training, that it was easy to get . . . enough people to make a ball team, so we had a lot of ball teams and we'd play baseball all summer long and have a tournament that would last all summer. Usually we'd have all of the diamonds at the park going at the same time. In the early days we used to play at Salt Lake Park in Huntington Park. And sometimes we'd just spend the whole . . . like in the early sixties, '61, '62, we'd play at Salt Lake Park and we'd be there all day on Saturday, playing game after game after game, getting sunburned, and then go home and play Monopoly, or Scrabble, or dominoes, until the wee hours of the morning. It was fun. We'd just all crash at the preacher's house and I'd fry chicken and play dominoes.[69]

The AIAA continued to expand and gain a reputation throughout Indian Country during the 1960s and into the 1970s. It experimented with a number of different sports, but the most popular remained softball, basketball, and bowling (which was under the auspices of the American Indian Bowling Association, an affiliated group that began in Los Angeles in 1966). The AIAA's annual tournaments also became increasingly popular. Thirty-four teams competed in the annual AIAA All-Indian Basketball Tournament in 1967; twenty were from the city, six from other parts of California, and eight from outside the state. Forty teams participated in the tournament two years later, with nineteen from the Los Angeles area, eight from other parts of California, and fifteen from out of state, mostly from Arizona and New Mexico.[70] Howard Yackitonipah, a Comanche Indian, was a consistent participant in AIAA activities for many years. Yackitonipah spoke about how he got involved and the diversity of Indian peoples who had come to participate in the leagues in 1970:

[The AIAA] gives [Indians in Los Angeles] something. That's an outlet. They can go somewhere and be among their own people. . . . Now, in our February [basketball] tournament we have teams coming from Oklahoma . . . Chicago, Oakland, 'Frisco, Phoenix, Flagstaff. . . . All these teams come out here and we have a big four-day tournament. Then on Saturday night . . . we have these big basketball games and afterwards we rent a hall and have a big dance. . . . That's just because I go around to all these agencies: the Indian Center, the BIA, the bars where the Indians hang out, and all the basketball games and all the churches and I put up posters saying that we're going to have a dance or come to our bowling or come to our ball games.

The AIAA was especially important to Yackitonipah, he went, on, because "when [he] was [first] here, there was nothing. I had no place to go."[71]

The composition of the teams in the AIAA and the group's activities reflected the layering of tribal and intertribal Indian identities. The very fact of the organization's existence suggested a larger Indian consciousness, as with the Los Angeles and Portland Indian Centers. Arthur Ketcheshawno, the AIAA president, noted that the organization was "a means for the American Indians to band together for unity, fellowship, and other common interests, such as group identity."[72] Many of the teams were organized along intertribal lines, such as the Huntington Park Indians, or the teams sponsored by the Nazarene Indian Church, Brighter Day Indian Mission, and Urban Indian Development Association. Others were based on tribal membership, such as the Papago Raiders and Raiderettes, the Choctaws, and a team sponsored by the Navajo Club. Even among intertribal groups certain tribes or regions predominated, such as the First Indian Baptist Church team that was composed mostly of Indians from Oklahoma.[73] The presence of Indians from throughout Indian Country at AIAA tournaments also reinforced both tribal and intertribal identities. The teams from outside Los Angeles added more tribes and more diverse experiences to the AIAA that strengthened the idea of a pan-Indian consciousness. They also provided Indians in the city with the opportunities to meet and reconnect with Indians from their own tribes who lived in different cities or back on the reservations.

Powwows were another venue that highlighted the persistence and development of both tribal and intertribal identities. In 1969 the PAIC sponsored an "Indian Encampment" that was Portland's first powwow. The event attracted a crowd of 1,000 that represented thirty-eight different tribes from around the Pacific Northwest. There were displays of Indian tepees, costumes, ornaments, beads, and traditional foods that reflected the distinctiveness of individual tribes. Much of the day was taken up by dancing contests, where Indian women, men, and children dressed in tribal regalia and performed tribal dances.[74] The powwow also acted as a crucible that mixed the different traditions together for all to take part in and enjoy. Powwow visitors could learn about, partake in, and incorporate the traditions of other tribes or participate in activities open to all Indian attendees. The Indian Encampment was renamed the Portland Indian Pow-Wow and Encampment, and in 1970 it became a satellite event of Portland's annual Rose Festival. The powwow included the dance contests and displays of Indian culture from the previous year that highlighted individual tribal traditions. Other activities were added and framed as intertribal or "Indian," such as softball games, church services, and a pageant to crown Miss Indian Northwest.[75] These activities were augmented in subsequent years by new features reflecting both tribal and intertribal Indian culture, including tepee-raising races, a "parade of chiefs," and additional displays and trading of Indian jewelry, arts, and crafts.[76]

Powwow clubs began forming as early as the 1930s in Los Angeles by drawing together Indians from many different tribes who met to drum, sign, and dance in Indian dress. Often these clubs were motivated by the need to develop forums for keeping Indian culture alive in the city. Dennis Tafoya recalled how, when he was growing up in the 1950s and 1960s, these groups allowed him and his family members to participate in an intertribal Indian community where they learned from other tribes and contributed their own tribal dances and songs:

> [We didn't find a lot of Pueblos] to participate with in our own tribal or traditional dance. But what was here in Los Angeles was an intertribal community. . . . I'd say after the first six months we made connection with the powwow community. . . . A contemporary Indian powwow here is . . . intertribal, with Pawnees, Otoes, Navajos, Hopi, Pueblo, Ute, Cherokee, Choctaw, it doesn't matter. You decide which form of dance you want to express as contemporary and you partake in it, as long as you understand the protocol of that dance, in that dance arena, or of that song. . . . [Later], in the mid-sixties, we had a whole group of the Orange County Oklahoma families, and our family and a number of others, we'd get together. . . We would teach all of them some of our Pueblo dances. . . . So it was kind of an example of the intertribal sharing of our own culture.[77]

These groups were intertribal in nature, but they also came to reflect the emphasis of certain regions of Indian Country. The all-male Roach Society met sporadically in Los Angeles from 1933 to 1954 and broadly emphasized the singing and dancing of the Great Plains and the Eastern Woodlands. Growing numbers of Indian migrants from Oklahoma joined the remnants of the Roach Society and reorganized it in 1954 as the Drum and

Feather Club. The group tended to favor the drumming, singing, dancing, and costumes of the Southern Plains and Oklahoma tribes. The Orange County Group was similarly made up of families of Oklahoma Indians living in Orange County, including many who worked at the Indian Village at Disneyland. They broke off from the Drum and Feather Club in 1957 and eventually began calling themselves the Roadrunners, while continuing to emphasize Oklahoma and Southern Plains styles in their performances. The Many Trails Indian Club formed in 1958 to fill the need for "Northern style" powwows, or those that showcased Indian culture of the Northern Plains. The core of the group was a contingent of Sioux singers that split from the Drum and Feather Club. The Little Big Horn Association was led by actor Iron Eyes Cody and was organized in 1964 to also emphasize the Northern style.[78]

The powwows put on by these clubs became important events for Indian people in Los Angeles. Powwows provided opportunities to gather, watch, participate, and meet with other urban Indians. Kenneth and Greta Yackitonipah, a Comanche Indian couple, noted that they rarely had a chance to see or associate with Indians in Los Angeles except for once a month when they went to a powwow. "Everybody has their different interests," Greta explained in 1970, "and the only time when everybody all gets together is when we have an Indian pow-wow. And if the pow-wow's to their liking, why everybody will go, and you see the same bunch of people." Kenneth had been dancing "since he was knee-high" and also liked to drum and sing. Greta, whose parents "were not powwow people," never danced when she was growing up, but after meeting Ken she began going to powwows and dancing in costume along with their daughter, Kimmy. "You know, I was an Indian," Greta recalled, "and it appealed to me, so I brought my kids up to know what it's all about."[79] A 1964 cartoon that ran in *Talking Leaf* expressed the abundance of powwow opportunities in Los Angeles. It pictured a group of Indians sitting around a fire and was captioned: "What do you mean no Pow-wow this month? Back in L.A. we have three different ones on one night!"[80] A weekly powwow schedule was coordinated and regularized by the late 1960s, so that roughly nine months a year there was a different powwow every Saturday night in the Greater Los Angeles area (the schedule was suspended during the summer when many Indian families and individuals traveled out of the city). Groups such as those mentioned above held powwows at community centers and school gymnasiums from Stanton in Orange County to the Indian enclave of Huntington Park and Eagle Rock near Pasadena. Other Indian organizations, such as the Indian student associations at Los Angeles–based colleges and universities, held powwows less regularly to promote their work.[81] Several groups also held multiday, outdoor powwows annually or to celebrate special events. Dennis Tafoya remembered the Many Trails Indian Club's three-day powwows at Corriganville, in the Santa Monica Mountains just north of the Los Angeles, as the best powwows on the West Coast.[82]

Some groups in the 1960s came to devote more time and resources to the welfare of the poorest Indians in the city, as urban Indian populations rapidly increased. These groups often scrambled to provide adequate services with monies obtained primarily through fund-raising and charitable contributions. The Voice of the American Indian Association in Portland (described above) fits this pattern. The Indian Welcome House (IWH) began in downtown Los Angeles in 1963, under the sponsorship of the United Presbyterian Church of Southern California. It was nonsectarian and was designed to help Indians who had recently arrived in the city from the reservation. The IWH provided temporary room and board, job counseling and referrals, and a friendly environment that included other Indians to whom newcomers could turn for support.[83] It merged with the Los Angeles Indian Center in 1970, as part of an effort to pool resources.[84]

The Los Angeles Indian Center attempted to meet the welfare needs of new migrants to the city, but it often struggled to secure a steady source of revenue. The AFSC came to the conclusion that the Indian Center needed to stand on its own, and it withdrew funding in 1955. This left the Indian Center without the means to cover even the $200 a month it paid in rent. Director Stevie Standingbear joined with Indian Center founder and longtime member Myra Bartlett to organize a "Wampum Club" for raising money. The Indian Center came to rely on membership dues, the sale of arts and crafts, rummage sales, and other fund-raising activities, such as powwows, holiday parties, buffalo dinners, and barbecues. Assistance from other local organizations and charities also was welcomed. Maintaining services remained difficult through the 1950s and early 1960s. The Indian Center was completely out of money at one point, so chairman Joe Vasquez moved its headquarters to his own home and listed his telephone as the contact phone number.[85]

The Indian Center experienced something of a rebirth in 1964. Members attempted to refocus its mission and find more effective ways of serving the Indian people of Greater Los Angeles. *Talking Leaf* was revived as the official newsletter of the Indian Center, and the Board of Directors pledged to undertake "a vast, energetic publicity campaign to make Indians and palefaces alike become aware of the *immediate* needs of our Indian population."[86] Vasquez stated:

> Down through the years, we of the Indian Center have tried to be of some service to the Los Angeles Indian Community. However, as time goes by the needs of our people are always changing, due mainly to the fact that our Indian population has rapidly mushroomed. Now as never before, we are desperately in need of a large building to house a Center which will meet our many demands. . . . Our one big fault up to this point is that we have not actively solicited the help and support of the Los Angeles Indians. We are going to correct that this time, as a matter of fact, let me at this time extend an invitation to all Indians, here in Los Angeles or anywhere else for that matter, to participate in our drive forward.[87]

Nonetheless, the next few years in some ways saw a return to the types of activities that were popular in the late 1940s and early 1950s. The Indian Center continued to collect donations of clothing, household goods, and food for needy Indians. The Indian Center also remained a social space for Indian people to gather. Glenna Amos remembered that in the 1960s the Indian Center "was just kind of run on donations and it was just a shabby old building. They had a pool table and pretty much I just went up there to look through the clothes and visit with people more than anything."[88] Other activities popular with more- established working- and middle-class Indians—such as dances and various outings by the Indian Center's Youth Club, dinners, and holiday parties—returned with more regularity. *Talking Leaf* took on added importance as a community billboard by publicizing the activities of Indian churches, powwow groups, and the AIAA.[89]

The Indian Center in this period also foreshadowed the changes and issues that were to dominate urban American Indian organizations throughout the country in the 1970s. It became the first urban American Indian organization in the country to earn a grant from the federal Office of Economic Opportunity (OEO) when it received funding under the OEO's Community Action Program in 1964. The grant allowed the Indian Center to pay administrative salaries, maintain a full-time paid staff of seven, move to a more suitable building, and begin to expand its social and recreational services.[90] The Indian Center and dozens of urban Indian organizations would receive millions of dollars in government funding over the next decade, as Indian activism exploded onto the national scene and the federal government took serious notice of urban American Indians for the first

Los Angeles Indian Centers, Inc. council members, ca. 1964. Left to right, back row: unknown, Joe Vasquez, Sam Kolb, Iron Eyes Cody, Fred Gabourie; center row: Ralph Coonfield, Rod Red Wing, John King, unknown, Bobby White; front row: Joseph F. Tafoya Jr., Mitch Murdock, unknown, unknown. Courtesy of Dennis Tafoya.

time. These funds would transform the work and composition of urban Indian organizations, as they began to do for the Los Angeles Indian Center in 1964.

The expansion of federally funded social service organizations and their involvement with the Indian activism of the period is the topic of the next chapter. This movement did not originate, however, with the occupation of Alcatraz Island by Indian protestors in 1969 or the highly publicized events staged by the American Indian Movement during the 1970s. Native people had long been organizing themselves to address community needs and to argue for the validity of maintaining Indian identities in the midst of modern American society. These groups provided many different ways to "be Indian" in the city, from the AIPA and the Four Winds Club in the 1930s to the Indian Centers in cities such as Los Angeles and Portland during the 1960s. Early-twentieth-century urban Indian organizations contributed to a nascent reimagining of Indian Country. The organizations of the postwar period and subsequent decades firmly claimed and defined the city as part of Indian Country.

CHAPTER 6

GRASSROOTS INDIAN ACTIVISM

The Red Power Movement in Urban Areas

O n Thanksgiving Day in 1977 about forty American Indian women and men ate their holiday meal at a drug and alcohol abuse treatment center near Los Angeles's skid row, run by United American Indian Involvement, Inc. (UAII). UAII was founded in 1973, with the assistance of the National Institute for Alcoholism and Alcohol Abuse, to provide hot meals, showers, beds, referrals, and emergency medical care to American Indians who walked in off the street. Its staff was made up entirely of Native people, because UAII director and cofounder Baba Cooper believed that "Indian [alcoholics] don't relate well to non-Indians." John Eagleshield, a twenty-eight-year-old Sioux Indian and the staff paramedic, was among the celebrants on this particular Thanksgiving. Eagleshield had recently received his degree from the Los Angeles Associated Technical College, with the help of a federal Comprehensive Employment and Training Act (CETA) grant administered through the Los Angeles Indian Center. He had spent the last few Thanksgivings involved with protests organized by the American Indian Movement, but he decided that this year the work he could do for UAII would be "more realistic and meaningful."[1]

Shifts in U.S. Indian policy and American Indian activism influenced the efforts by UAII to serve the Indian community of Los Angeles, the funding and training of its staff, and decisions by individuals including Eagleshield to forgo public protest in favor of community service. American Indian historians have recently begun to study the most public protests of the "Red Power" movement, such as the occupation of Alcatraz Island and the activities of the American Indian Movement. They have shown how such high-profile events drew attention to the challenges faced by American Indians and encouraged federal policymakers to support "self-determination," or the efforts by Native people to address their own needs after decades of both paternalism and neglect by government officials.[2] A few scholars also have examined how Native people in cities received attention in this period and were awarded millions of dollars in local, state, and federal funding.[3] Urban American Indian groups such as UAII were empowered by these grants to provide a myriad of social services, train a generation of Indian professionals, and develop institutional models that continue to be used today.

Yet to be studied is how these local struggles to serve urban Indian populations were influenced by the public protests of the Red Power movement beyond the influx of new funds. Addressing this question reveals much about American Indian life in cities during the 1970s. It also contributes to new directions in scholarship on the civil rights movement that seeks to understand the relationships between local and national activism. Over a decade ago scholars such as John Dittmer and Charles M. Payne offered a corrective to the "top-down" approach that focused on Martin Luther King Jr. and other national leaders to the exclusion of local people. These studies showed that the foundation for the civil rights movement was established through decades of grassroots activism by unheralded individuals and was carried on during the 1950s and 1960s in localities all over the country.[4] Recent work in American Indian history has similarly argued that the Red Power movement was predicated on a long history of political activism by Native people through early-twentieth-century Progressive organizations, reservation struggles to fight assimilation, and Cold War–era political debates, among other efforts.[5] Some authors also have embraced a "bottom-up" approach to pay attention to how local people received and adapted national movements to particular conditions on the ground. A newly opened chapter of the Black Panthers in a Midwestern city, for example, might show considerable variation from the founding chapter in Oakland, Calif., because of the local population's unique historical experiences and traditions of activism that shaped its understanding of Black Power.[6] All of this work dovetails with that of scholars who have been thinking about a "long civil rights movement" that dates to the 1930s and was developed through various strains and trajectories of activism well into the 1970s.[7] Scholars can gain a better understanding of how movements for social justice are reinterpreted and transform over time by understanding the connections between the local and the national within this extended, multilayered civil rights movement. The patterns that can be gleaned might hold clues for those seeking to understand both the causes preceding and the reverberations following surges of public protest and activism, from the best known nonviolent actions of the 1950s through the Red Power movement of the 1970s.

American Indians in cities who were already operating within a tradition of political activism were encouraged by a national movement that gained publicity through public protests. They then transformed the movement by tailoring its goals and tactics to meet their specific needs. Urban American Indians took advantage of increasing opportunities for serving their communities during the 1970s, as Red Power activists moved Indian concerns into the national spotlight and government officials responded with new policies. The organizations controlled by local activists applied the concepts endorsed by the Red Power movement to the particular issues affecting urban Indian people, such as employment, housing, education, health care, recreation, and cultural development. The mass protest that constituted the public face of the Red Power movement maintained some support and continued to be used selectively around the country. Activists increasingly, however, turned their attention to local urban American Indian organizations and in doing so shifted the location of the Red Power movement from street demonstrations to grassroots Indian activism. At the same time, they made the most forceful and public case to date for their visions of a reimagined Indian Country, one in which cities were understood to be places where Indian people could both survive and thrive.

❖ ❖ ❖

American Indians in cities have been involved in political activism since the early decades of the twentieth century. Scholars Daniel M. Cobb and Loretta Fowler have persuasively argued that the Red Power movement should be understood as an especially visible moment in a long history of Native political action.[8] The urban context is no exception. As early as the 1920s, groups such as the Twin Cities Chippewa Council in Minneapolis–St. Paul and the American Indian Progressive Association in Los Angeles were interested in reforming federal Indian policy, extending citizenship rights to American Indians, and providing services to the poorest of the city's Indians. American Indian actors also were advocates for Native people and sought to influence their working conditions and the depictions of Native people in film, beginning with the first Hollywood Westerns. Certain prominent individuals such as Luther Standing Bear critiqued the ways that the United States had treated Indian peoples throughout its history and argued on behalf of American Indians more generally.

The civil rights movement of the 1950s and 1960s profoundly shifted the nature of political and social activism in America for all groups. African American freedom workers brought attention to the racism and discrimination that permeated day-to-day life and underlay persistent poverty. The federal government responded in the 1960s with legislation and federal policies meant to end racial discrimination. It also created government programs to address the root causes of inequality, such as the Lyndon B. Johnson administration's War on Poverty. These government programs helped politicize community activism by empowering grassroots organizations to serve local needs. Being an "activist" in the 1960s and into the 1970s could mean going out and marching in protests and demonstrations designed to call attention to inequalities or to make demands on public officials. Activism also could mean working with groups and organizations that sought to harness federal poverty funds to serve local communities affected by years of racism and discrimination.

American Indians were within the constituency of the War on Poverty. The bulk of government antipoverty efforts directed at Native people went to reservation communities, however, until the Red Power movement emerged in the early 1970s.[9] A few exceptions included a 1965 Office of Economic Opportunity (OEO) grant for the Central Presbyterian Church in Phoenix, Ariz., to run preschool, day-care, and Head Start programs for the city's American Indians.[10] The newly formed American Indian Study Center in Baltimore, Md., received funding from the OEO's Community Action Agency in 1968 to nurture "Indian culture, Indian life, history and craft" among Lumbee Indians living in the city.[11] The Los Angeles Indian Center received its second War on Poverty grant in 1967 (the first is described in Chapter 5) to pay salaries and to support the center's social services and recreation program.[12]

Native people also took advantage of government efforts in the late 1960s to encourage university attendance by students of color, and they became active on campus in establishing ethnic studies programs. An American Indian Students Association was organized in the fall of 1968 at the University of Minnesota for the forty-five or so Indian students attending the school on state-funded minority scholarships. African American students occupied a university building for forty-eight hours the following January and relented only after plans were made to develop an African American Studies department. American Indian students followed on the demands of these black students, and two weeks later met with university administrators to form an American Indian Studies department that began offering courses and advising students the following year.[13] Native students brought to campus through minority recruitment programs similarly joined African American, Chicano, and Asian American students in successful strikes for the establishment of ethnic studies departments at San Francisco State University (SFSU) and University of California, Berkeley.[14]

Several campuses in the Los Angeles area in these years began recruiting American Indian students and developing programs to assist them as they matriculated. The High Potential Program (HPP) and the Equal Opportunity Program (EOP) both began in 1969 at the University of California, Los Angeles (UCLA) to enroll members of racial groups that were underrepresented in the student body. The HPP sought to recruit and mentor students who would not otherwise have met the university's academic requirements for admission, and the EOP provided funding to promising students with financial need.[15] The American Indian student population at UCLA increased under these programs from seven to seventy for the 1969–70 academic year.[16] Dennis Tafoya (Santa Clara Pueblo) remembered attending UCLA in 1971 as a transfer student from El Camino Junior College in Torrance, Calif., and joining a cohort of Native students.[17] These initiatives to enroll more American Indian students also included developing courses to "give relevance and meaning to the contemporary Indian" on the theory that this would help with the retention of American Indian students. Five instructors of Native descent were hired at UCLA for the fall of 1969 to teach courses such as "Liberation of the American Indian," "American Indian Community Development and Interaction," and "American Indian Studies in Literature."[18] Edward D. Castillo (Cahuilla/Luiseño) taught "Survey in Native American History" and reflected:

> I had always wanted to take a course in American Indian history, and now, ironically, I was assigned to teach the class I had so desperately sought as an undergraduate. I worked fifteen hours a day preparing my lectures and discussion groups. In retrospect, I realize that the entire faculty of our program was seeking to forge a Native American perspective in our various specialties of history, literature, art, and other fields. It was a challenging and powerful reorientation for our students, many of whom were exposed for the first time to a systematic grounding in the national American Indian experience.[19]

This group of students, instructors, and courses became the core of UCLA's research unit, founded in 1970 to promote research, education, and community service related to American Indians and called the American Indian Cultural Center (later renamed the American Indian Studies Center).[20]

This activism by American Indian students and teachers on college campuses and the growing recognition of Native people in cities by government officials set the context for the Red Power movement. There were public demonstrations by American Indians in the 1950s and 1960s that were part of a longer history of political action by Native people that went back decades. American Indian activism did not gain widespread publicity and develop into a national movement, however, until the November 1969 occupation of Alcatraz Island in San Francisco Bay. Eighty-nine American Indians landed on the island and claimed it for a group they called the "Indians of All Tribes." Almost all of the original protestors were students from the American Indian programs at SFSU, Cal-Berkeley, and UCLA. They were led by Richard Oakes (Mohawk), an SFSU student who had traveled from the San Francisco Bay area to UCLA and had recruited almost half of the original occupiers out of Edward Castillo's class (including Castillo).[21] The occupation of Alcatraz soon became a platform for airing Indian grievances and a symbol of renewed pride in Indian identity. The protesters planned to develop the island into a center for the teaching of Indian history, culture, and spirituality and cited a history of abuse, stolen lands, and broken promises. Extensive media coverage publicized the occupation and brought support from around the world. The messages of pride in Indian ancestry and examples of Indian militancy resonated with Indian people, and thousands journeyed to the Bay area to join the protests. Jack Forbes (Powhatan/Delaware) noted that Alcatraz got so much positive publicity that it finally made it "all right to be Indian, headbands and all." The American Indian Movement (AIM), a group organized in Minneapolis in 1968 on the model of the Black Panthers, followed Alcatraz by staging a series of protests that also used confrontational methods and received national attention. Many Indians across the country continued to embrace these protests as a way to focus concern on the problems of Native people and to demand fundamental structural changes in government programs and federal Indian policy.[22]

Cities with American Indian populations became sites of support for the national protests by raising money and staging public demonstrations to draw additional notice to national actions. AIM developed a presence in Los Angeles and depended on both local Indians and a wider leftist coalition to promote its agenda. AIM's national leadership formed an alliance in 1973 with a faction of leaders on the Pine Ridge Reservation in South Dakota. This alliance culminated in a ten-week occupation of Wounded Knee, a reservation hamlet and the site of the infamous 1890 massacre of

Sioux women, men, and children by the U.S. Army. The Wounded Knee occupation drew national attention and helped publicize American Indian issues, such as the poverty, government mismanagement, and continuing loss of land and resources on Indian reservations. AIM members and supporters in Los Angeles rallied in support and worked to collect donations during the occupation. Mark Banks (Anishinaabe) was AIM's press secretary and the older brother of AIM cofounder Dennis Banks. He spent much of the siege in Los Angeles raising money and generating publicity through connections in the local media, whom he had cultivated during several years as a Los Angeles radio and television personality known as "Johnny West."[23] A group calling itself the United People for Wounded Knee (UPWK) began a series of demonstrations in support of the protesters with a mass rally at the downtown Federal Building in March 1973.[24] The same group staged another rally in Griffith Park the following month and organized a "pilgrimage" to Wounded Knee.[25] A benefit for Wounded Knee was held at the University of Southern California and sponsored by the school's Ethnic Studies Department, Asian American Student Alliance, Black Student Union, Movimiento Estudiantil Chicano de Aztlan (MEChA), and Vietnam Veterans against the War.[26] AIM found support in Los Angeles after the occupation ended for its members who were indicted and brought to trial for their participation the following year. Mark Banks continued to raise money in Los Angeles and counted on donations from sympathetic Hollywood stars.[27] Director of the Los Angeles Indian Center Randy Edmonds (Kiowa) remembered: "I used to have AIM people come to the LA Indian Center when I was there . . . Just to stop by, you know, and try to get some money. And I'd help them raise a few bucks here and there, and they'd have a meeting somewhere around, and they'd move on. . . . And [once when they were here] we went and met with Marlon Brando and he gave us $25,000 for an AIM defense fund, up at his house."[28] UPWK sponsored its first postoccupation Wounded Knee benefit in July, featuring "Native American speakers on sovereignty, health conditions, law, the Indian Movement" and a "special message from Dennis Banks." Well-known American Indian musicians Jessie Ed Davis and Floyd Westerman also performed at the event.[29] UPWK held a rally at the downtown Federal Courthouse in October.[30] The group finally celebrated with a victory party after the charges against the Wounded Knee defendants were dropped in the fall of 1974.[31]

Other urban Indians staged their own protests, inspired by the Red Power movement, that were tailored to address local concerns. These protests did not always garner the same amount of attention as the Alcatraz occupation and AIM activities, but they nonetheless drew on the Red Power movement for tactics and ideology. A group of Chicano and Native American activists in Portland, Ore., were encouraged by the atmosphere of Indian empowerment and the renewed pride in Indian identity to begin making plans for the Chicano Indian Studies Center of Oregon (CISCO). They followed the example of Deganawidah-Quetzalcoatl University (DQU), which began near Davis, Calif., in 1971, after a group led by Jack Forbes occupied an unused parcel of federal land and forced negotiations that yielded plans for an indigenous university under the control of Indian and Chicano administrators.[32] CISCO organizers sought a similar program that was based on the "intrinsic value of Chicano and Indian culture." This program would offer "high school or high school equivalency work, college preparatory courses, college level courses, and vocational training, as well as health care and child care." The group particularly hoped to address high dropout rates and target young men who were returning from Vietnam.[33] CISCO organizers proposed establishing the new center at a vacant military base in the town of Corvallis, eighty miles south of Portland, named Adair Air Force Station. They filed a proposal to fund the endeavor and began writing letters to petition Governor Tom McCall and Senator Mark Hatfield.[34]

CISCO leaders turned to the protest tactics of the Red Power movement after months of effort yielded few results. A caravan of Indians from across the county converged on the BIA's national offices in Washington, D.C., in November 1972 as part of an event that AIM organized to publicize the history of U.S.-Indian relations, called the Trail of Broken Treaties. The protesters occupied the BIA's national offices and renamed the building the "American Indian Embassy" when efforts to meet with BIA officials failed.[35] A group of Native people in Portland demonstrated in support at the local BIA office. The occupation in Washington, D.C., soon ended, but CISCO organizers maintained the spirit of protest. They led a group from the Portland protest to the city of Salem and were joined by students at the Chemawa Indian School (a federal boarding school) to number 200 in all. They continued on to Adair Air Force Station in Corvallis, where they occupied a building and clustered in a gymnasium to beat drums, sing, dance, and wave signs that read "American Indian Embassy, Camp Adair Division" and "Custer Had it Coming—Now It's Time for the BIA."[36] The protesters included Sidney Stone (Blackfeet), who was attending graduate school at Oregon State University in Corvallis. Stone jumped at the chance to go, after having been politicized by a summer spent working and seeing the injustices of daily life on the Blackfeet Reservation.[37] John Spence (Blackfeet/Gros Ventre), an assistant professor of Indian Education at Portland State University and an alcohol rehabilitation worker with the city, was a protester who joined a bit more reluctantly. Spence was concerned that authorities would react violently, as they had at other Indian protests around the country. He managed to put aside these worries because of his belief in the importance of the cause.[38] County, state, and federal officials were quick to negotiate with the protesters, and after twenty-four hours an agreement was made to transfer ten buildings to CISCO within thirty days.[39]

A number of other cities were sites of similar protests that applied the tactics, ideology, and general spirit of the Red Power movement to local issues. About one hundred Native people descended in December 1970 on the Southwest Museum of the American Indian, the largest repository of American Indian items outside the Smithsonian Institute and the oldest museum in Los Angeles. They demanded the removal of American Indian remains and sacred relics that were on display. Thirteen people locked themselves in the auditorium, another group went to confront the museum director, and the remainder stayed outside with signs that read "Dig Up Your Own Dead" and "Indian Power." The standoff ended two hours later, after the director covered the exhibits in question with sheets and agreed to meet with the group the following week.[40] Forty Indians returned for a meeting with the director that turned into a two-hour shouting match. The leader of the group presented the museum with a list of fourteen demands that included permanently removing sacred items and giving Indian people more control over the museum. The two sides finally agreed to the removal from public display of a Cheyenne scalp and a medicine bag.[41] Twelve Indian demonstrators were arrested at the museum a few weeks later for locking themselves in the auditorium to protest another exhibit.[42] A group called the Native American Committee organized a protest at the 1970 National Conference of Social Welfare in Chicago where the BIA was to report on its work among Indians. The group was joined by AIM leaders from Milwaukee and Cleveland, who disrupted the conference by rearranging exhibits and commandeering the podium during a plenary session. Another group set up an encampment it called the Chicago Indian Village, outside Wrigley Field, later that year to protest the housing conditions of Native people in the city. The group then moved to occupy a former Nike missile base on Lake Michigan that it planned to convert into housing and a cultural and educational center.[43] Additional protests in the early 1970s by urban Indians included the occupations of Fort Lawton in Washington State, Ellis Island in New York harbor, the Twin Cities Naval Air Station in Minneapolis, and a vacant coast guard lifeboat station in Milwaukee.[44]

Significant numbers of Native people in cities remained skeptical or had mixed feelings about the Red Power movement. Older and more established urban Indians in particular looked upon the occupations and the high-profile protests with disdain. A forty-nine-year-old Indian from Oklahoma named Wayne Miller, who worked as a janitor and was active in Los Angeles Indian community events, stated, "Well, I don't think much about Alcatraz or what they're doing. . . . The younger kids, I think the younger kids, it's just what they see other people doing and they follow in their footsteps, they say, 'Well if they can do that, why can't I,' [they copy] the Chicano and Black militants."[45] Arlene Poemoceah, a Comanche Indian from Oklahoma living in Los Angeles, noted that she was "more involved with my family and my community more or less in my area and just, I just don't know, I really just don't have the time to stop and look at what purpose [Indian protestors are] going for and why."[46] Her husband, Elmer Poemoceah, said, "Well, my way of thinking is that these are not really our ways, you know, the Indian way back home. Personally, I don't think that they are all real Indians [protesting at Alcatraz]."[47]

Sometimes the differing attitudes about the Red Power movement led to public confrontations. Many advocates of Red Power charged that Indians who were in opposition to the movement were "too middle class" and had relinquished their Indian identity and absolved the United States of past injustices. Those opposed to the movement often responded by further scorning the behavior of Red Power supporters. A member of a group called United Native Americans (UNA) caused a stir in 1970 at a meeting of a short-lived effort to create a coordinating body for the different Indian organizations in Los Angeles, called the United American Indian Council (UAIC). The UNA member declared that his organization was "the closest thing to a militant organization" while the UAIC "amounted to no more than a group of middle-class Indians who didn't really represent anyone."[48] Another UNA member attended an event organized at a Los Angeles area cultural center by the local branch of the federal Kennedy Action Corps, titled "An Afternoon of Rapping about the Indian-American." An Indian businessman stated during the event that "Indians had to concentrate on adapting themselves to the white man's world of commerce." This led the UNA member to respond, "You're nothing but a white man," which set off a shouting match.[49] An effort to unite urban American Indian organizations in Portland was beset by similar disagreements in 1971. Members of the Portland American Indian Center (PAIC) pejoratively described some of the younger and angrier delegates as "militants and hippies." John Spence argued in response that the PAIC was too interested in "stressing the positive aspects of Indian life" at the expense of social issues and struggles for Indian rights. Spence further charged that PAIC members tried "to be more white than Indian" and were like "blacks that use hair straighteners."[50]

Most urban Indians were probably somewhere in the middle of this rancorous debate. They may have been troubled by the national protests and images of Indian militancy. Nonetheless, they formed an appreciation for the attention the Red Power movement brought to Indian problems, and they hoped that it would lead to some good. Diane Daychild, a Tohono O'odham Indian living in Phoenix, stated simply, "I agree with [AIM], but I don't agree with how they're approaching [Indian problems]."[51] Tom Knifechief, a twenty-three-year-old Pawnee Indian in Los Angeles, noted in 1971 that he personally did not associate with "militant Indians," but he thought that "Alcatraz was a good thing. I didn't like some of the ways they was doing it, but I think it had to be done that way . . . it got a lot of attention, and it shocked a lot of people because it told them, 'We're tired of being pushed around, and we're tired of being made fun of and we're here.'"[52] Wanda Big Canoe Adamson, who grew up on a reservation in Canada before moving to Los Angeles, had a similar observation: "You sometimes wonder why people are upset with the Black explosion [in social activism], but sometimes that's what it takes, to wake people up. Our Alcatraz situation, a lot of us didn't like it. . . . But out of it came a national awareness that things are bad."[53] The occupation of Wounded Knee in 1973 by AIM protesters brought a fresh round of similar comments. Nancy Herrod, an Indian student at California State University, Los Angeles, thought that the Wounded Knee occupation was "good because it helped Indian people by making the public aware of our problems, but it went on too long and got violent, which turned the public off." Harvey Wells, the coordinator of the HPP at UCLA, believed that the occupation was "inevitable considering government and social oppression against Indians." He could not sanction "placing young Indian lives in danger," but he added that he "supports what [AIM] tries to stand for."[54] A number of veterans of the era maintained ambivalent feelings, looking back on the Red Power movement more than thirty years later. Dennis Tafoya remembered that "there was conflict even amongst my peers, both Indian individuals that I knew who lived in Indian Country, as well as a lot of my Indian friends here [in Los

Angeles, over Red Power protest]." He was especially troubled by his observation that members of AIM "didn't appreciate education" and "really were down on people who went to college." Yet, Tafoya was quick to add: "Don't get me wrong, what was going on in Indian Country was terrible. There was a lot of oppression, a lot of subjugation, there were real problems with authorities and law enforcement, and Indians were dying. So I think AIM did some good work in trying to raise the consciousness of the American people to serious problems."[55] Randy Edmonds also saw AIM and its legacy as somewhat contradictory:

> AIM was trying to bring some notice to Indian problems and I think they did a pretty good job of it. But they turned a lot of people sour too. Even other Indians didn't like it. Alcatraz, again, they're trying to get someone to pay attention to them, to Indian issues. . . . I think it did work to some degree, but it also just pissed a lot of people off. . . . Yeah, that AIM movement was somewhat beneficial, but [it also wasn't] favorable to many Indians because of the tactics that they used. Yet they still brought attention to the Indians, the plight of the Indians.[56]

Most urban Indians could agree that Indians had suffered injustices and that contemporary issues affecting Indian people needed more attention. Many people recognized that the Alcatraz occupation and the AIM protests had helped force the issue, regardless of their shortcomings. Even those Native people involved in these confrontations probably would have agreed, when not being publicly called out as middle class, "apples (red on the outside, white on the inside)," or militants. Mahonta Bad Horse, a Seminole Indian who grew up in Oklahoma and lived in Los Angeles, made just this argument by suggesting that "militants" and those that oppose them "aren't too far apart, they have some of the same concerns."[57]

The full impact of the Red Power movement can ultimately be seen in the tremendous influence it exerted on these grassroots community activists who raised doubts about or even repudiated it but nonetheless were empowered by it and came to espouse and implement its goals. Raymond Sprang, a Northern Cheyenne Indian from Montana who served on the council of the American Indian Student Association at UCLA, said of himself and his fellow Native students: "No, we're not militant. But we're bucking the administration for more recognition and we want an Indian studies department. We're also working for changes in our High Potential Program, we want more student input of ideas and dynamics."[58] American Indian students and Red Power militancy had evolved together and were intricately linked, even though Sprang differentiated them. One of the most important legacies of the Red Power movement was that it led to more support for programs such as those that encouraged university attendance by Native students and curricula designed to meet their particular needs. Local, state, and federal officials were already moving toward addressing the problems facing urban Indians in the late 1960s—through OEO funds and students scholarships, as we have seen. But the occupation of Alcatraz and the activities of groups such as AIM helped prod the Richard M. Nixon administration to take even greater action for Indians and to focus on urban populations. Federal funds for American Indians in cities dramatically increased in the 1970s to support a wide range of new organizations, social services, and educational programs. These organizations reflected many of the ideals of the Red Power movement. They believed that previous efforts to address Indian issues had woefully neglected Indian culture and identity, and that only by foregrounding "Indianness" could Indian problems be solved. Social activists including Sprang and his fellow students also kept up the pressure on officials and policymakers to continue support for their work, even if they were not always as confrontational as some protesters or AIM members. Such local adaptations of the Red Power movement during the 1970s continued long after the high-profile demonstrations faded from the daily news. These adaptations marked the movement's transition from national protest to grassroots Indian activism. The Red Power movement also provided urban Indians with the tools they needed to forcefully claim the social and cultural geography of the city as urban space.

Health care for urban Indians was one of those areas in which there was both an expansion of federal support and an increase in Indian social activism with the rise of the Red Power movement. Native-run health clinics targeting urban Indians were opened in the 1970s in cities across the country, including Chicago; Dallas; Denver; Detroit; Green Bay, Wis.; Los Angeles; Milwaukee; Minneapolis; Oakland; Oklahoma City; Omaha; Portland, Ore.; Seattle; Spokane, Wash.; Tulsa, Okla.; and Wichita, Kans.[59] Inadequate medical and dental care had long been an issue for Native people in cities, and especially since the expansion of urban Indian populations following World War II. On arriving in urban areas, Indians were often ill prepared to negotiate the private health care system after having received free (albeit generally poor) health care services on reservations or in boarding schools from the Indian Health Service (IHS). Some Indians living in cities returned to the reservation to attend to medical needs, but others let conditions go untreated, neglected preventive procedures, and remained

uninformed on a variety of health care issues. Urban Indian poverty intensified these trends. The result was that American Indian health indicators
were among the worst of any urban group in such areas as life expectancy,
infant mortality, diabetes and other preventable diseases, alcoholism, nu-
trition, psychiatric issues, and dental health.[60] The establishment of public
health care facilities offering free services to urban American Indians thus
filled a tremendous need.

The staff that ran these health care centers also might be thought of
as activists working to address historically rooted poverty, to advocate for
self-determination, and to cultivate ethnic identity. Urban Indian health
practitioners believed that these clinics were able to create a more meaningful health care experience for their clients because they were directed
by Native people. Director Juanita Connors of the Indian Free Clinic, Inc.
(IFC) in Huntington Park (an area of Los Angeles with a large Indian population) argued that her organization filled a "social as well as a medical
function," because she had found that urban Indians were reluctant to approach non-Indian health agencies.[61] The IFC maintained an all-Indian
board of directors and employed several Indian doctors and nurses. It
opened in 1971 and was funded by the federal Economic Youth and Opportunities Agency. Its staff of thirty-two volunteer doctors and dentists
saw nearly 150 patients each month during the two nights a week that it
was open. The clinic expanded its patient load, services, and budget over
the next few years through grants that it won from the federal Office of Native American Programs, the federal Women, Infants, and Children (WIC)
Nutritional Program, the California State Health Department, and the California Urban Indian Health Council. The IFC offered a wide range of basic
medical and dental care, prescription medicines, family planning, prenatal
care, and pediatrics; a WIC Nutritional Program; and an Indian Women's
Health Clinic every Tuesday night that included physical checkups, pelvic
examinations, Pap smears, breast examinations, blood tests, and diabetes
testing. The clinic also offered free transportation. The IFC developed a
cultural component that included classes in Native language, culture, and
religion to help get clients in the doors and also to reinforce its programs.
The staff estimated that by 1973 it served 7,000 outpatients per year. The
most common medical conditions it treated among its Indian clientele in
its first year and a half of operation were diabetes, dysentery, venereal disease, tuberculosis, influenza, trachoma, chicken pox, mumps, hepatitis,
pinworms, and skin diseases.[62] The goal of Indian health care workers at
the IFC and in other cities was to heal the Indian sick and ailing. Being able

to do so meant harnessing funds and developing programs that cultivated Indian identity and culture.

The development of programs to treat alcoholism was closely related to the establishment and expansion of health care services for American Indians in cities. These organizations also were focused on the unique experiences and needs of American Indians and sought to cultivate Indian culture as a way of helping its patients. Programs to treat Indian alcoholics and train Indians as alcohol rehabilitation counselors were fueled by federal funding. They opened in many cities during the 1970s, including Albuquerque; Baltimore; Dallas; Denver; Detroit; Los Angeles; Portland, Ore.; Sacramento, Calif.; Salem, Ore.; San Francisco; Seattle; and Sioux City, Iowa.[63] The Native American Rehabilitation Association (NARA) formed in Portland in 1970 and opened a halfway house specifically for Indian people with drinking problems. Steve Askenette, a Menominee Indian, began the group after obtaining start-up funds from St. Vincent de Paul and the Catholic Archdiocese of Portland. Askenette had seen a good deal of the hardships of Indian life and had experienced the failures of general alcohol recovery programs firsthand through the course of a difficult life that included a stint at the Oregon State Penitentiary. Askenette hired an Indian staff, because he believed that "[o]nly another Indian [can] deal with an Indian alcoholic." The staff worked to help its clients by establishing a foundation of ethnic identification and building a program of recovery that incorporated Indian culture and contemporary treatment methods. NARA members fostered pride in Native ancestry by traveling to powwows, where they established a "sobriety tent," hosting alcohol-free powwows, encouraging the sharing of Indian culture between members of the group, and practicing arts and crafts. The group's strong belief in the value and importance of Native ancestry also was reflected in the attitude of the staff. When NARA established its office, its members decided that the telephones, the coffeepots, and the group van would be painted red. NARA also used more mainstream methods of treatment, such as the standard twelve-step program and group counseling popularized by Alcoholics Anonymous and other recovery groups and professionals. Some staff members felt that even more attention to Native culture was warranted, and they splintered off to work with organizations that placed additional emphasis on the development of Indian identity as a path to sobriety. A Lakota man named Devere "Papason" Eastman began a group in 1974 that he named Anpo (a Lakota word translated as "daybreak," "dawn," or "new day"). Anpo leased twenty acres in Mt. Hood National Forest, where the group established a camp that could house about thirty people for ceremonies to treat Indian alcoholics. A similar group named Sweat House Lodge began in the late 1970s in Corvallis, Ore., and was staffed by many members of Portland's Indian community. The group took on live-in clients with alcohol problems and treated them with sweats, drumming, singing, dancing, and the study of Native American spirituality. The lines between NARA, Anpo, and Sweat House Lodge were never clearly fixed. Together they constituted an alcohol recovery community that took Indian identity as a starting point to and an essential ingredient in recovery. NARA brought its clients to Sweat House Lodge and Anpo for regular visits; clients switched programs or were placed according to their specific needs; and staff members moved back and forth between the various groups.[64] One Umatilla Indian man named Vincent Wannassay explained how he first sought treatment from NARA in the late 1970s and then eventually enrolled in Sweat House Lodge after fifteen years of living as an alcoholic on the streets of Portland. He found that he had to find something to replace alcohol, and for him that was Native culture. Wannassay achieved sobriety, went to college, obtained a degree in art, and returned to Portland to become a traditional dancer and leader in Portland's Indian community.[65]

The establishment of alcohol rehabilitation programs for American Indians followed remarkably similar patterns in Los Angeles. Indian Lodge became the city's first Indian alcohol program as part of the social service organization Indian Welcome House. Indian Lodge began operating as a halfway house by 1972 in a private home near downtown, under the oversight of the Los Angeles Indian Center and with grants from the OEO and the Intertribal Council of California. The Indian Lodge was served by an all-Indian staff. It housed about fifteen clients who were contacted on skid row or referred from hospitals, jails, welfare agencies, and health departments. Clients had to be sober for forty-eight hours and were issued a blanket, a sheet, a pillowcase, a towel, soap, a toothbrush, clothes, and aspirin and were given a mandatory shower and enema. They were asked to stay two weeks and to perform household chores that paid twenty dollars a week to help build self-esteem. They also were assisted in finding work and were visited on the job by staff members.[66]

The staff members at Indian Lodge felt that they were uniquely able to understand the problems of their clients and to help Indians get sober, because they were both recovering alcoholics and Indians themselves. Counselor Melvin Chiloquin, a Klamath and Shasta Indian who had been sober for three years, described the Indian Lodge's clients and his ability to relate to them: "These are men from off the streets and from out of courts and hospitals, men who are down and out and don't have even the price of a down payment on a postage stamp. These are men who are sick and shaky and miserable and ready to throw in the sponge if they could only find out how to throw in the sponge. I've been there many times myself so they can identify with me as having given up booze and making a go of everyday life moment by moment. Slowly but surely they come around to it too."[67] Director Edward Olivas, a Chumash Indian with twelve years of sobriety, more specifically addressed the function of an all-Indian alcohol treatment center and its ability to succeed where other programs had failed: "[Many alcohol programs] are run by the white man and sometimes Indians feel more at home with their own people. They feel like they could probably accomplish more amongst themselves. They feel like there's more understanding, there's more communication, that they belong more when they're amongst themselves."[68] Frank DuPoint, a Kiowa Indian, Indian Lodge's house manager, and a recovering alcoholic, echoed Olivas's thoughts: "Among alcoholics, there's a lot of compassion involved toward one another, in relationship with one another. And being an Indian, it seems as though it's the companionship and the relationships working throughout the building here are in better harmony than they would be working with the white institutions."[69] The Indian Lodge used methods of treatment adapted from AA and complemented it with a program of Indian culture and identity in ways that were similar to NARA's. House residents attended outside AA meetings, hosted an AA meeting open to the public, heard educational lectures, watched films, and learned about Indian arts and crafts. The Lodge held a closed AA meeting for house members on Friday night, called the "Saddle-Up Group," which included a "rap session on alcoholism and the problems of urban Indians." DuPoint noted that "[the residents are better able to] relax there during those [Friday] meetings, because they're all Indians. They chat and they more or less let their hair down and talk." Lodge members often went on weekends as a group to local powwows or played as a team in the American Indian Athletic Association softball league. Graduates of Indian Lodge could still get help from its staff through an outpatient clinic after being discharged.[70] The Indian Lodge began a separate program for women by 1974. Around this same time, the American Indian Free Clinic in Compton, Calif., established a thirty-day residential alcohol program with funding from Los Angeles County, called the Main Artery Alcohol Recovery Program.[71] Indians could also get treatment for alcoholism through UAII beginning in 1973 (as described at the beginning of this chapter). UAII required only that its clients be in need of a safe place to get away from the streets and regroup among other Indians and did not require them to be sober to be admitted. UAII often referred its clients in need of more intensive treatment to Indian Lodge or Main Artery.[72]

Education for urban Indians was another long neglected area that got attention in the early 1970s. Studies found that urban American Indians consistently ranked at the bottom of performance testing when compared with other groups and maintained some of the highest dropout rates. A rise in Indian advocacy and increased funding led to a rethinking of the ways that Indians in cities experienced the educational system from preschool through higher education. Advocates for Indian education specifically placed importance on the need for Indian instructors and the foregrounding of Indian identity and culture. The Milwaukee Indian Community School began in 1970 when three American Indian mothers began home-schooling local Indian children, and it later moved to a local church to accommodate more students. The school was then able to acquire part of an abandoned Coast Guard station near the city after AIM occupied the site. The school focused on the remedial needs of Indian students in grades K–12. It also maintained an "Indian core" that included visiting instructors from local reservations and classes in five Native languages. By 1976 a total of 102 students had attended the school, and six of the nine teachers were of Native descent. Grants from the Indian Education Act and the Department of Agriculture allowed twice as much spending on each student as was the national average in public schools. Federal funds similarly helped establish in 1971 the Heart of the Earth Survival School in Minneapolis, which stressed Indian culture through much of its curriculum. It was followed by another alternative school in Minneapolis, called the Red School. It sought to "offer an alternative system to provide [Indian] children and future leaders with tools of survival . . . and give them a good, relevant education which does not cost them their identity, religion, music, heritage, or pride."[73] The Little Big Horn School was begun as an alternative public American Indian school in Chicago in 1971. It hired a staff of five and enrolled eighty Indian high school students with a $250,000 federal grant.[74]

Los Angeles during the 1970s was a particularly active site of reform and activism in Indian education. Tribal American Consulting Corporation opened Tribal American Preschool in Bell Gardens, Calif., in September 1972. Tribal American was funded by a grant from the state Department of Education and began in an old church building with a class of ninety children. It received federal funding over the next couple of years under a Title IV grant that allowed it to add a day-care center and develop programs for parents on topics such as how to create learning environments at home and other issues related to American Indian education. Glenna Amos, a Cherokee Indian, remembered how important Tribal American was to her as a place where she could take children and also interact with other Indian parents:

> My two younger children both were in pre-school and day care with [Tribal American]. Both of them went through kindergarten there . . . that really made me able to work, because I had no one to baby-sit for me. . . . So for me, Tribal American worked perfectly, it made a big difference, and as a single mother at that time . . . it gave me a place to see people, to talk to people, to talk to other single parents that were having the same kind of problems that I was. We had our annual parent meetings where we'd go to Kellogg West [Conference Center in Pomona] or something and stay for the whole weekend and hear speakers, and have steak dinners, for me it was a real treat. It was also exciting because we'd hear the good things about what was out there for our kids and how we could guide them and that was really important.

Tribal American's programs emphasized active learning, with a particular focus on developing an awareness of Indian culture and its contributions to American society. Amos recalled: "[Tribal American] had a cultural van that would come and the kids could either do tutorials or cultural activities, depending on whether they were behind in school and needed help with reading or math, otherwise they could do cultural activities. . . . The kids really looked forward to that because they got a snack and they got to do their beadwork or grow a plant or whatever they were doing, it meant a lot to them." Cultural activities included Indian arts and crafts, Indian dancing, Indian storytelling and music, and learning about Indian life. Tribal American's board of directors and staff were mostly Indian, and it received a federal Comprehensive Employment and Training Act grant to hire and train Indian staff.[75]

There also were efforts in Los Angeles to adjust the curriculum and policies of public schools to account for the needs of American Indian students, parents, and employees. The American Indian Education Commission (AIEC) was established in February 1976 by the Los Angeles City Unified School District as a component and advisory board to the Board of

Education. The AIEC was composed of two paid staff members and thirty volunteer "Indian Community Commissioners" who met once a month to address a variety of issues, such as defending the rights of Indian students, representing Indian parents in school disputes, and assisting Indian teachers in personnel matters. The AIEC also provided training to non-Indian school personnel on how to work with Indian students, with emphasis on developing respect for Indian culture and values in the classroom. The group reviewed and evaluated books, films, and other classroom materials, developed curriculum and resource materials, and worked for the hiring of more Indian teachers and staff. Indian parents and educators also could follow the work of the AIEC and other educational news through its publication *The Moccasin Telegraph*.[76]

The initiative to develop American Indian Studies programs and recruit Native students into higher education that began in the late 1960s intensified on the campuses of Los Angeles area colleges and universities during the early 1970s. California State University, Long Beach (CSULB) began implementing the Educational Opportunities Programs and planned to admit seventy-five Indian students for the fall 1972 semester, so as to more than double the number on campus. CSULB offered five American Indian Studies classes, supported a Native American Student Council to provide input on the American Indian Studies program, and had plans to develop all-Indian student housing and day care.[77] Native students at CSULB also worked within a larger organization of American Indian college students in Southern California, called the Native American Student Alliance. It included members from the University of California campuses at Los Angeles, San Diego, Irvine, Santa Barbara, and Berkeley, in addition to Los Angeles City College and East Los Angeles College.[78]

UCLA's American Indian Cultural Center (AICC) and its population of Indian students were especially active throughout the 1970s. Nine additional American Indian Studies courses were submitted for approval by the spring of 1972 to enhance the five already being taught, as part of a larger effort to develop the curriculum. The AICC also was working with other departments, such as history, art history, and foreign languages, to create cross-listed classes. The School of Library Science began helping with the AICC Library, and by the end of 1974 it contained 6,000 volumes and maintained 250 serial subscriptions.[79] Enrollments of American Indian undergraduate and graduate students continued to climb, as UCLA implemented new recruitment and retention programs. Indians became eligible for the UCLA Academic Advancement Program (UAAP), which targeted groups that were underrepresented in the student body for socioeconomic reasons. Fifty-two Native students were admitted to UCLA in 1973 under UAAP, and an Indian counselor was hired to advise them on academic, financial, housing, and personal issues.[80] The leaders of certain graduate programs also worked to increase their Indian enrollments. The Masters of Public Administration Program received a grant for that purpose from the federal Office of Economic Opportunity, and the Masters of Library Science Program received funding from the federal Health, Education, and Welfare Department.[81] American Indian enrollment at UCLA was up to 195 students by the fall of 1973 and included thirty-two graduate students.[82]

Many of these students participated in an especially vibrant American Indian Student Association that provided peer counseling, sponsored Indian speakers and musicians, and organized an Indian Culture Week every May.[83] The 1973 festivities featured lectures, concerts, a powwow, films, and guests that included activist Vine Deloria Jr., musicians Paul Ortega and Floyd Westerman, and actors Tom Laughlin and Iron Eyes Cody.[84] Such activities were essential for nurturing and retaining Indian students. Anthony F. Purley, the AICC director in 1971, noted that in the past Indian students had always had to "stop being Indian essentially" or give up their ethnic identification and hereditary culture in order to succeed in college.[85] That changed dramatically under the higher education programs of the early 1970s. James Monroe, a Blackfeet and Yakama Indian, noted: "[When I enrolled as a student at UCLA, it was] the first time that I really can remember relating to Indians, as something that, I don't know how you would say it . . . as an identity. . . . The Indians in Cut Bank [near the Blackfeet Reservation in Montana] that I would talk to, play sports, whatever, we didn't really talk about our Indian heritage that much. . . . At UCLA I took some Indian culture classes, some Indian history."[86] This ability to "be Indian" socially, culturally, and intellectually while attending college helped thousands of American Indian students graduate from Los Angeles area universities during the 1970s and beyond.

The organizations that benefited the most from the Red Power movement and the new attention to urban Indian concerns were "Indian centers" located in cities throughout the country. Indian centers were in many cases established during the 1950s as recreational and charitable organizations in response to the burgeoning postwar urban Indian populations. In the 1970s they developed into well-funded, multifaceted, Indian-run social service agencies with the help of federal funds. There are examples in many cities—including Baltimore; Chicago; Cleveland; Dallas; Denver;

Detroit; Fairbanks, Alaska; Lincoln, Nebr.; Oakland; Omaha; Minneapolis; Phoenix; Portland, Ore.; San Diego; San Francisco; Seattle; Sioux City, Iowa; and Toronto—but no other group exemplifies the empowerment of Indian activism as fully as the Los Angeles Indian Center. It was one of four urban Indian centers across the country to receive a grant in 1971, under the Model Urban Indian Centers Program funded by the departments of Health, Education, and Welfare; Labor; and, Housing and Urban Development, in addition to the Office of Economic Opportunity. (The other cities were Denver, Omaha, and Phoenix.) The program was intended to allow the Los Angeles Indian Center to significantly expand its range of services to the local Indian population and to develop models that would be studied for use by Indian centers in other cities.[87] Six departments were established by Indian Center staff in the first year of the grant, and each was headed by a full-time employee. The Employment Department set up interviews, counseled, made referrals, contacted government agencies and corporations about jobs, developed work-study programs, and helped get Indian students enrolled in local colleges through the new recruitment programs. Indian students also received help through the Tutorial Department, which served elementary through secondary school students, enrolled Indians in General Educational Development (GED) classes, offered free piano classes, and organized trips to museums, beach parties, and picnics. The Social Services Department provided free tax-preparation classes, coordinated potluck dinners, spoke for local groups to raise money, created exhibits and booths for local exhibitions, and held weekly "rap sessions" for Indian girls. The Youth Department built on the traditions that dated back to the 1950s by organizing outings to movies, puppet shows, baseball games, county fairs, and circuses. It also helped Indian youths to attend summer camps and offered Indian cultural classes. The Community Services Department distributed money, clothing, and household goods to families, in addition to providing counseling and referrals. The Public Information Department revived the publication of *Talking Leaf*, kept updated lists of Indian organizations in Los Angeles, wrote grants for new programs, met with television networks and movie studios to advise on images of Indians in the media, compiled a photo library, and contributed to local public affairs television and radio productions.[88] Two new satellite centers also were opened and were fully staffed through the grant funds. Indians could receive services through Indian Center West in West Los Angeles or through Indian Center Southeast in Huntington Park, in addition to the main location near downtown.[89]

The future of the Indian Center seemed in jeopardy, and all three locations were slated to close when the Model Urban Indian Centers grant ran out in 1974.[90] Two new funding sources were later secured that allowed the Indian Center to continue the expansion of its services and programs until the end of the decade. The Greater Los Angeles Community Action Agency gave almost $60,000 to the Indian Center for its education programs.[91] The Indian Center received an even more important grant under the federal Comprehensive Employment and Training Act (CETA) that was designed "to provide job training and employment opportunities to economically disadvantaged, unemployed, under-employed populations." The Indian Center's CETA grant was for the development of a "comprehensive manpower program to raise the employment potential of Indians in Los Angeles." It was to create youth programs, on-the-job training, classroom training, remedial educational counseling, career planning, cultural projects, transportation services, health care programs, and child care services, with the assistance of an advisory council composed of representatives from the Department of Labor, Bureau of Indian Affairs, and Los Angeles County and City governments.[92]

The parameters of the CETA grant turned out to be sufficiently broad so that the Indian Center was able to use it to fund virtually all of its ongoing programs and its expansion into other areas. Indian Center's Executive Director Lincoln Billedeaux marveled after a year at the rapid growth enabled by the CETA grant and noted that the Indian Center had evolved into a "comprehensive, multi-purpose socio-economic delivery agency offering an array of programs and services to the Los Angeles Indian Community."[93] It added a new location in the San Gabriel Valley city of El Monte, and the home branch of the Indian Center moved into a three-building complex with a parking lot on Washington Boulevard in downtown Los Angeles.[94] Indian Center Southeast in Huntington Park also was moved to larger facilities in Bell Gardens because of the demand for services in Southeast and South Los Angeles.[95]

The Indian Center's increased budget also better enabled it to serve the kinds of community functions that had been a basis for the organization since its founding in the 1930s. The Indian Center's newsletter, *Talking Leaf*, became more polished, first as a magazine and later as a newspaper. It was published with more regularity and sent to subscribers in Los Angeles and in other cities, as well as on Indian reservations throughout the country. *Talking Leaf* continued to print news of births, deaths, weddings, and the activities of local Indian organizations, churches, sports leagues, and powwow groups. All of the new resources available to Indians in Los Angeles in the realms of health, recreation, education, employment, and other areas were advertised, along with the programs and services of the Indian Center. *Talking Leaf* also prominently featured national Indian news, including the major protests and issues brought about by the Red Power movement and profiles of Indian professionals, entertainers, and athletes of national reputation.[96]

The physical locations of the Indian Center served as centers of community where Indian people felt welcome to take advantage of the services or simply gather to socialize. All four Indian Center branches developed their own unique character that reflected the specific interests of the staff and their clients in that part of the city. Indian Center West had its own team within the American Indian Athletic Association softball league and ran a popular boxing program. It also sponsored silversmith classes taught by a local Navajo master silversmith, who worried that young Indians in the city were missing out on the traditional arts taught on the reservation.[97] Indian Center Southeast was the site of the Drum and Feather Club powwow every third Saturday of the month and the weekly meeting place for an all-Indian Boy Scout troop and an Alcoholics Anonymous group.[98] It sponsored a Career Day in April 1975 to make Indian students aware of educational and career opportunities available in Los Angeles. It featured an address by Vine Deloria Jr., representatives from twenty-five area colleges, universities, and trade schools, and a powwow in Ford Park. Free transportation was provided for the event from the other Indian Center locations.[99] The Los Angeles County Department of Parks and Recreation also contributed to Indian Center Southeast by sponsoring a ten-week workshop on Indian dancing and singing, and the Greater Los Angeles Community Action Agency gave Indian Center Southeast a special grant for youth programs.[100] A variety of other unique activities and programs were available at Indian Center headquarters, Indian Center West, Indian Center Southeast, and Indian Center San Gabriel Valley.

Overall, the tremendous range of services provided by the Los Angeles Indian Center and other urban American Indian organizations in the 1970s is a testament to the influence of the national Red Power movement; the importance of local, state, and federal antipoverty programs; and the willingness of local activists to harness these newly available resources to better serve the social and cultural needs of urban Indian communities— thereby laying claim to urban areas as part of a reimagined Indian Country. Thousands of Indian people benefited from these services, whether the services were emergency food and shelter, training for better-paying and more-fulfilling jobs, opportunities for expressing Indian culture, comprehensive health care, or education that embraced Indian identity. These programs nurtured working-class urban Indian communities and trained a generation of professionals in ways that enabled many Indian people to move from the depths of poverty to more comfortable lives and increasingly into the middle class. A few examples help illustrate the efficacy of these programs. Victor Hill came to Los Angeles in 1974 as an alcoholic who was separated from his family and possessed few job skills. He checked into the Indian Lodge and got sober, then started taking classes at UCLA and joined the Indian Lodge staff through the CETA program. "For a guy like me with no training," Hill reflected, "[Indian Lodge] sets you up and makes things happen. . . . My life and this place have helped me make this 180 degree turn."[101] Gloria Sanborn left the Navajo Reservation for Los Angeles in the late 1960s to find a better life for herself and her young daughter. Nine years later she had worked at several part-time jobs, depended on welfare, and could not afford the tuition to finish stenographer school. Sanborn went to the Indian Center for help in 1976 and enrolled in an employment training program that enabled her to finish school and find professional work. She expressed her appreciation for the Indian Center's help and said, "I'm tired of being poor and hungry . . . it's a lot easier being an Indian if you've got the bucks behind you."[102] Dennis Tafoya grew up in a more financially secure household in Hermosa Beach, Calif., but also benefited from the programs at UCLA. In 1975 he began a job with the Los Angeles County Department of Social Services as a welfare eligibility worker and the department's liaison to the city's Indian community. Tafoya eventually rose up through the ranks to become the director of the Los Angeles County Office of Affirmative Action Compliance and the highest-ranking American Indian in Los Angeles County government.[103] Hill, Sanborn, Tafoya and thousands of other American Indians in cities would have encountered many more obstacles along their way without the social service programs of the 1970s. These programs and their focus on Indian self-determination, Indian nationalism, and Indian cultural identity were a positive step in what had been a long and devastating history of relationships between Indian people and local, state, and federal governments.

The history of social service programs for American Indians in urban areas during the 1970s also illuminates a type of grassroots activism that should be considered part of the Red Power movement as much as the highly publicized protests and demonstrations of the era. Local leaders in cities around the country seized on the opportunities created by the new attention placed on Indian concerns and kept the pressure on public officials to fund the work they were doing serving their communities. Sidney Stone reflected on the importance of the Red Power era after a career spent as a social worker for American Indians. Stone believed that during the 1970s the new prominence of Native people helped counter the hopelessness that had developed through decades of failed government policies. Stone went on to say that Indian people were taught throughout their lives to look the other way and that they could not do anything to change the status quo. The activist movement turned this around. Stone participated in demonstrations to publicize American Indian issues in the early 1970s and then took that same ethos and applied it to her community service.[104] Native activism had never before attainted the level of a national movement that reached so many Indian people and gained such support across American society. The transition from these high-profile protests to the types of grassroots, community-based activism practiced by Stone and thousands of others reveals a great deal about how national movements can reverberate in localities throughout the country. It also makes the case for more investigations of how local populations relate to national movements. These studies should emphasize the importance of national actions. Researchers may ultimately find, however, that the real work of changing people's lives is located more squarely in grassroots activism. Such activism also both drew on and perpetuated the reimagining of Indian Country by forcefully claiming the social and cultural geography of the city as Indian. It is a reimagining that continues to the present day—although not uncontested—as is discussed in the Conclusion.

INDIAN COUNTRY, REIMAGINED

Cities, Towns, and Indian Reservations into the Twenty-First Century

The American Indian Resource Center (AIRC) at the County of Los Angeles Library in Huntington Park celebrated its twenty-fifth anniversary in 2004. It was established as one of four ethnic studies resource centers in 1969, and it has since developed the largest county library collection of American Indian materials in the country. Local schoolchildren, American Indian community members, and scholars regularly take advantage of the AIRC's books, periodicals, microfilm, newspapers, videotapes and DVDs, audiocassettes and compact disks, vertical file of more than 800 subject folders, and the only complete sets of the Indian Census Records and Records of the Indian Claims Commission outside of the National Archives and Records Administration. The AIRC also bills itself as an "information referral center" to American Indians in Greater Los Angeles that helps urban Native people stay informed on contemporary issues relating to health, education, employment, law, economic development, politics, culture, and community activities.[1]

The library also has faced a number of serious challenges. Library administrators consistently failed to find qualified Indian librarians or even directors familiar with issues in Indian Country between the mid-1970s and the mid-1990s. Budget cuts in the 1980s eliminated funding for the center's only two staff positions, a library assistant and a library aide to the director, as well as for a county-level ethnic resource center coordinator, who had worked to make sure that each center was being properly served by the county. The distance between the county library management and the AIRC grew, and some of the most basic library and archival management practices were neglected. Michael McLaughlin (Winnebago) later served as AIRC director. He noted, for instance, that collection development lagged for years at a time, so that "there were a lot of dissertations and theses from the late 1970s to [about] 1985 and then suddenly you have no dissertations for ten years." McLaughlin was nonetheless hopeful following a 2005 meeting with the directors of the other County of Los Angeles Public Library ethnic resource centers and the county librarian that included discussions of issues such as funding, classification of materials, collection development, and preservation. It was the first time that the county librarian had visited an ethnic resource center outside of a public event, as far as anyone could remember.[2]

The history of the AIRC helps illustrate the inroads American Indians have made into urban areas across the United States and also how challenges still face their communities. The AIRC came about in an atmosphere of rising urban Indian populations, national and grassroots Indian activism, and government and public support for urban Indian programs, including many of the social service organizations that served Indian people. That support began to fade over subsequent decades even as urban Indian populations continued to grow. Indians in cities have increasingly been forced to regroup and seek creative ways to address their needs, while learning from their experiences and those of earlier generations of urban migrants. All of the themes that have helped define the American Indian populations of the country's urban areas—migration to the city, the diversity of life and work experience, the creation of urban Indian organizations, struggles for visibility, and social mobility—persist as the new millennium continues to unfold.

The AIRC also exists within a much larger network of places important to Native people that expands throughout the city, the region, and even the country. Much of this book has focused on the experiences of American Indians *within* urban, metropolitan areas. It has examined the migrations of Indians to U.S. cities, the experiences of urban Indian life, and the formation of groups and organizations that fostered urban Indian identity, culture, and community. In doing so, it follows patterns long established by histories of immigrant communities that focus on the new lives established by migrants at their destination points.[3] Such an approach also resembles the vast majority of scholarship on postconquest Indian history that regards Indian reservations, boarding schools, and cities as bounded and all-encompassing.[4] The increasingly complex relationships that have developed between cities, towns, rural areas, and Indian reservations throughout the country are unaccounted for in this model. Cities have not simply become destinations to Native people. They also are important points on networks across which Indians move with regularity.

In other words, reimagining Indian Country to include the cities of the United States means more than just shifting the location of Indian Country to urban areas for the majority of American Indians. Cities, towns, rural areas, and Indian reservations altogether make up an Indian Country reimagined for the twenty-first century.

◆ ◆ ◆

U.S. census numbers have always been problematic but nonetheless show that urban American Indian populations have continued to rise in past decades. American Indian activists and organizations have long claimed that the census dramatically undercounts Native people in cities. The 1990 census reported that the number of American Indians in Greater Los Angeles decreased from almost 61,000 in 1980 to fewer than 58,000, even as the urban American Indian population nationwide rose by approximately 275,000. A group of American Indian social service providers, business leaders, artists, educators, and entertainers responded by forming the American Indian Complete Count Committee of Los Angeles and Orange Counties in the year 2000 to encourage Indian participation in the census and to avoid what they called the mistakes of 1990.[5] The 2000 federal census numbers for urban American Indians were again higher for Greater Los Angeles, and they also continued to climb nationwide. A new option on the 2000 census further complicated these statistics, however. Census participants could check more than one category as they self-identified by race. This meant that non-Indians who checked the "American Indian or Alaska Native" box as a secondary identifier because of a belief in indigenous ancestry were included in the "American Indian and Alaska Native alone or in combination with one or more other races" category with people of mixed ancestry who identified strongly as Native American. Nonetheless, the "American Indian and Alaska Native Alone" category still indicates a significant increase in urban populations throughout the country. Even when viewed critically, the 2000 census is thus consistent with the trends of the past century. In other words, urban Indian populations have continued to grow and represent a greater majority of all American Indians (see Table 3).

This also continues to be an economically stratified population. Indian poverty persists, both in the homes of urban American Indian families and on the city streets. A study by the National Urban Indian Policy Coalition published in 1996 found that mental health patients served by urban Indian health clinics increased by 200 percent from 1988 to 1990; urban

TABLE 3 American Indian and Alaska Native Population of Select U.S. Urbanized Areas, 1980–2000

			2000	
Urbanized Area	1980	1990	American Indian and Alaska Native Alone	American Indian and Alaska Native Alone or in Combination with One or More Other Races
Los Angeles–Long Beach	60,893	57,624	94,320	169,511
San Francisco–Oakland	16,959	20,611	16,324	41,257
Seattle	13,868	19,879	27,849	57,348
New York–Northeast New Jersey	19,745	42,245	62,500	140,630
Chicago–Northwest Indiana	9,216	13,142	22,251	50,420
Minneapolis–St. Paul	14,895	22,451	19,339	33,557
Denver	7,864	12,058	18,713	34,458
Oklahoma City	17,035	21,948	25,208	41,831
Albuquerque	8,436	13,681	39,992	47,280
United States	827,075	1,100,534	1,487,386	2,954,411
(% of Total American Indian and Alaska Native Population)	(54%)	(56%)	(61%)	(69%)

Source: U.S. Bureau of the Census, *1980 Census of Population: Volume I, Characteristics of the Population; Chapter B: General Population Characteristics; Part 6: California* (Washington, D.C.: GPO, 1983), 172, 177; U.S. Bureau of the Census, *1980 Census of Population: Volume I, Characteristics of the Population; Chapter B: General Population Characteristics; Part 7: Colorado* (Washington, D.C.: GPO, 1983), 50; U.S. Bureau of the Census, *1980 Census of Population: Volume I, Characteristics of the Population; Chapter B: General Population Characteristics; Part 15: Illinois* (Washington, D.C.: GPO, 1983), 122; U.S. Bureau of the Census, *1980 Census of Population: Volume I, Characteristics of the Population; Chapter B: General Population Characteristics; Part 25: Minneapolis* (Washington, D.C.: GPO, 1983), 71; U.S. Bureau of the Census, *1980 Census of Population: Volume I, Characteristics of the Population; Chapter B: General Population Characteristics; Part 33: Albuquerque* (Washington, D.C.: GPO, 1983), 36; U.S. Bureau of the Census, *1980 Census of Population: Volume I, Characteristics of the Population; Chapter B: General Population Characteristics; Part 34: New York* (Washington, D.C.: GPO, 1983), 159; U.S. Bureau of the Census, *1980 Census of Population: Volume I, Characteristics of the Population; Chapter B: General Population Characteristics; Part 38: Oklahoma* (Washington, D.C.: GPO, 1983), 56; U.S. Bureau of the Census, *1980 Census of Population: Volume I, Characteristics of the Population; Chapter B: General Population Characteristics; Part 49: Washington* (Washington, D.C.: GPO, 1983), 55; U.S. Bureau of the Census, *1990 Census of Population; General Population Characteristics: United States* (Washington, D.C.: GPO, 1992), 3; U.S. Bureau of the Census, *1990 Census of Population; General Population Characteristics: Urbanized Areas* (Washington, D.C.: GPO, 1992), 54, 87, 101, 165, 176, 188, 192, 226, 232; U.S. Bureau of the Census, *2000 Census of Population and Housing, United States: 2000, Summary Population and Housing Characteristics* (Washington, D.C.: GPO, 2002), 294, 341; "American FactFinder," U.S. Census Bureau, http://factfinder.census.gov (accessed 15 February 2010).

Indians exhibited three times the rate of all other racial groups for diabetes and heart disease; and suicide rates for urban Indians were four times greater than for all other racial groups. The study then focused on Chicago and stated that 25 percent of the city's American Indian population lived below the poverty line, and 38 percent of American Indian households earned less than $15,000 a year.[6] In a 2000 study, researchers at the University of California, Los Angeles (UCLA) similarly examined three decades of census data and came to the conclusion that American Indians in Los Angeles faced a crisis of poverty, education, and housing. Approximately 25 percent of Native children in the city were living below the federal poverty line, and 45 percent were in families headed by a single parent. Native students also were less likely to go on to postsecondary education, and those who did had higher than average dropout rates. Another 2000 UCLA study compared the Los Angeles County American Indian population with non-Hispanic whites. It found that the poverty rate among Native people was more than two and half times greater; Native families were eight times more likely to live in the poorest neighborhoods; the unemployment rate was almost twice as high for Native people; and Native men and women earned 45 percent less and 31 percent less, respectively.[7] A national study by the Seattle Indian Health Board's Urban Indian Health Initiative found that, compared with the rest of the population, urban American Indians suffered higher rates of chronic illness and were more likely to die from accidents and alcoholism.[8]

There also are signs that urban American Indians persist in moving solidly into the middle class. American Indian professionals who came of age in the 1970s and 1980s are among the leaders of today's city Indian organizations, work as lawyers, doctors, and educators, and serve in city and county government.[9] American Indians are still concentrated in the working-class communities of American cities, but they also have moved in greater numbers to more affluent middle-class neighborhoods.[10] Glenna Amos (Cherokee) noted while reflecting back on over fifty years of life in Los Angeles: "We've come a long way. . . . I know that I'm almost 62 and most of us that came out on relocation, most of our kids have moved from the neighborhoods that we came into when we relocated, to the next better neighborhood. Like the people who lived in Bell Gardens now live in Norwalk and Downey and are buying homes rather than renting." Amos believed that "employment-wise a greater majority of our people are able to find jobs, have skills, and work" in contrast to when she was growing up in Los Angeles. Amos also found in her work as a social service provider that even people newly arrived in the city from the reservation "have a much higher level of education and they don't have as much trouble . . . because they've been off to smaller cities and have more experience with non-Indian people."[11]

Access to higher education in particular has remained a focus of American Indian community leaders and plays an important role in this social mobility, even if Native people are attending at rates lower than those of other ethnic groups. Portland State University (PSU) boasts the largest enrollment of American Indian students in Oregon and built a $4.5 million Native American Students and Community Center at its downtown campus in 2003. University administrators explained that the student center was unique, in that it was meant to provide student services and also to welcome American Indians from the larger community, such as tribal elders living in or visiting the city. Francene Ambrose (Yakama), a twenty-four-year-old graduate student, welcomed the center for the chance to meet with other Native people of various generations and from different tribes, noting, "Now we have someplace to get together." PSU's President Daniel Bernstine argued that, in combination with a newly established Native American Studies minor, the center would foster American Indian community and help students toward graduation.[12] Colleges and universities throughout Greater Los Angeles also continue to recruit and nurture Native students on campus by developing relevant curriculum and support services. The American Indian Studies Center at UCLA offers a master's program, colloquiums, and support for advanced research. American Indian students at UCLA play a particularly active role in sponsoring speakers and cultural events, such as the annual powwow, and mentoring and tutoring both current and prospective students. Indian students making their way through college have more Native faculty as role models, even if as a whole it is yet another area where Indian people are underrepresented.[13]

Urban Indian organizations that have supported Native people and helped to define a reimagined Indian Country in U.S. cities since the early twentieth century have faced a number of challenges in recent decades. Federal funding to urban Indian groups was scaled back in the late 1970s and plummeted in the 1980s. Oftentimes, allegations of financial mismanagement and embezzlement by some groups exacerbated funding woes. A number of cases involved inexperienced administrators and bookkeepers, while in others blatant malfeasance occurred. The 1970s saw the growth of the Urban Indian Program (UIP) in Portland. UIP operated at a budget of almost $1.5 million a year by 1975. Grants from various local, state, and federal sources allowed it to hire a full-time staff of forty-three and 108 program trainees. Its programs included a full-time health clinic that provided diagnosis and treatment for 15,000 patient visits a year; a day-care center for Native children; classes that taught urban skills, such as balancing a checkbook and understanding landlord-tenant laws; and counseling for former convicts of Indian ancestry. UIP received recognition from the federal Department of Housing and Urban Development and the Department of the Interior in 1979, when the agencies jointly funded a project that took the UIP as a model for presentations to other urban Indian groups across the nation. Federal budgets for Indian affairs and other social spending were slashed drastically, however, during the 1980s and thus UIP's major sources of funding were cut off. Internal consensus was at times tenuous during the 1970s and disintegrated under this new stress. Mismanagement and embezzlement served as the final death knell, and by the mid-1980s UIP ceased to exist. Other groups in Portland disappeared or reduced their services and got by on budgets of only a small fraction of those a few years earlier.[14] Similar events occurred in Los Angeles. Several Los Angeles area Indian groups closed their doors for good in the 1980s and 1990s, including the Los Angeles Indian Center. It had been the oldest urban Indian organization in the country and had served Native people in the city for more than fifty years.[15]

Other Indian organizations have found new ways to survive, adapt, and prosper, as they have continued to define and support a reimagined Indian Country into the twenty-first century. Indians across the country worked creatively after the worst of the budget cuts were over in the 1990s to secure funding sources, rebuild their programs, and create new ones to meet the evolving needs of their communities. By the turn of the twenty-first century, a number of Indian groups continued to operate in Portland, supported by a combination of federal, state, local, private, and tribal funds. The Native American Rehabilitation Association boasted almost thirty years of experience in alcohol and drug rehabilitation and expanded its range of services. It assumed a place at the center of Portland's Indian community, along with organizations such as Pi Nee Waus (a group for Indian elders), the United Indian Students in Higher Education, and the American Indian Association of Portland (a consortium group).[16] The Orange County (California) Indian Center changed its name to the Southern California Indian Center, Inc. (SCIC) in 1987, and it came to serve Indian people in Los Angeles, Orange, Riverside, and San Bernardino counties by taking over many of the programs of the defunct Los Angeles Indian

Center. United American Indian Involvement (UAII) lost its main source of federal funding in 1996. It expanded by offering a wider variety of health care services and new programs on a grant-by-grant basis. The UAII provided a place for Indian people, to get out, have lunch, and socialize during the week—which was especially important for older residents living nearby. Recent initiatives include child and family counseling, cultural activities for Indian foster children, a veterans group, and workforce training for recovering alcoholics. Both SCIC and UAII developed a diverse funding base that includes a number of county, state, and national grants, instead of relying on single, major sources of funding that could be withdrawn at any time.[17]

Indians in the city still face public policy that is formulated without their needs in mind. Reverberations were felt across the country in 2006 when the George W. Bush administration proposed eliminating funds for thirty-four urban American Indian clinics that had served 106,000 Indians the previous year. The proposal justified the move by stating that, "Unlike Indian people living in isolated rural areas, urban Indians can receive health care through a wide variety of federal, state, and local providers." This position failed to recognize the ways that urban Indian health clinics have catered to the specific needs of the populations they have served to significantly improve health care delivery. Julie Gardipee-Chriske, a forty-nine-year-old Cree Indian dealing with chronic pain from diabetes, reflected the testimonies of urban Indians from the 1970s when she noted that she relied on the Pocha Clinic in Helena, Mont., and was averse to using non-Indian hospitals and medical facilities. "If I lose this place," Gardipee-Chriske said, "I'm someone that will probably die." These sentiments were put into broader context by Marjorie Bear Don't Walk, the executive director for the Indian Health Board in Billings. "We have helped a lot of people," Bear Don't Walk said, "but these are the very people we worry about now, the kind of people who could disappear into the system, or perhaps maybe never make it into the system at all."[18] The cuts proposed in 2006 were not an anomaly but could be considered part of a regular pattern of underfunding of urban Indian services health clinics that in 2006 received only 1 percent of the Indian Health Service budget.[19] Local and state agencies also remain either woefully ignorant of urban Indian needs and experiences or make few provisions for them. A 1996 study found that a city ordinance prohibited American Indians in Chicago from participating in the city's Minority Business Enterprise program, because the required statistics and data needed to prove discrimination had never been compiled. American Indian business owners in Houston were similarly excluded from city programs designed to promote minority businesses for lack of a "disparity study."[20] More anecdotally, Tanya Renne George sued Contra Costa County in 2002, because a county worker told her that she had to seek tribal benefits before she would be eligible for welfare benefits from the suburban San Francisco county.[21] Such practices and policies vividly illustrate the lack of government response to the migratory trends and resulting needs of American Indians throughout the twentieth century.[22]

University academics also could do more to explore the relationships between American Indians and cities. The few policy-oriented studies and the handful of historical works produced over the last two decades on urban American Indian population are encouraging. The vast bulk of scholarship on American Indian people in all disciplines, however, still falls short of seriously confronting and exploring the realities of American Indian urbanity. Such omissions have implications for our understandings of American Indian life. They also preclude numerous potentially fruitful conversations that could link American Indians to major trends distinguishing twentieth- and now twenty-first-century North American culture and society.

Even American Indian leaders at times resist shifting focus from reservations and reimagining Indian Country to include urban communities. Randy Edmonds, a Kiowa/Caddo Indian born in Oklahoma, reflected in 2005 on some of the changes he had seen in California over the past fifty years, during which he had worked for various federal programs and non-profit organizations serving American Indians in Los Angeles, Madera, and San Diego. Edmonds noted with some satisfaction that several California tribes had become "very rich" through "gaming, hotels, and other kinds of business development," which enabled them to invest in the types of reservation infrastructure, health care, and other improvements that had been promised yet neglected for so many years by the federal government. Edmonds was less pleased when asked whether these newly empowered tribes had reached out to urban Indian communities and organizations. He said: "I've tried to get the tribes to fund [the Indian Human Resource Center in San Diego]. But their feelings are now that we're not a viable organization. And so they just don't fund us. They might give us a little, maybe $1000, $2000, $3000 here or there, you know, for this and that . . . but they haven't given us any big money. . . . We're out of state Indians in their eyes." Edmonds went on to note that even those Indians who in earlier decades received help from the Indian Human Resource Center and later returned to their reservations seemed to forget what the organization was doing for the intertribal community of Indians in the city. They instead preferred to use gaming profits and resources to concentrate on tribal issues.[23] It is of course critical to protect tribal sovereignty and the reservation land base, but such policies also neglect very real American Indian needs.

Other American Indian people are working with renewed energy to incorporate the concerns of their urban populations as they formulate and influence policy for a reimagined Indian Country. American Indian leaders and community members from around the country gathered in Phoenix in 2005 for the National Urban Indian Family Coalition Summit, which was promoted as an opportunity to "develop new strategies to deal with the challenges of Indian child welfare, employment and housing while developing financial literacy and maintaining culture and identity." The coordinator of the summit proclaimed it "historic" and "important" for having brought together "executive directors, key policymakers, and decision makers to begin developing a national agenda for urban Indians."[24] The editors of *Indian Country Today*, the country's leading American Indian newspaper, praised the conference for helping to define common goals and identities across urban and reservation boundaries and argued that it provided a "much-needed service and forum for Indian country."[25] A more concrete example of reservation and urban cooperation has been the transfer of Temporary Assistance to Needy Families (TANF) programs (more commonly known as federal welfare services) to tribal administrators. The Torrez Martinez Desert Cahuilla Indian tribe began running "Tribal TANF" out of offices near downtown Los Angeles, Commerce, and Lancaster, Calif., to serve urban American Indians. American Indians in cities have always lagged behind other groups in utilizing non-Indian welfare programs, so government officials and Native leaders hoped that Indian-run TANF programs could more effectively deliver social services and generally stay better attuned to reaching urban Indians.[26] Other tribes throughout the country also have thought creatively about how to reach all of their members, whether rural or urban. Navajo Nation President Joe Shirley Jr. in 2006 began urging tribal members living in Albuquerque to form their own chapter so that it could represent their interests and ensure that they receive funds and services from the tribe.[27] The Navajo Nation also sponsored polling locations in both Albuquerque and Phoenix in the tribal elections of 2011.[28] The Cherokee Nation similarly supports the group Tsalagi LA, a "A Cherokee Nation Satellite Community of Los Angeles," for the purpose of connecting to tribal members living in Los Angeles.[29]

Closing the reservation-urban divide in favor of a more expansive sense of Indian Country is not a new trend, but it is one that has intensified in recent years. Native people have long moved between cities, towns, rural areas, and reservations with regularity, so as to create a social geography sometimes regional in scope and at other times national that defies the notions of bounded urban and reservation Indian communities.[30] Some of these trends were described in Chapter 1, and they involve Native people's labor migrations through the cities, towns, rural areas, and reservations in regions throughout the country. Other Indians have moved between these spaces for recreation, education, intertribal gatherings, and tribal business or Indian advocacy, among other purposes. For instance, students of the Sherman Institute, the Bureau of Indian Affairs boarding school in the town of Riverside, Calif., had extensive contact with Los Angeles and San Diego for extracurricular purposes through the first half of the twentieth century. Hardly a month went by from the 1920s through World War II that Sherman athletes did not visit these cities to compete in sports such as basketball, football, baseball, cross country, track, boxing, wrestling, and handball.[31] Indians living on reservations have also historically visited cities for more casual recreation. For example, *The Warm Springs Reservation Tomahawk*, a tribal newspaper published by the Confederated Tribes of the Warm Springs Reservation, commented between 1963 and 1971 on movements between the reservation and Portland, Ore., 100 miles to the west, noting trips to the city to attend Portland Trailblazers basketball games, watch drag races, go shopping, participate in Boy Scouts events, and visit museums.[32] Indians living on reservations also increasingly joined intertribal gatherings held in urban areas after World War II. They were among the thousands who annually traveled to the Greater Los Angeles area for the celebration of Indian Day, the National Orange Show, the American Indian and Western Relic Show, All American Indian Week at the Los Angeles County Fairgrounds, and the tournaments of the American Indian Athletic Association.[33] Indians from reservations also journeyed to urban areas for hearings and conferences related to tribal affairs, or to conduct tribal business during the 1960s and 1970s, when the civil rights movement and Indian activism encouraged the involvement of Indian people in the formation of policy. Members of the Warm Springs tribal government, for example, traveled to Portland during this period to meet with the Oregon Fish Committee, Oregon Historical Society, Oregon Health Sciences Center, National Congress of American Indians, National Tribal Chairman's Association, Oregon State Intergroup Human Relations Council, Affiliated

Tribes of Northwest Indians, Oregon Indian Education Conference, and Northwest Portland Area Indian Health Board.[34] All of these examples of Native people regularly traveling from reservations to cities and towns and back again hint at what have likely been much more widespread histori-cal patterns of Indian movement throughout the many spaces making up Indian Country.

These movements have both intensified and grown more complex with the advent of tribal gaming on some Indian reservations in recent years.[35] Some tribal members whose families have resided in cities for generations have moved back to reservations to work for gaming tribes on everything from running casinos and hotels to establishing social service and educa-tional institutions. Many of these returnees have college educations and other experiences that have prepared them for vital roles in guiding the tribes to take advantage of their newfound wealth. One example is the Pechanga Reservation, where the population increased from less than 100 in the 1960s to 346 in 2000, primarily because of jobs made available by the growing reservation economy. Individual cases serve as further illustration. Gary DuBois grew up in nearby San Bernardino County, Calif., during the 1970s and occasionally visited the Pechanga reservation for tribal meetings. DuBois left for graduate school in St. Louis and then worked in Oklahoma and Washington, D.C. He returned to California and moved onto the reser-vation for the first time in 1999, when he took a new position as cultural re-sources director. Russell "Butch" Murphy was raised on the Pechanga reser-vation and went to school in nearby Riverside before settling down to teach in San Diego. He was able to move back to the reservation in the late 1990s, when he took a job as tribal spokesman. Marc Macarro also grew up on the Pechanga reservation and left for college in Santa Barbara. He returned to serve the tribe and assumed the office of tribal council chairman after graduation.[36] These new migration patterns have been made possible by casino revenues and the choices that gaming tribes have made with them. They add to a long history of Native people moving across the network of cities, towns, and reservations that make up Indian Country.

The increasing social and cultural impact of Native people on cities and towns that has followed from the advent of tribal gaming also has made it more obvious than ever before that these spaces are part of Indian Country. Gaming tribes in California have contributed billions of dollars to dozens of local, state, and national elections and political campaigns to influence everything from pro-gaming initiatives on statewide ballots to mayoral and city council races in the city of Los Angeles.[37] Gaming tribes also have amassed new influence in the social and cultural life of the state. They have been the sponsors of numerous events and annual festivals, from the Riverside County Fair to Beverly Hills awards shows; endowed chairs in history departments; donated to the construction of new buildings at major universities; and competed to take over management of the oldest museum in Los Angeles.[38] Advertisements for tribal casinos are now ubiquitous on television and billboards, and within major metropolitan institutions, such as along the outfield wall at Petco Park, the home stadium of Major League Baseball's San Diego Padres (considering the team's name, a situation rife with irony). Gaming tribes have even paid for public relations commercials that argue for "tribal self-sufficiency" (a euphemism for the rights to continue casino gaming) by contextualizing contemporary conditions for Native people within tribal histories. Casino profits have clearly allowed some Indian people to become major players in the cultural life of towns and cities.

These kinds of social and cultural connections between Indians on reservations and cities and towns are likely to increase with time, as Indian people continue to make various uses of the many spaces composing Indian Country, furthering the reimagining of Indian Country in the process. This is consistent with the history of Native people throughout the twentieth century. Constant movements by Indian people for more than the past 100 years have built networks between cities, towns, rural areas, and Indian reservations. Cities have been especially important for Native people, despite the absence in the popular consciousness of virtually any association between Indians and urban areas. Indians have long lived in and otherwise used cities. They have struggled alongside other migrants and peoples of color to negotiate the demands of urban life. The reimagining of Indian Country was in a nascent state in the early twentieth century and proceeded in a slow and halting way, as Indians only began to define the city as "Indian space." Community institutions nonetheless helped to establish a permanent Indian presence in the city, to define what it meant to be both "urban" and "Indian," and to stoke a reconceptualization of the broader Indian world. The federal government began to incorporate cities into its Indian policy with the relocation program after World War II, in ways that abetted the reimagining of Indian Country, even as the government tried to stamp it out. The 1960s and 1970s saw greater non-Indian acceptance of an expanded Indian Country, as more attention was paid to the needs of urban Indians. There has been a lag in this consciousness over the past few decades after funding for social service programs and government spending in general was drastically cut during the 1980s. The focus by Indian tribes on reservation-based issues such as self-determination and tribal sovereignty also has often worked to define Indian Country narrowly for pragmatic political purposes. This tendency has increased at times with the ascendency of Indian gaming. Ironically, even as Indian people continue to become more urban, the reimagining of Indian Country seems to have taken several steps back.

Nevertheless, many Indian-run organizations in cities have persevered, urban Indian populations continue to rise, and cities have taken on particular importance for Native people with the rise of Indian gaming. A renewed effort by Indian leaders and government officials to think creatively about what cities and towns mean to Indian people is reflected by developments such as the National Urban Indian Family Coalition Summit, the creation of Tribal TANF, urban polling places for tribal elections, and the changes that have come with the rise of Indian gaming. The realities of modern American Indian life demand that more policymakers, scholars, and American Indian leaders, and the American public, follow suit, by reimagining Indian Country to include the urban areas of the United States.

Regardless, it seems assured that many Native people themselves will continue to reimagine and define Indian Country with cities in mind. They have been doing so for many generations, whether or not this imagining makes its way into the consciousness of scholars, the general public, and tribal leaders on reservations. One final story can further illustrate these connections. Sidney Stone took a job as an employment counselor on the Blackfeet Reservation in Montana in 1972. This was her first trip back since her family had left in 1955 when she was a child. This experience somewhat unexpectedly became a homecoming for Stone, who suddenly found herself in the middle of an enormous web of relations. She went around introducing herself to people, and many turned out to be relatives or to have some connection to her family. Stone said that it was a good deal like "leaving a foreign country and coming home." Stone then assumed a thoughtful expression and quickly added that just because Indians reside in the city it does not mean that they do not have that same sense of belonging. She went on to explain that many Indians create that sense in urban areas by developing complex networks that work to foster a sense of responsibility for each other and build community even as they maintain connections to reservations.[39] A history of American Indians and cities reveals this process. In the end, it is Indian people who have created an Indian Country, reimagined; judging by the past 100 years of North American history, they will continue to do so, well into the twenty-first century.

NOTES

ABBREVIATIONS

BRL, ANC	Braun Research Library Collections, Autry National Center
ISAW, ANC	Institute for the Study of the American West Collections, Autry National Center
RG 75, NARA, PAR	Record Group 75, National Archives and Records Administration, Pacific Alaska Region
RG 75, NARA, PR	Record Group 75, National Archives and Records Administration, Pacific Region

INTRODUCTION

1. John and Lois Knifechief interview; Ahhaitty interview.

2. U.S. Bureau of the Census, *Sixteenth Census of the United States: 1940*, 21; U.S. Bureau of the Census, *1950 Census of Population*, 88; U.S. Bureau of the Census, *1960 Census of Population*, 144; U.S. Bureau of the Census, *1970 Census of Population*, 262; U.S. Bureau of the Census, *1980 Census of Population*, 12; Shoemaker, *American Indian Population Recovery in the Twentieth Century*, 77. Although these population statistics are useful for conveying a sense of Indian urbanization over time, they also are problematic. On the one hand, they tend to undercount the number of Indians living in the city by a wide margin. On the other hand, changes in methodology from one federal census to the next, such as the introduction of self-reporting race in 1970 and the option of choosing multiple races in 2000, make the very definition of "Indian" variable.

3. Throughout this work I use the terms "American Indian," "Indian," "Native," and "Native American," as well as tribal designations whenever possible. There is little consensus about the best terms to use, as scholars and Native peoples find all

of these terms both preferable in some ways and problematic in other ways. See Yellow Bird, "What We Want to Be Called," 1–21.

4. In using a case study to argue for national trends, albeit with supporting evidence from other localities, this book follows the model provided by Cohen, *A Consumers' Republic*, which explores the centrality of mass consumption in twentieth-century American society from the vantage point of suburban New Jersey.

5. Richter, "Whose Indian History?"; Iverson, "American Indians in the Twentieth Century." Lately, American Indian scholars have moved in still more innovative directions, covering a wide variety of topics that cast new light on Indian lives, show the complexity of their interactions with other peoples, and merge American Indian history with developments in other fields. See, for example, O'Brien, *Dispossession by Degrees*; Hosmer, *American Indians in the Marketplace*; Deloria, *Indians in Unexpected Places*; Hosmer and O'Neill, eds., *Native Pathways*; Shoemaker, *A Strange Likeness*; Miles, *Ties That Bind*; Raibmon, *Authentic Indians*; O'Neill, *Working the Navajo Way*; Cobb, *Native Activism in Cold War America*; Rosier, *Serving their Country*; Bauer, *We Were All Like Migrant Workers Here*; Harmon, *Rich Indians*. For a more in-depth discussion of the New Indian History and recent work in American Indian history, see Rosenthal, "Beyond the New Indian History."

6. Danziger, *Survival and Regeneration*; Fixico, *The Urban Indian Experience in America*; Vicenti-Carpo, "'Let Them Know We Still Exist'"; LaGrand, *Indian Metropolis*; Thrush, *Native Seattle*; Amerman, *Urban Indians in Phoenix Schools, 1940–2000*.

7. Yu, "Los Angeles and American Studies in a Pacific World of Migrations," quotation on p. 33; Gabaccia, "Is Everywhere Nowhere?"; Delgado, "In the Age of Exclusion"; McKeown, *Chinese Migrant Networks and Cultural Change*; Ngai, *Impossible Subjects*.

8. Scott, *Domination and the Arts of Resistance*.

9. Kelley, *Race Rebels*; Lipsitz, *Dangerous Crossroads*; Garcia, *A World of Its Own*.

CHAPTER 1

1. Romaldo LaChusa Folder, Student Case Files, 1903–1980, Sherman Institute, RG 75, NARA, PR; "Record of Graduates," Box 38, Outing System, 1932–1933, Central Classified Files, 1907–1939, Records of the Superintendent, Sherman Institute, RG 75, NARA, PR; Federal Manuscript Census for Los Angeles County, 1910, NARA, PR; "Census Roll of the Indians of California under the Act of May 18, 1928," NARA, PR; Federal Manuscript Census for Los Angeles County, 1930, NARA, PR.

2. For the emphasis on post–World War II Indian urbanity, see Prucha, *The Great Father*, 1191–96; Philp, "Stride Toward Freedom"; Burt, "Roots of the Native American Urban Experience"; White, *"It's Your Misfortune and None of My Own*," 582–83; Weibel-Orlando, *Indian Country, L.A.*; Parman, *Indians and the Ameri-*

can West in the Twentieth Century; Fixico, *Urban Indian Experience in America*; and LaGrand, *Indian Metropolis*. For a few rare pre–World War II accounts of American Indians in cities, see Shoemaker, "Urban Indians and Ethnic Choices"; Einhorn, "The Warriors of the Sky"; Peters, "Continuing Identity"; and Thrush, *Native Seattle*.

3. In writing this chapter I have been especially influenced by both the contributions and the omissions in the last two decades of scholarship on the history of Los Angeles during the early twentieth century. Much of this work is rooted in social history and deals with migrant groups who came to the city, both influencing and participating in developing patterns of work, housing, leisure, gender, politics, and culture. See Sanchez, *Becoming Mexican American*; Davis, *Company Men*; Garcia, *A World of Its Own*; Sitton and Deverell, eds., *Metropolis in the Making*; McGirr, *Suburban Warriors*; Nicolaides, *My Blue Heaven*; Sides, *L.A. City Limits*; and Wild, *Street Meeting*.

4. In fact, American Indians established the first urban centers in North America, long before European arrival. Forbes, "The Urban Tradition Among Native Americans."

5. McWilliams, *Southern California*, 21–48; Shipek, *Pushed into the Rocks*; Fogelson, *The Fragmented Metropolis*, 5–23; Philips, "Indians in Los Angeles, 1781–1875"; Carrico and Shipek, "Indian Labor in San Diego County, California, 1850–1900"; Magliari, "Free Soil, Unfree Labor"; Street, *Beasts of the Field*, 3–157.

6. Shipek, *Pushed into the Rocks*, 34–54. Also see Hyer,*"We Are Not Savages,"* for a rare look at the history of specific Southern California Indian groups during this period.

7. "General Information on the School," *The Purple and Gold* [yearbook of the Sherman Institute, Riverside, Calif.], 1930, 15–16; "Index to Mission Indian Agency Records," RG 75, NARA, PR.

8. American Indian presence in the cities and towns of North America before 1900 and in the first decades of the twentieth century is a topic that requires a great deal more attention, but see Ronda, "Generations of Faith"; Calloway, ed., *After King Philip's War*; O'Brien, *Dispossession by Degrees*; Knight, *Indians at Work*; Raibmon, *Authentic Indians*; Thrush, *Native Seattle*; Usner, "American Indians on the Cotton Frontier"; and Knack, "Nineteenth-Century Great Basin Indian Wage Labor." For studies of colonial Latin America, see Chance, *Race and Class in Colonial Oaxaca*; Wightman, *Indigenous Migration and Social Change*; Zulawski, "Social Differentiation, Gender, and Ethnicity"; Pescador, "Vanishing Woman"; and Powers, *Andean Journeys*.

9. Shipek, *Pushed into the Rocks*, 55–56; Hyer, *"We Are Not Savages,"* 129–90.

10. "Reservation News," *The Indian* [publication of the Mission Indian Federation, Riverside, Calif.], November 1921.

11. "Under the Lodge Pole," *The Indian*, 10 March 1922.

12. "Under the Lodge Pole, *The Indian*, May 1922.

13. "Los Coyotes Items," *The Indian*, October 1922.

14. "Indians of Backcountry in Need," *The Indian*, May 1922.

15. Meeks, "The Tohono O'odham, Wage Labor, and Resistant Adaptation, 1900–1930"; O'Neill, *Working the Navajo Way.*

16. Clark, *Roots of Rural Capitalism.*

17. Meriam, *Problem of Indian Administration*, 680–99.

18. Knight, *Indians at Work*; Arnold, "Work and Culture in Southeastern Alaska."

19. LaGrand, *Indian Metropolis*, 24–26.

20. Prins, "Tribal Network and Migrant Labor."

21. Bauer, *We Were All Like Migrant Workers Here.*

22. *The Moravian* [published by the Northern Province of the Moravian Church in America, Bethlehem, Pa.] 55 (2 February 1910): 68.

23. James E. Jenkins, Banning, Calif., to Commissioner of Indian Affairs, Washington, D.C., 11 February 1919, Box 4, William H. Weinland Collection, Henry H. Huntington Library, San Marino, Calif.

24. Drown, "Indian Grape Pickers in California."

25. "Reservation News."

26. "Under the Lodge Pole," *The Indian*, February 1922.

27. "Under the Lodge Pole," *The Indian*, 10 March 1922.

28. "Under the Lodge Pole," *The Indian*, August 1922.

29. "Under the Lodge Pole," *The Indian*, October 1922.

30. Costo interview.

31. "Under the Lodge Pole," *The Indian*, 10 March 1922.

32. "Under the Lodge Pole," *The Indian*, February 1922.

33. Fogelson, *Fragmented Metropolis*, 43–78, 123–31.

34. Ibid., 63–134; Tygiel, "Metropolis in the Making."

35. Fogelson, *Fragmented Metropolis*, 75.

36. Sitton and Deverell, eds., *Metropolis in the Making.*

37. Beck, "The Chicago American Indian Community."

38. Shoemaker, "Urban Indians and Ethnic Choices"; Danziger, *Survival and Regeneration*, 71–72; Harmon, *Indians in the Making*, 106, 148–49; Meriam, *Problem of Indian Administration*, 705–42.

39. Einhorn, "The Indians of New York City"; Einhorn, "Warriors of the Sky"; Mitchell, "The Mohawks in High Steel."

40. Peters, "Continuing Identity."

41. Meriam, *Problem of Indian Administration*, 705–13.

42. Ibid.; Patterson, "Indian Life in the City."

43. "Census Roll of the Indians of California under the Act of May 18, 1928," NARA, PR.

44. Ibid.; "Oral History: Ethel Rogoff."

45. Federal Manuscript Census for Los Angeles County, 1900, NARA, PR.

46. Federal Manuscript Census for Los Angeles County, 1920, NARA, PR. See discussion below for the discrepancies between the 1928 California State Census and the decennial federal censuses.

47. Ortiz, "Foreword," xvii.

48. Federal Manuscript Census for Los Angeles County, 1920, NARA, PR.

49. Federal Manuscript Census for Los Angeles County, 1930, NARA, PR.

50. Underwood interview.

51. Lee Shippey, "Lee Side o' LA," *Los Angeles Times*, 3 August 1929, sec. 2, p. 2; Lee Shippey, "Lee Side o' LA," *Los Angeles Times*, 7 November 1929, sec. 2, p. 4; Thorne, "The Indian Beverly Hillbillies: The Migration of Oklahoma's Wealthy Indians to Southern California in the 1920s." I am grateful to Professor Thorne for sharing her research with me.

52. Federal Manuscript Census for Los Angeles County, 1920, NARA, PR; Federal Manuscript Census for Los Angeles County, 1930, NARA, PR.

53. Federal Manuscript Census for Los Angeles County, 1930, NARA, PR; Wild, *Street Meeting*, 13.

54. Federal Manuscript Census for Los Angeles County, 1920, NARA, PR; Federal Manuscript Census for Los Angeles County, 1930, NARA, PR. This picture of Indians in Los Angeles concentrated in lower- skilled and domestic work but moving into higher-paying occupations is supported by the findings of Lewis Meriam, who in 1928 led a government-sponsored investigation into the conditions of Indians throughout the country. See Meriam, *Problem of Indian Administration*, 714–16.

55. The methodology of the federal census stipulated that enumerators traveled from door to door, assessing the occupants of each home and recording data, including "race," a category that was limited to a single descriptor. Ultimately, the final assessment belonged to the census taker, who might be influenced by various factors, including the occupants' phenotype, language and speech patterns, neighborhood, and any information offered by the occupant.

56. For the 1928 census California Indians self-registered at the OIA office in Riverside or on any California Indian reservation. Another conclusion that might be drawn is that many ethnic Indians in Los Angeles primarily identified or were consciously passing as non-Indians, but nonetheless wanted to be included on the 1928 census rolls, either for financial reasons, or because the political process of land settlement awakened a new ethnic consciousness. For the latter argument in regard to Orange County, see Haas, *Conquests and Historical Identities in California, 1769–1936*, 130. Regardless, it is likely that the 1928 census provides a more accurate count than the decennial censuses of Los Angeles County residents who were ethnically California Indians.

57. "Census Roll of the Indians of California under the Act of May 18, 1928," NARA, PR; Federal Manuscript Census for Los Angeles County, 1930, NARA, PR.

58. "Census Roll of the Indians of California under the Act of May 18, 1928," NARA, PR; Federal Manuscript Census for Los Angeles County, 1920, NARA, PR; Federal Manuscript Census for Los Angeles County, 1930, NARA, PR; P. Narcha, President, American Indian Progressive Association, to Mr. C. L. Ellis, Superintendent, Mission Indian Agency, 30 Nov 1927, Folder 9.1, Box 17, Central Classified Files, 1870–1953, Mission Indian Agency, RG 75, NARA, PR; "Redskins Today Regular Folks," *Los Angeles Times*, 23 April 1928, sec. 2, p. 10; *California Indian News* (n.p., 1937), Folder 94, Box 16, Central Classified Files, 1870–1953, Mission Indian Agency, RG 75, NARA, PR; Thomas Largo and Stella Von Bulow, California Indian Rights Association, Inc., to Indian Friends and Friends of Indians, September 1942, Folder 94, Box 16, Central Classified Files, 1870–1953, Mission Indian Agency, RG 75, NARA, PR.

59. Gregory, *American Exodus*, 40–41.

60. Nash, *American West Transformed*.

61. Prucha, *Great Father*, 1006–7; Nash, *American West Transformed*, 128–47.

62. Richard LaCourse, "The Last Four Decades," *Confederated Umatilla Journal* [publication of the Confederated Tribes of the Umatilla Reservation, Umatilla, Ore.], October 1976, p. 12.

63. John Dady, Superintendent, Mission Indian Agency, to Mrs. Susan Coonradt, 5 July 1945, Education Folder, Box 520, Mission Indian Agency, RG 75, NARA, PR.

64. Paul Jackson, Superintendent, Chemawa Indian School, to Ralph Fredenberg, Superintendent Grande Ronde-Siletz Agency, 6 August 1941, Folder 995, Box 92, Grande Ronde/Siletz Decimal Files, RG 75, NARA, PAR; R. Abeita, Assistant Guidance and Placement Officer, Bureau of Indian Affairs, Portland Area Office, to Carl Stevens, Branch Representative, State Welfare Division, 9 September 1941, Folder 996, Box 92, Grande Ronde/Siletz Decimal Files, RG 75, NARA, PAR; Carl Stevens, Superintendent Indian Education, to Ralph Fredenburg, Superintendent Grande Ronde-Siletz Agency, 7 October 1941, Folder 996, Box 92, Grande Ronde/ Siletz Decimal Files, RG 75, NARA, PAR; George Batterson, NYA Field Youth Personnel Officer, to Ralph Fredenburg, Superintendent Grande Ronde-Siletz Agency, 25 September 1942, Folder 994, Box 92, Grande Ronde/Siletz Decimal Files, RG 75, NARA, PAR.

65. Paul Jackson, Superintendent, Chemawa Indian School, to Earl Wooldridge, Superintendent Grand Ronde-Siletz Agency, 16 February 1943, Folder 995, Box 92, Grande Ronde/Siletz Decimal Files, RG 75, NARA, PAR; Jackson to Fredenberg, 6 August 1941.

66. Abbott, *Portland*, 125–26, 148–49; Nash, *American West Transformed*, 75–78.

67. Robert Olmos, "Couple's Transition to City Life Problem-Free," *Oregonian*, 28 April 1970, p.11.

68. Indian Service Teacher Now O.S.C. Shipwright," *Bo's'ns Whistle* (Oregon

Shipyard Edition) [publication of the Oregon Shipbuilding Corporation] (Portland, Ore.), 17 March 1944, p. 5. This article does not give Mrs. Reifel's first name, but I have taken liberties to provide one for the purposes of this narrative.

69. "Comanches," *Bo's'ns Whistle*, 9 December 1943, p. 7.

70. "Heroic Indian, 63, Gives Life in Rescue of 6 Adults, 5 Children in Cottage Fire," *Oregonian*, 28 February 1943, p. 1.

71. *Bo's'ns Whistle* (Oregon Shipyard Edition) 18 May 1945, 2.

72. Danziger, *Survival and Regeneration*, 29–30, 71–73; LaGrand, *Indian Metropolis*, 37; Albon, "Relocated American Indians in the San Francisco Bay Area," 297.

73. "Permanent Employment Found by Many Grads," *Sherman Bulletin* [publication of the Sherman Institute, Riverside, Calif.], 27 September 1940, 3.

74. "Vocations," *Sherman Bulletin*, 25 October 1940, 3.

75. "Three Shermanites Off to U.S. Army Service," *Sherman Bulletin*, 21 February 1941, 3.

76. "Several Students are Placed on Jobs in Industry," *Sherman Bulletin*, 4 April 1941, 1.

77. "Douglas Features All-Indian Employees in Magazine Article," *Sherman Bulletin*, 7 November 1941, 1–3.

78. "Memorandum: 6 December 1941," *Sherman Bulletin*, 19 December 1941, 2.

79. "Sherman to Commence Defense Training Course," *Sherman Bulletin*, 13 January 1942, 1; "Defense Training Classes," *Sherman Bulletin*, 27 March 1942, 2.

80. "Defense Training Classes."

81. "Twenty-two Welding Graduates Placed in Employment," *Sherman Bulletin*, 13 October 1942, 1.

82. "Aircraft Company Likes Indian Students' Work," *Sherman Bulletin*, 5 February 1943, 1.

83. "Welding News," *Sherman Bulletin*, 19 March 1943, 2.

84. "Thirty Sherman Boys Enter Armed Services During Summer Months," *Sherman Bulletin*, 15 October 1943, 3.

85. "Student Enrollment Short of Previous Years at Sherman," *Sherman Bulletin*, 29 October 1943, 1.

86. U.S. Census Bureau, *Sixteenth Census of the United States: 1940*, 564; U.S. Census Bureau, *1950 Census of Population*, 179.

87. Gibbs interview.

88. Wills interview.

89. Rainwater interview.

90. Ortiz, "Foreword," xvii–xviii.

91. Iverson, *"We Are Still Here,"* 103–13; Nash, *American West Transformed*, 139–47; Parman, *Indians and the American West in the Twentieth Century*, 107–22; Deloria, "This Country Was a Lot Better Off When the Indians Were Running It."

CHAPTER 2

1. Press Kit, *For the Service* (1936), ISAW, ANC.

2. "Chief Thunderbird," *Internet Movie Database*, http://www.imdb.com/name/ nm0862083 (accessed 1 September 2011).

3. See, for example, Bataille and Silet, eds., *The Pretend Indians*; Churchill, *Fantasies of the Master Race*; Rollins and O'Connor, eds., *Hollywood's Indian*; and Kilpatrick, *Celluloid Indians*.

4. Moses, *Wild West Shows and the Images of American Indians, 1883–1933*; Black, "Picturing Indians: American Indians in Movies, 1941–1960"; Raibmon, "Theatres of Contact"; Patterson, "'Real' Indian Songs"; Gleach, "Pocahontas at the Fair"; Raheja, "Screening Identity"; Spencer, *The New Negroes and Their Music*; Garcia, *A World of Its Own*; Imada, "Aloha America"; Ellis, "Five Dollars a Week to Be 'Regular Indians'"; Watkins, *Stepin Fetchit*. My thinking also has been influenced by a 2002 conference at UCLA, titled "Selling Race: The Limits and Liberties of Markets," organized by Henry Yu and John Giggie.

5. Much of this work begins with the important study by anthropologist Scott, *Domination and the Arts of Resistance*. See also Kelley, *Race Rebels*; Lipsitz, *Dangerous Crossroads*; Sanchez, *Becoming Mexican American*; and Garcia, *A World of Its Own*.

6. Wallis, *The Real Wild West*. Also see Ellis, "Five Dollars a Week to Be 'Regular Indians.'"

7. Meriam, *The Problem of Indian Administration*.

8. Moses, *Wild West Shows and the Images of American Indians*; Ellis, "Five Dollars a Week to Be 'Regular Indians.'"

9. Standing Bear, *My People, the Sioux*.

10. Ellis, "Five Dollars a Week to Be 'Regular Indians,'" 200–201.

11. Raibmon, "Theatres of Contact," quotations on pp. 158 and 173, respectively. For other accounts of American Indians performing at expositions, see Ryckman, *Story of an Epochal Event in the History of California*; Wallis, *Real Wild West*, 339; Meyn, "Cincinnati's Wild West"; Thrush, *Native Seattle*; and Raibmon, *Authentic Indians*.

12. Buffalo Tiger and Kersey, *Buffalo Tiger*, 53–77.

13. Cattelino, "Casino Roots."

14. Imada, "Hawaiians on Tour."

15. Balshofer and Miller, *One Reel a Week*, 2–80; Brownlow, *The War, the West, and the Wilderness*; Wallis, *Real Wild West*, 357–75. Currently this area is part of Topanga State Park and is located just east and north of where the Pacific Coast Highway (California Highway 1) and Sunset Boulevard meet.

16. "Looking Back: Noted Director Tells How He Made His Start in Motion Pictures," *Moving Picture World*, 10 March 1917, 1506; "Memoirs of Thomas H. Ince," *Exhibitor's Herald*, 20 December 1934, 31–32; Balshofer and Miller, *One Reel a*

Week, 2–80; Brownlow, *The War, the West, and the Wilderness*, 253–63; Wallis, *Real Wild West*, 357–75.

17. De Rockbraine interview.

18. Tuska, *The Filming of the West*, 89–96; McCoy, *Tim McCoy Remembers the West*; Cody, *Iron Eyes*; "Indian Pow-wow Called Tonight for Hollywood," *Los Angeles Times*, 3 March 1925, sec. 2, p. 2; Souvenir Program for *Iron Horse* (1925), ISAW, ANC.

19. McCoy, *Tim McCoy Remembers the West*, 183–84.

20. De Rockbraine interview.

21. Bruner interview.

22. "William Eagle Shirt," *Internet Movie Database*, http://www.imdb.com/name/nm/0794405 (accessed 1 September 2011); Broadside for *Custer's Last Fight* (1912), ISAW, ANC; Tuska, *Filming of the West*, 25.

23. Howard McClay, "'Bravo' 200th Role for Him," *Daily News* 20 November 1953, 38; "Charles Stevens (I)," *Internet Movie Database*, http://www.imdb.com/name/nm0828314 (accessed 1 September 2011).

24. McBride, *Molly Spotted Elk*; "Spotted Elk," *Internet Movie Database*, http://www.imdb.com/name/nm0819492 (accessed 1 September 2011).

25. "Chief Yowlachie," *Internet Movie Database*, http://www.imdb.com/name/nm0950385 (accessed 1 September 2011); "Hopi Master Singer Found," *Los Angeles Times*, 6 Sep 1928, sec. 2, p. 11; Lee Shippey, "Lee Side o' LA," *Los Angeles Times*, 3 August, 1929, sec. 2, p. 2; Ryckman, *Story of an Epochal Event in the History of California*; "Museum Sunday Lecture Series," *Masterkey* [publication of the Southwest Museum of the American Indian, Los Angeles, Calif.] 15 (1941): 212; [Photograph], *Wild West* (1946), ISAW, ANC; Press Kit, *Dude Goes West* (1948), ISAW, ANC.

26. Richard Davis Thunderbird, "Secret Rites and Ceremonies of the Ancient Cheyenne," Folder 35, MS 641, BRL, ANC; [Various dated and undated newspaper clippings], Folder 40, MS 641, BRL, ANC; "Program for Hotel Del Coronado, 24 July 1926," Folder 38, MS 641, BRL, ANC; Merton Albee, to Chief Thunderbird, 3 February 1928, Folder 35, MS 641, BRL, ANC; Agent's Contract, 9 July 1930, Folder 29, MS 641, BRL, ANC; [Various clippings and correspondence], Grace Slaughter Correspondence Folder (unnumbered), MS 641, BRL, ANC; *Masterkey* 2 (1929), front cover, 10, 16; "To the Museum, Uncovered," *Christian Science Monitor*, 25 January 1930, 10; Cody, *Iron Eyes*, 79; "Thunderbird," *Internet Movie Database*.

27. Standing Bear, *My People, the Sioux*; Ehrheart, "Chief Luther Standing Bear II."

28. Standing Bear, *My People, the Sioux*, 278.

29. Standing Bear, *My People the Sioux*; Ehrheart, "Chief Luther Standing Bear II"; Lee Shippey, "Lee Side o' LA," *Los Angeles Times*, 25 June 1933, sec. 1, p. 16; "The Southwest Museum Indians," *Masterkey* 1 (1928): 29; "The Children in the Museum," *Masterkey* 2 (1928): 13–15; "Sunday Lectures," *Masterkey* 2 (1929): 30; "To the Museum, Uncovered"; "Indian Prowess Shown in Song and Dance Fete," *Los*

Angeles Times, 1 August 1932, sec. 2, p. 5; Chief Standing Bear to Frederick Webb Hodge, 20 July 1931, Frederic Webb Hodge/Chief Standing Bear Correspondence Folder (unnumbered), MS 7, BRL, ANC; Luther Standing Bear to William S. Hart, 3 August 1925, and William S. Hart to Luther Standing Bear, 7 August 1925, Folder 6, Box 5, William S. Hart Collection, Seaver Center for Western History Research, Los Angeles Natural History Museum; Luther Standing Bear to William S. Hart, 28 March 1927, William S. Hart to Luther Standing Bear, 30 March 1927, and Luther Standing Bear to William S. Hart, 31 March 1927, Folder 5, Box 5, Hart Collection, Seaver Center for Western History Research, Los Angeles Natural History Museum; Luther Standing Bear to William S. Hart, 5 April 1927, Folder 5, Box 5, Hart Collection, Seaver Center for Western History Research, Los Angeles Natural History Museum; Wallis, *The Real Wild West*, 373; "Chief Standing Bear," *Internet Movie Database*, http://www.imdb.com/name/nm0822052 (accessed 1 September 2011).

30. Moses, *Wild West Shows*, 227; Wallis, *Real Wild West*, 375.

31. William S. Hart to Henry Makes Enemy, 19 October 1926, Folder 6, Box 5, Hart Papers, Seaver Center for Western History Research, Los Angeles Natural History Museum.

32. Robert Joseph, "A Closed Shop Is the Reward of the Indian," *New York Herald Tribune*, 4 June 1939, sec. 6, pp. 2, 4.

33. Brownlow, *The War, the West, and the Wilderness*, 290.

34. Black, "Picturing Indians," 84–138.

35. Joseph, "A Closed Shop Is the Reward of the Indian."

36. Red Fox, *The Memoirs of Chief Red Fox*.

37. Standing Bear, *My People the Sioux*, 285.

38. This analysis is offered by Churchill, Hill, and Hill, "Examination of Stereotyping"; Keshena, "The Role of American Indians in Motion Pictures"; and Singer, *Wiping the War Paint off the Lens*, 14–21. More generally, over the last thirty years "the new Indian history" and the field of ethnohistory have brought much needed attention to Native peoples' agency, yet earlier works that focus on victimization continue to influence the public's historical imagination. See, for example, Brown, *Bury My Heart at Wounded Knee*; Jennings, *The Invasion of America*; and Limerick, *The Legacy of Conquest*, 179–221.

39. For related discussions, see Jay Silverheels, "Lo! The Image of the Indian!!!"; Owens, *Mixedblood Messages*; Garcia, *A World of Its Own*, 121–54, especially 153–54; Gary Giddins, "What Made Sammy Run?," *New York Times*, 28 December 2003, sec. 7, p. 11.

40. Garcia, *A World of Its Own*, 125.

41. "First Arapaho Student Here for Pow-wow," *Los Angeles Times*, 28 Nov 1926, sec. 2, p. 2; Meriam, *Problem of Indian Administration*, 717–23; Lee Shippey, "Lee Side o' LA," *Los Angeles Times*, 21 May 1932, sec. 2, p. 4; Iron Eyes Cody, "Little Big Horn News," *Talking Leaf* [publication of the Los Angeles (Calif.) Indian Center], June 1975, 11.

42. Quoted in Friar and Friar, *The Only Good Indian . . . The Hollywood Gospel*, 254.

43. Ibid.

44. "Beauty Contest Will Feature Powwow," *Los Angeles Times*, 13 Sept 1938, sec. 1, p. 22; Joseph, "A Closed Shop Is the Reward of the Indian."

45. "Indians Pay Honors to Chief Bear," *Los Angeles Times*, 18 April 1926, sec. 1, p. 15.

46. "Indians Hold Weird Rites," 26 Dec 1932, *Los Angeles Times*, sec. 2, p. 13. Also see "Scalp Will Be on Display for Indian Session," *Los Angeles Times*, 26 November 1926, sec. 2, p. 12; Joseph, "A Closed Shop Is the Reward of the Indian."

47. Lee Shippey, "Lee Side o' LA," *Los Angeles Times*, 3 August, 1929, sec. 2, p. 2. For additional Indian powwows and gatherings, see "First Arapaho Student Here for Pow-wow"; Lee Shippey, "Lee Side o' LA," *Los Angeles Times*, 27 March 1930, sec. 2, p. 4; and Joseph, "A Closed Shop Is the Reward of the Indian."

48. Meriam, *Problem of Indian Administration*, 722–23; "Thousand Indians Picnic," *Los Angeles Times*, 1 Oct 1928, sec. 2, pp. 1–2; "Wigwam Club Has Pow-Wow," *Los Angeles Times*, 30 September 1929, sec. 2, p. 9; Iron Eyes Cody, "Little Big Horn News," *Talking Leaf*, November 1976, p. 8.

49. Iron Eyes Cody, "Little Big Horn News," *Talking Leaf*, November 1976, 8; Iron Eyes Cody, *Iron Eyes*, 127, 239–40.

50. Jean Ward, "Indian Center in Heart of LA," *Los Angeles Examiner*, 10 June 1956, sec. 5, pp. 1, 16; Indian Center Aided," *Los Angeles Examiner*, 24 September 1956, sec. 2, p. 1.

51. "Indians in Organization," *Los Angeles Times*, 17 May 1931, sec. 4, p. 12.

52. Thunderbird, "Secret Rites and Ceremonies of the Ancient Cheyenne."

53. "Strongheart, An American [publicity brochure for Chautauqua Circuit]," 1929 [?], Series 1, Box 47, Ms C150, Redpath Chautauqua Collection, Special Collections, University of Iowa, Iowa City, Iowa; "Indian Center Aided"; "League to Aid Indian Files Incorporation," *Los Angeles Times*, 12 January 1932, sec. 2, p. 20.

CHAPTER 3

1. Howard Yackitonipah interview.

2. Ibid.

3. For Indians and assimilation, see Prucha, *The Great Father*, 609–758; Hoxie, *A Final Promise*; McDonnell, *The Dispossession of the American Indian, 1887–1934*; and Lomawaima, *They Called It Prairie Light*. On Americanization, see Gerstle, "Liberty, Coercion, and the Making of Americans."

4. Fixico, *Termination and Relocation*; Burt, "Roots of the Native American Urban Experience"; Philp, "Stride Toward Freedom"; Nash, "Relocation."

5. U.S. Department of the Interior, *Annual Report of the Secretary of the Interior* [1951]; U.S. Department of the Interior, *Annual Report of the Secretary of the Interior* [1952]; U.S. Department of the Interior, *Annual Report of the Secretary of*

the Interior [1958]; U.S. Bureau of Indian Affairs, *The Bureau of Indian Affairs Voluntary Relocation Service Program,* 3–7; U.S. Bureau of Indian Affairs, *Handbook*; Fixico, *Termination and Relocation,* 134–56.

6. Fixico, *Termination and Relocation,* 143; Sorkin, *The Urban American Indian,* 27.

7. Sorkin, *The Urban American Indian,* 25–27.

8. Application for Relocation, Folder: General Information, 1956, Box 7, Central Classified Files, 1948–62, Los Angeles Field Employment Assistance Office (hereafter Los Angeles Field Office Central Classified Files), RG 75, NARA, PR. This process also is apparent from my examination of the individual case files of applicants from the jurisdiction of the Portland Area BIA Office (Washington, Oregon, and Idaho). See Boxes 1691–1977, Individual Case Files for Relocation, Training and Employment, 1955–68, Portland Area Office, RG 75, NARA, PAR.

9. Charles Miller to All Field Relocation Officers, 3 February 1956, Folder—Relocation Services Eligibility Requirements, 1957–58, Box 12, Los Angeles Field Office Central Classified Files, RG 75, NARA, PR.

10. Mary Nan Gamble to Charles Miller, 3 February 1955, Folder—General Information, 1956, Box 7, Los Angeles Field Office Central Classified Files, RG 75, NARA, PR; Mary Nan Gamble to Charles Miller, 13 April 1956, Folder—Relocation Services Eligibility Requirements, 1957–58, Box 12, Los Angeles Field Office Central Classified Files, RG 75, NARA, PR.

11. L. Bear, 28 May 1956, Folder—Scheduling, 1955–58, Box 7, Los Angeles Field Office Central Classified Files, RG 75, NARA, PR. Also see several letters contained in Folder—Success Stories and Problem Stories, Box 21, Los Angeles Field Office Central Classified Files, RG 75, NARA, PR.

12. Individual Case Files for Relocation, Training and Employment, 1955–68, Portland Area Office, RG 75, NARA, PAR. Because these files remain classified, I was granted permission to view them only upon agreeing not to disclose personal information. Thus, I have not provided citations to individual files, and for all examples of Indian experience taken from these files I have employed pseudonyms and in some cases changed key identifiers, such as tribal affiliation.

13. Kessler-Harris, *In Pursuit of Equity.*

14. AVT Services, Questions and Answers, 15 October 1957, Folder—Policy Relating to Adult Training Services, Box 1674, Branch of Relocation Services Administrative Files, (hereafter Los Angeles Administrative Files), RG 75, NARA, PR; Assistant Commissioner, Economic Development, to All Area Directors, 15 April 1959, Folder—Relocation (Policy), 1959–61, Box 13, Los Angeles Field Office Central Classified Files, RG 75, NARA, PR.

15. Assistant Commissioner of Indian Affairs to Area Directors, 14 August 1958, Folder—Policy Relating to Adult Training Services, Box 1674, Los Angeles Administrative Files, RG 75, NARA, PR.

16. Individual Case Files for Relocation, Training and Employment, 1955–68, Portland Area Office, RG 75, NARA, PAR.

17. Ibid.

18. Ibid.

19. C. W. McCall, Employment Assistant Officer, to Donald Spaugy, Field Employment Assistance Officer, 5 April 1963, Folder—FY 1963, Box 14, Los Angeles Field Office Central Classified Files, RG 75, NARA, PR; Donald Spaugy to Paul Nelson, Area Field Representative, 10 April 1963, Folder—FY 1963, Box 14, Los Angeles Field Office Central Classified Files, RG 75, NARA, PR.

20. Glenn, "From Servitude to Service Work."

21. Individual Case Files for Relocation, Training and Employment, 1955–68, Portland Area Office, RG 75, NARA, PAR.

22. George Felshaw, to Charles Miller, 27 July 1961, Folder—Field Offices 1960–61, Los Angeles Field Office Central Classified Files, RG 75, NARA, PR.

23. Reuben Fuher, Relocation Officer, to George Felshaw, 19 August 1959, Folder—1958–1961 AVT Inquiries Concerning Applicants, Box 12, Los Angeles Field Office Central Classified Files, RG 75, NARA, PR; Carroll Donlavy, to Reuben Fuher, 21 August 1959, Folder—1958–1961 AVT Inquiries Concerning Applicants, Box 12, Los Angeles Field Office Central Classified Files, RG 75, NARA, PR.

24. Dale Wing to George Sheer, Art Instruction Incorporated, 17 February 1959, Folder—General Correspondence, 1958–59, Box 1675, Administrative Records of the Relocation and Employment Assistant Branch, 1958–1966 (hereafter Portland Administrative Files), RG 75, NARA, PAR.

25. White, *"It's Your Misfortune and None of My Own,"* 282–84, 506–7; Barrera, *Race and Class in the Southwest*; Blauner, *Racial Oppression in America*, 23–25, 57–65.

26. Felshaw to Miller, 27 July 1961; Individual Case Files for Relocation, Training and Employment, 1955–68, Portland Area Office, RG 75, NARA, PAR.

27. Jack W. Womeldorf, Relocation Officer, to Rudolph Russell, Field Relocation Officer, 3 December 1957, Folder 6, Box 1, Bureau of Indian Affairs Relocation Records, Newberry Library.

28. Jack Womeldorf, Relocation Officer, to George Felshaw, 10 October 1957, Folder—Intermountain School Correspondence, 1957–58, Box 10, Los Angeles Field Office Central Classified Files, RG 75, NARA, PR; Jack Womeldorf to George Felshaw, 3 December 1957, Folder—Intermountain School Correspondence 1957–58, Box 10, Los Angeles Field Office Central Classified Files, RG 75, NARA, PR; Thomas Tommaney, Superintendent, to George Felshaw, 15 June 1958, Folder—Intermountain School Correspondence 1957–58, Box 10, Los Angeles Field Office Central Classified Files, RG 75, NARA, PR. During the same period, a similar relationship existed between LAFRO and the Sherman Institute in nearby Riverside. See "Graduate News," *Sherman Bulletin*, 10 November 1960, 4; "Few Jobs Available for Graduates," *Sherman Bulletin*, 9 December 1960, 1.

29. Asst. Commissioner, Economic Development, to All Field Relocation Officers, 12 March 1959, Folder—Field Offices, 1960–61, Box 8, Los Angeles Field Office Central Classified Files, RG 75, NARA, PR.

30. Community Adjustment "Hello" Booklet, 19 January 1956, Folder—Hello Booklet, Box 9, Los Angeles Field Office Central Classified Files, RG 75, NARA, PR.

31. Folder 4, Box 32A, Church Federation of Greater Chicago Collection, Chicago Historical Society.

32. Welfare Planning Council, Los Angeles Region, Family and Adult Services Division, Summary, Committee on the Study of the Needs of the Newcomer Indians, 1 October 1959, Folder—Welfare Planning Council, Box 11, Los Angeles Field Office Central Classified Files, RG 75, NARA, PR.

33. Los Angeles Indian Churches and Indian Clubs, 1964[?], Folder—Indian Councils, Box 1, Los Angeles Field Office Central Classified Files, RG 75, NARA, PR.

34. Arthur Stoneking to George Felshaw, 2 May 1961, Folder—Organizations Interested in Indians, 1959–61, Box 2, Los Angeles Field Office Central Classified Files, RG 75, NARA, PR; George Felshaw to Mr. And Mrs. Edward M. Spencer, 8 December 1961, Folder—Organizations Interested in Indians, 1959–61, Box 2, Los Angeles Field Office Central Classified Files, RG 75, NARA, PR; George Felshaw to Geneieve Cazarea, 8 December 1961, Folder—Organizations Interested in Indians, 1959–61, Box 2, Los Angeles Field Office Central Classified Files, RG 75, NARA, PR.

35. George Felshaw to Judge Robert Clifton, 24 June 1960, Folder—Law and Order, 1957–61, Box 4, Los Angeles Field Office Central Classified Files, RG 75, NARA, PR.

36. Folders 1–3, Box 32A, Church Federation of Greater Chicago Collection, Chicago Historical Society.

37. George Felshaw to Staff, LAFRO, 20 July 1961, Folder—Office Methods and Memos 1952–62, Box 2, Los Angeles Field Office Central Classified Files, RG 75, NARA, PR; George Felshaw to Staff, LAFRO, 11 August 1961, Folder—Office Methods and Memos 1952–62, Box 2, Los Angeles Field Office Central Classified Files, RG 75, NARA, PR.

38. George Felshaw to Vocational Training Applicants, 28 January 1959, Folder—Relocation (Policy) 1959–61, Box 13, Los Angeles Field Office Central Classified Files, RG 75, NARA, PR.

39. Leonard C. Allen, Portland Area Office, to AVT Trainees, 1959, Folder—Letters to Trainees and Concerning Trainees, Box 1973, Portland Administrative Files, RG 75, NARA, PAR.

40. Individual Case Files for Relocation, Training and Employment, 1955–68, Portland Area Office, RG 75, NARA, PAR.

41. Ibid.

42. Ibid.

43. Record of Counseling Contact, 1960, Folder—Allied Welding School, Box 15, Los Angeles Field Office Central Classified Files, RG 75, NARA, PR.

44. Individual Case Files for Relocation, Training and Employment, 1955–68, Portland Area Office, RG 75, NARA, PAR. For Yackitonipah, see the beginning of this chapter.

45. Individual Case Files for Relocation, Training and Employment, 1955–68, Portland Area Office, RG 75, NARA, PAR.

46. Report, Adult Vocational Training, 19 October 1962, Folder—Portland Dropout Study, 1958–1961, Box 1679, Portland Administrative Files, RG 75, NARA, PAR.

47. Portland Area Director to Agency Superintendents, undated, Folder—Memorandum to Agencies, 1958–1959, Box 1673, Portland Administrative Files, RG 75, NARA, PAR.

48. Peters interview; Paul Houston, "Indian Discovers Life in City is Good—But It's Terrifying," *Los Angeles Times*, 3 March 1968, sec. C, pp. 1, 3.

49. M. M. interview.

50. Fixico interview.

51. Bad Horse interview.

52. Kimmis Hendrick, "Minorities Bear Brunt of Layoffs," 24 February 1958, Folder—Newspaper Clippings, 1956–1961, Box 10, Los Angeles Field Office Central Classified Files, RG 75, NARA, PR.

53. Individual Case Files for Relocation, Training and Employment, 1955–68, Portland Area Office, RG 75, NARA, PAR.

54. National Council on Indian Opportunity, *Public Forum before the Committee on Urban Indians*, 93–96.

55. Allan Parachini, "The Indians: Frustration Still the Same," *Los Angeles Herald-Examiner*, 21 Nov 1971, sec. A, p. 6.

56. Young interview; National Council on Indian Opportunity, *Public Forum before the Committee on Urban Indians*, 266–69.

57. Brown interview.

58. Goodvoice, "Relocation."

59. MacKenzie, dir., *The Exiles* (1961); Trillin, "New Group in Town"; Jean Murphy, "The Urban Indian: Agonizing Transition from Old Ways to New," *Los Angeles Times*, 22 March 1970, sec. E, pp. 1, 15, 17; Penelope McMillan, "The Urban Indian—LA's Factionalized Minority," *Los Angeles Times*, 26 October 1980, sec. 2, pp. 1, 4, 6; A. Carruth-Cocopah, "One Man's Opinion, *Talking Leaf*, April 1969; Bell, "The Rules and Regulations of Aggression and Violence among the American Indian Men of Skid Row, Los Angeles"; Graves, "Drinking and Drunkenness Among Urban Indians."

60. Strouse interview.

61. Caroline Martinez to LARFO, 15 September 1956, Folder—Scheduling 1955–58, Box 7, Los Angeles Field Office Central Classified Files, RG 75, NARA, PR.

62. Tafoya interview; Weibel-Orlando, *Indian Country, L.A.*, 205–8.

63. Benjamin James to H. T. Borden, Relocation Officer, 13 June 1955, Folder—Success Story Cases 1953–56, Box 8, Los Angeles Field Office Central Classified Files, RG 75, NARA, PR.

64. Individual Case Files for Relocation, Training and Employment, 1955–68, Portland Area Office, RG 75, NARA, PAR.

65. Boyer, "Reflections of Alcatraz."

66. National Council on Indian Opportunity, *Public Forum before the Committee on Urban Indians*, 91.

67. Amos interview.

68. Means, *Where White Men Fear to Tread*.

69. Ibid., 141–48, quotation on p. 142.

70. Tafoya interview; Weibel-Orlando, *Indian County, L.A.*, 209; Mary Nan Gamble, Field Relocation Officer, Los Angeles Field Office, to Guy C. Williams, Superintendent, United Pueblo Agency, 25 July 1956, Folder—Success Story Cases 1953–56, Box 8, Los Angeles Field Office Central Classified Files, RG 75, NARA, PR.

71. Leonard C. Allen, Portland Area Office, to Victor E. Hill, Chemawa Indian School, 14 August 1958, Folder—General, Chemawa, Box 1675, Portland Administrative Files, RG 75, NARA, PAR; H. B. Jenkins, Bureau of Indian Affairs, to Don C. Foster, Portland Area Office, 12 September 1958, Folder—Letters to Trainees and Concerning Trainees, Box 1673, Portland Administrative Files, RG 75, NARA, PAR.

72. Memorandum, Reports on Graduates on Relocation, Phoenix Indian School, 6 July 1959, Folder—Schools (Pupils and Graduates), Box 13, Los Angeles Field Office Central Classified Files, RG 75, NARA, PR.

73. Individual Case Files for Relocation, Training and Employment, 1955–68, Portland Area Office, RG 75, NARA, PAR.

74. Ibid.

75. Ibid.

76. Houston, "Indian Discovers Life in City is Good—But It's Terrifying."

77. Forcia interview.

78. Lamore-Choate, "My Relocation Experience," 38–39.

79. Yellow Eagle, "Oral History: Glen Yellow Eagle."

80. John and Lois Knifechief interview.

81. Tafoya interview.

82. These groups will be discussed in greater detail in Chapter 5.

83. Garbarino, "The Chicago American Indian Center: Two Decades."

84. *Talking Leaf*, n.d. [1972?], Folder—Publications, Box 23, Los Angeles Field Office Central Classified Files, RG 75, NARA, PR; Resolution of the Council of the Indian Center, 28 March 1956, Folder—Indian Center 1956–58, Box 11, Los Angeles Field Office Central Classified Files, RG 75, NARA, PR; Jean Ward, "Indian Center in Heart of LA," *Los Angeles Examiner*, 10 June 1956, sec. V, pp. 1, 16.

85. Ward, "Indian Center in Heart of LA"; Bob Houser, "Suddenly There Were

10,000 Indians Here," *Independent Press Telegram*, 19 August 1956, sec. B, p. 16; Houston, "Indian Discovers Life in City is Good—But It's Terrifying"; "'Shooting Star' Agency Helps Indians Adjust," *Los Angeles Times*, 3 March 1968, sec. C, p. 2; Carruth-Cocopah, "One Man's Opinion"; Parachini, "The Indians: Frustration Still the Same"; Sandra Osawa, "To Be Indian in LA," *Talking Leaf*, October–November 1972, 3.

86. "Supervisor Ernest E. Debs on Indian Relocation Program," *Talking Leaf*, 15 May 1968.

87. National Council on Indian Opportunity, *Public Forum before the Committee on Urban Indians*, 123.

88. Albert Lerner, Acting Director, to Carolyn Morgan, 5 June 1971, Folder—Requests for Information 1970–71, Box 22, Los Angeles Field Office Central Classified Files, RG 75, NARA, PR; Form Letters, Titus Wilson, Acting Director, to Indian Community Organizations, 15 July 1971, Folder—Requests for Information, 1970–71, Box 22, Los Angeles Field Office Central Classified Files, RG 75, NARA; Aurelia Wick, Guidance Specialist, to Betty Dobratz, 25 June 1971, Folder—Requests for Information 1970–71, Box 22, Los Angeles Field Office Central Classified Files, RG 75, NARA, PR; National Council on Indian Opportunity, *Public Forum before the Committee on Urban* Indians, 124.

89. Roy Haynes, "Awarding of Indian Contract Stirs Dispute," *Los Angeles Times*, 7 March 1971, sec. F, pp. 4–5; Lester interview; Edmunds [*sic*] interview; Amos interview.

90. Johnson, Nagel, and Champagne, "American Indian Activism and Transformation: Lessons from Alcatraz," in Johnson, Nagel, and Champagne, eds., *American Indian Activism*; Forbes, *Native Americans and Nixon*, 26, 28–29, 36–37; Prucha, *Great Father*, 1098; Clarkin, *Federal Indian Policy in the Kennedy and Johnson Administrations, 1961–1969*; Cobb, "Philosophy of an Indian War"; Cobb, "'Us Indians Understand the Basics'"; Nixon, "Message to Congress on Indian Affairs"; Sorkin, *Urban American Indian*, 59–63, 78–79, 111–14; Kotlowski, "Alcatraz, Wounded Knee, and Beyond."

91. Edmonds interview.

CHAPTER 4

1. Young interview.

2. Sugrue, *The Origins of the Urban Crisis*; Self, *American Babylon*. Also see Cowie and Heathcott, eds., *Beyond the Ruins*.

3. Lemke-Santangelo, "Deindustrialization, Urban Poverty and African American Community Mobilization in Oakland, 1945 through the 1990s," quotation on p. 346.

4. Sides, *L.A. City Limits*, 169–97, quotation on p. 180.

5. Although deindustrialization has been ignored by scholars in American Indian Studies, it might be made part of recent efforts to merge American Indian

Studies with U.S. economic history: Hosmer, *American Indians in the Marketplace*; Hosmer and O'Neill, eds., *Native Pathways*; O'Neill, *Working the Navajo Way*; Harmon, "American Indians and Land Monopolies in the Gilded Age."

6. Fixico interview; U.S. Department of the Interior, *Annual Report of the Secretary of the Interior* [1945], 249–50; Nash, *American West Transformed*, 128–47; Albon, "Relocated American Indians in the San Francisco Bay Area"; Fortunate Eagle, *Alcatraz! Alcatraz! The Indian Occupation of 1969–1971*, 23; Johnson, Nagel, and Champagne, "American Indian Activism and Transformation," 21–22; Deloria, "This Country Was a Lot Better Off When the Indians Were Running It."

7. Bill Murphy, "Navahos Find Success on Leaving Reservation," *Los Angeles Times*, 15 January 1956, sec. A, p. 1.

8. Gordon Grant, "Relocated Indians Find Haven Here," *Los Angeles Times*, 31 January 1955, sec. 2, pp. 2–4.

9. Skenandore interview.

10. Strouse interview.

11. Lynch, "In the Urban Spirit," 22–25, 70.

12. Charley interview.

13. "News of 1953 Graduates," *Sherman Bulletin*, 1 December 1953, 15.

14. Thomas Bush and Ed Cony, "Indians and Industry," *Wall Street Journal*, 28 December 1955, 1, 4.

15. "A Cup of Coffee With the Edmund Whites," *Sherman Bulletin*, 1 February 1956, 15.

16. Art Ryon, "North American Indians Work at North American," *Los Angeles Times*, 13 October 1952, sec. 2, pp. 1, 28; Bush and Cony, "Indians and Industry."

17. Grant, "Relocated Indians Find Haven Here."

18. Goodvoice, "Relocation."

19. "Few Jobs Available for Graduates Next Summer," *Sherman Bulletin*, 9 December 1960, 1.

20. Kimmis Hendrick, "Minorities Bear Brunt of Layoffs," *Christian Science Monitor*, 24 February 1958, 3.

21. Pinto interview.

22. Tafoya interview.

23. National Council on Indian Opportunity, *Public Forum before the Committee on Urban Indians*, 64.

24. Hendrick, "Minorities Bear Brunt of Layoffs."

25. Fastwolf interview.

26. Fixico interview.

27. Haberman interview.

28. Penn interview.

29. Liz McGuinness, "Peaceful Indians Forced to Fight," *Los Angeles Evening Mirror News*, 5 April 1960, sec. 2, p. 3.

30. M. M. interview.

31. Bowen interview.

32. National Council on Indian Opportunity, *Public Forum before the Committee on Urban Indians*, 118.

33. Olivas interview.

34. Brown interview.

35. Sandra Osawa, "Police Backlash in L.A.," *Talking Leaf*, February 1973, 7–8.

36. Kenneth Reich, "Police Dept. Reports to Bradley About Indian Group's Accusation of Harassment," *Los Angeles Times*, 16 September 1975, sec. 2, p. 8.

37. Bell, "The Rules and Regulations of Aggression and Violence among the American Indian Men of Skid Row, Los Angeles"; Albon, "Relocated American Indians in the San Francisco Bay Area," 298–99; Graves, "Drinking and Drunkenness Among Urban Indians"; Price, "U.S. and Canadian Indian Ethnic Institutions"; Makofsky, "Tradition and Change in the Lumbee Indian Community of Baltimore."

38. Brown interview.

39. Reyes, *Bernie Whitebear*, 64–79.

40. Danziger, *Survival and Regeneration*, 34–35.

41. Goodvoice, "Relocation," quotations on pp. 135 and 145, respectively.

42. MacKenzie, dir., *The Exiles* (1961).

43. Jack Slater, "Caught Between Two Cultures," *Los Angeles Times*, 29 February 1976, sec. 10, pp. 1, 6, 7, 8.

44. Reyes, *Bernie Whitebear*, 81.

45. M. M. interview.

46. Allan Parachini, "The Indians: Frustration Still the Same," *Los Angeles Herald-Examiner*, 21 November 1971, sec. A, p. 6.

47. Gabourie, *Justice and the American Indian*, 5; National Council on Indian Opportunity, *Public Forum before the Committee on Urban Indians*, 113–19.

48. Jean Murphy, "The Urban Indian: Agonizing Transition from Old Ways to New," *Los Angeles Times*, 22 March 1970, sec. E, pp. 1, 15, 17.

49. Goodvoice, "Relocation," 139.

50. Olivas interview.

51. Parachini, "The Indians: Frustration Still the Same."

52. Svensson, *The Ethnics in American Politics*, 35–36; American Indian Policy Review Commission, *Report on Urban and Rural Non-Reservation Indians*, 57–80; Sorkin, *The Urban American Indian*.

53. Patrick Borunda, "Native Americans in Portland," Commissioner Jordan Series, Stanley Parr Archives and Records Center; City Club of Portland, "Report on the Urban Indian in Portland," 61–64; Bohanan, "The Urban Indian Program in Portland, Oregon"; Red Bird and Melendy, "Indian Child Welfare in Oregon."

54. Murphy, "The Urban Indian."

55. A. David Lester, "The Neglected Poor: Los Angeles' Growing Community of American Indians, *Los Angeles Times*, 22 August 1974, sec. 2, p. 7.

56. Osgood Caruthers, "L.A. Indians Seek Their Own Hospital," *Los Angeles Times*, 25 April 1976, pp. 1, 8, 9.

57. Edmunds [sic] interview; Chet Barfield, "Indian Resource Director to Retire After Two Decades of Activism," *San Diego Union-Tribune*, 29 April 1999, sec. B, pp. 1, 7–8.

58. John Fleischman, "Going Home: The Great Indian Dream," *Los Angeles Times*, 17 September 1972, sec. E, pp. 1, 4. Additional examples in Los Angeles include Glover Young, whose story began this chapter, and Ernie Peters, discussed in Chapter 3.

59. Berryhill, "Memories of Growing Up in the Oakland Community, circa 1952–66."

60. Robert Olmos, "Couple's Transition to City Life Problem Free," *Oregonian*, 28 April 1970, p. 11.

61. Fastwolf interview.

62. John and Lois Knifechief interview; Tom Knifechief interview.

63. Tafoya interview; Sando, *Pueblo Profiles: Cultural Identity through Centuries of Change*, 65–69; Weibel-Orlando, *Indian Country L.A.*, 205–15.

64. McGuinness, "Peaceful Indians Forced to Fight."

65. Jay Gourley, "There's an Indian Behind Every Rock in Los Angeles: Since the Relocation Act of 1954, L.A.'s Indian Population Has Skyrocketed," *Los Angeles Herald-Examiner*, 8 July 1968, sec. A, p. 16.

66. Gridley, *Indians of Today*, 52; "Land, Justice, Awards Make the News," *Talking Leaf*, February 1976, 5; "Fred Gabourie: Bringing Perspective to the Bench," *Talking Leaf*, March 1976, 4; Gabouri [sic] interview.

67. Chapters 5 and 6 discuss the expansion and development of Indian organizations in greater detail.

68. "Indian Center Evaluation Underway," *Talking Leaf*, July/August 1972, 4; "Indian Grapevine," *Talking Leaf*, July/August 1972, 18–19.

69. "Health Care Jobs for Indians," *The First People* [publication of the American Friends Service Committee, Pacific Southwest Region, Pasadena, Calif.], July 1974.

70. Norma and Jim Johnstone, "ICI Manpower Director Has Survived Many Battles," *Talking Leaf*, August 1975, 4.

71. "Introducing Staff: 'Sandy' Osawa," *Talking Leaf*, May/June 1972, 7–8.

72. Spence interview.

73. Lamore-Choate, "My Relocation Experience."

74. Jack Jones, "Indian Businessmen's Goal Is to Aid Brothers," *Los Angeles Times*, 18 January 1971, sec. 2, p. 4; "Pre-Business Workshop Planned to Help Indian Men and Women Succeed in Business—June 17," *UIDA Reporter* [publication of the Urban Indian Development Association], June 1972; "How to Succeed in Business by Really Trying, *UIDA Reporter*, September 1972; "UIDA's X-Mas Shopping Guide to American Indian Business," *UIDA Reporter*, December 1972; Urban Indian Development Association, *American Indian Business Directory*.

75. Urban Indian Development Association, *American Indian Business Directory*.

76. "Experience Pays off for Eagle Fire Protection," *UIDA Reporter*, April 1977; "Jacques' Rest Makes the 3rd for Cookes," *UIDA Reporter*, April 1979.

CHAPTER 5

1. "Indian Day," *Talking Leaf*, October 1964.

2. Hoxie, "Exploring a Cultural Borderland," quotation on p. 969. Also see Hoxie, "Introduction," for a further articulation of these arguments.

3. In this sense, urban American Indians were going through similar types of negotiations and adaptations as Native people working to "be Indian" while living on reservations and in rural areas through the twentieth century, a trend that has been better documented by American Indian Studies scholars. See Fowler, *Shared Symbols, Contested Meanings*; Foster, *Being Comanche*; Meyer, *White Earth Tragedy*; Hoxie, *Parading Through History*; Harmon, *Indians in the Making*; Hosmer, *American Indians in the Marketplace*; Rosier, *Rebirth of the Blackfeet Nation, 1912–1954*; O'Neill, *Working the Navajo Way*; Bauer, *We Were All Like Migrant Workers Here*; and Fisher, *Shadow Tribe*. Moreover, urban American Indians can be considered part of a larger conversation among Ethnic Studies scholars that understands ethnicity as something that is destabilized and fluid, with boundaries that are continually being negotiated and redrawn, largely to meet the needs of the actors. See Sanchez, *Becoming Mexican American*; Gutiérrez, *Walls and Mirrors*; Lemke-Santangelo, *Abiding Courage*; Escobar, *Race, Police and the Making of a Political Identity*; Garcia, *A World of Its Own*; Pitti, *The Devil in Silicon Valley*; Oropeza, *¡Raza Sí! ¡Guerra No!*; and Alamillo, *Making Lemonade out of Lemons*.

4. Meriam, *The Problem of Indian Administration*.

5. Deloria, *Playing Indian*.

6. Patterson, "'Real Indian Songs.'"

7. "What Is the American Indian Progressive Association," *The Okeh: Official Publication of the American Indian Progressive Association* [Los Angeles, Calif.], January 1926, 1.

8. "Articles of Association," *The Okeh: Official Publication of the American Indian Progressive Association*, January 1926, 1–2.

9. Pablo Narcha, "Editorial," *The Okeh: Official Publication of the American Indian Progressive Association*, January 1926, 2.

10. Meriam, *Problem of Indian Administration*, 721.

11. Narcha, "Editorial."

12. Shoemaker, "Urban Indians and Ethnic Choices."

13. "Redskins Today Regular Folks," *Los Angeles Times*, 23 April 1928, sec. 2, p. 10.

14. Meriam, *Problem of Indian Administration*, 720.

15. Patterson, "Indian Life in the City."

16. Meriam, *Problem of Indian Administration*, 723.

17. "Indians Plan Curtis Rally," *Los Angeles Times*, 28 September 1928, sec. 1, p. 9; "Thousand Indians Picnic," *Los Angeles Times*, 1 October 1928, sec. 2, pp. 1–2, including quotation.

18. *Quarterly Journal of the Society of American Indians* 1 (January–April 1913): 72–73.

19. *American Indian Magazine* [publication of the Society of American Indians] 4 (January-March 1916), 60–64.

20. Chief Red Fox (Skiuhushu), "Why Nation Should Honor 'Original Landlords' American Indian Day," *American Indian Advocate* [publication of the Tepee Order] 4 (Winter 1922), 8.

21. "American Indian Day [1926]," Graphics Collection, Chicago Historical Society; Beck, "The Chicago American Indian Community."

22. "Tiny Indian Chief Is Dance Winner," *New York Times*, 1 October 1934.

23. "War-Whoops Echo at Pow-Wow Here," *New York Times*, 30 September 1935.

24. "50 Indians Dance in Tribal Day Here," *New York Times*, 28 September 1936.

25. "Indians Smoke Peace Pipe, Stage War Dance in Annual Ceremonies in Prospect Park," *New York Times*, 27 September 1936.

26. "Cupano [*sic*] Thunderbird Flag Waves Beside Old Glory," *Los Angeles Examiner*, 30 September 1940; "State Indian Day Observed Here Sunday," *Los Angeles Examiner*, 22 September 1941; "Indians at Outing Go on Warpath," *Los Angeles Examiner*, 29 September 1941; "Warren to be Speaker at Indian Parley Today," *Los Angeles Examiner*, 27 September 1942. For a fuller treatment of American Indian Day, see Rosenthal, "American Indian Day."

27. Shoemaker, "Urban Indians and Ethnic Choices."

28. "Indian Center of Los Angeles" [promotional flyer], May 1958, *Talking Leaf* bound file, BRL, ANC.

29. "Indian Center—Background," *Talking Leaf (Special Edition: Indians in the City, Meeting the Challenges in Los Angeles)*, February 1975, 3.

30. Iron Eyes Cody, "Little Big Horn News," *Talking Leaf*, November 1976, 8.

31. Austin, *Around the World in San Francisco*, 9–10; Albon, "Relocated American Indians in the San Francisco Bay Area," 297–99.

32. "Indians' Plight Stressed," *Oregonian*, 15 May 1961, sec. 1, p. 15.

33. Ibid.; Peter Thompson, "Rummage Sales Slack So Indian Women Lose Center," *Oregon Journal*, 8 November 1961, sec. 1, p. 4; Kay Bollam, "Blackfeet Women Appeal for Presents for Needy," *Oregonian*, 14 Dec 1961, sec. 2, p. 2.

34. Linda Lapman, "Indian Center Haven for Homeless," *Oregonian*, 3 February 1962, sec. 2, p. 7.

35. "Indian Fete to Aid Fund," *Oregonian*, 24 August 1961, sec. 1, p. 22.

36. "Portland Indian Center Works for Success," *Oregonian*, 14 July 1962, sec. 2, p. 2.

37. Ibid.

38. "Rummage Sales Slack."

39. *American Indians of Today* [publication of the Portland American Indian Center]; *Tipi News* [publication of the Portland (Ore.) American Indian Center] July–October 1970, 1–3; *Tipi News*, April 1971, 1–9.

40. *American Indians of Today*; "1970 Indian Pow-wow and Encampment," *Tipi News*, July–October 1970, pp. 1, 3; *Tipi News*, November 1970, pp. 1–4; *Tipi News*, April 1971, 2; *Northwest Native American News* [publication of the Native American Rehabilitation Association, Portland, Ore.], 1972.

41. "Indian Center of Los Angeles."

42. "Report on the Indian Center in Los Angeles," September 1949, *Talking Leaf* bound file, BRL, ANC.

43. *Talking Leaf*, May 1951 through March 1954; Jack Forbes, personal communication with author.

44. "Welcome South Dakota Sioux!," *Talking Leaf*, June [July] 1951.

45. *Talking Leaf*, December 1951.

46. "Welcome Sherman Students," *Talking Leaf*, June 1951.

47. "Happenings in Our Indian Center Village," *Talking Leaf*, August 1951.

48. "Whispering Leaves," *Talking Leaf*, April 1952.

49. "Letters From Our Boys in the Armed Forces," *Talking Leaf*, February 1953.

50. *Talking Leaf*, June 1951; *Talking Leaf*, June [July] 1951.

51. *Talking Leaf*, May 1951 through March 1954.

52. *Talking Leaf*, February 1952.

53. Ibid.

54. *Talking Leaf*, January 1953.

55. "Letters From Our Boys in the Armed Forces."

56. *Talking Leaf*, May 1952.

57. Arguments for the eclipsing of tribal identity by pan-Indian identity include Weibel-Orlando, *Indian Country, L.A.*, 132–52; and Hirabayashi, Willard, and Kemnitzer, "Pan-Indianism in the Urban Setting."

58. *Talking Leaf*, October 1951.

59. "Indian Youth Club," *Talking Leaf*, May 1951.

60. "Indian Powwow, *Talking Leaf*, February 1952.

61. "April Diary," *Talking Leaf*, May 1951.

62. *Talking Leaf*, May 1951.

63. Ibid.

64. "Tribes Ready Authentic Indian Feast to Finance Summer Powwow," *Oregonian*, 9 March 1972, sec. 2, p. 1; "Dinner Aids Indian Center," *Oregon Journal*, 14 March 1972, sec. 2, p.1.

65. "Indian Powwow," *Talking Leaf*, January 1952.

66. *Talking Leaf*, March 1953.

67. *Talking Leaf*, March 1954.

68. "Origin of All Indian Sports Leagues of Los Angeles," *Talking Leaf,* September 1964, including quotation; "The Indian Scene," *Talking Leaf,* September 1964.

69. Amos interview.

70. Bramstedt, "Corporate Adaptations of Urban Migrants," 349–50.

71. Howard Yackitonipah interview.

72. National Council on Indian Opportunity, *Public Forum before the Committee on Urban Indians,* 257.

73. "AIAA Los Angeles Indian Girls' Softball Standings," *Talking Leaf,* September 1964; Bramstedt, "Corporate Adaptations of Urban Migrants," 130.

74. "Of the Indians in Our City," *Oregonian,* 8 June 1969, sec. NW, p. 8; "NW Indians to Convene in Park Tepee [*sic*] Village," *Oregonian,* 4 June 1970, sec. 1, p. 24; "1970 Portland Indian Pow-Wow and Encampment" [powwow program], Multnomah County Library.

75. "1970 Portland Indian Pow-Wow and Encampment"; *American Indians of Today*; "Indians Open Dancing Test: 1,500 Gather at Delta Park," *Oregonian,* 13 June 1970, sec. 1, p. 4; "Indian Dance Awards Won," *Oregonian,* 17 June 1970, sec. 2, p. 6; Barbara Jordon, "Indian Maiden Wins Title," *Oregonian,* 17 June 1970, sec. 2, p. 1.

76. "Tribes Ready Authentic Indian Feast"; "Indians Plan Rose Powwow," *Oregonian,* 7 June 1973, sec. 1, p. 23; "Grandiose Grin," *Oregonian,* 10 June 1973, sec. C, p. 11; "Hope Rises for Indian Center Here," *Oregon Journal,* 12 June 1973, sec. 1, p. 6; "Pendleton Girl Wins Miss Indian Crown," *Oregonian,* 17 June 1974, sec. A, p. 20; "Indians Begin Festival Dancing," *Oregonian,* 14 June 1975, sec. A, p. 8; "Indians Carry on Thanksgiving Tradition Started Before Pilgrims Landed," *Oregonian,* 24 November 1975, sec. B, p. 8.

77. Tafoya interview.

78. Bramstedt, "Corporate Adaptations of Urban Migrants," 85–89.

79. Kenneth and Greta Yackitonipah interview.

80. "Powwow News," *Talking Leaf,* September 1964.

81. "Powwow Schedule," *Talking Leaf,* May 1974; Bramstedt, "Corporate Adaptations of Urban Migrants," 447–59.

82. Tafoya interview.

83. "Helping Hand for American Indians," *Christian Science Monitor,* 27 April 1966, p. 17; Bramstedt, "Corporate Adaptations of Urban Migrants," 429; "Program Description: 8 December 1969," Indian Welcome House Folder, Jack Forbes Collection, University of California, Davis, Shields Library.

84. Jeppsen interview.

85. "Indians Wage Struggle to Keep Center Going," *Los Angeles Times,* 30 January 1955, sec. 1, p. 3; Jean Ward, "Indian Center in Heart of LA," *Los Angeles Examiner,* 10 June 1956, sec. V, pp. 1, 16; "News from the Indian Center," *Many Smokes: The Voice of the American Indian* [Los Angeles, Calif.], March 1962; "News from the

Indian Center," *Many Smokes: The Voice of the American Indian*, July 1962; Cody interview.

86. "Talking Leaf Reborn," *Talking Leaf*, September 1964.

87. "IC Methods Revamped," *Talking Leaf*, September 1964.

88. Amos interview.

89. *Talking Leaf*, September 1964-March 1969.

90. "Thanks to Donors," *Talking Leaf*, December/January 1967; "Indian Center Given EYOA Grant: Your Support is Needed," *Talking Leaf*, February 1967. These developments will be discussed in more detail in Chapter 6.

CHAPTER 6

1. Amos interview; Rambeau interview; Elaine Woo, "Indians on Skid Row 'Celebrate' Thanksgiving," *Los Angeles Herald Examiner*, 24 November 1977, sec. B, p. 2; "Eagleshield Uses CETA Program to Gain Profession and Honors," *Talking Leaf*, August 1976, 10.

2. Smith and Warrior, *Like a Hurricane*; Johnson, *The Occupation of Alcatraz Island*; Johnson, Nagel, and Champagne, eds., *American Indian Activism*; Kotlowski, "Alcatraz, Wounded Knee, and Beyond."

3. Hoikkala, "Feminists or Reformers?"; Rosenthal, "Repositioning Indianness"; Amerman, "'Let's Get In and Fight!'"

4. Dittmer, *Local People*; Payne, *I've Got the Light of Freedom*. More recently the case for local studies has been made persuasively both in the editors' introduction and by the collective weight of the individual essays contained in Theoharis and Woodard, eds., *Groundwork*.

5. Cobb and Fowler, eds., *Beyond Red Power*; Cobb, *Native Activism in Cold War America*.

6. Jones, "'Not a Color, but an Attitude'": Father James Groppi and Black Power Politics in Milwaukee"; Anderson, "Practical Internationalists: The Story of the Des Moines, Iowa, Black Panther Party"; Williams, "Black Women, Urban Politics, and Engendering Black Power."

7. Self, *American Babylon*, esp. 254–55; Von Eschen, *Race Against Empire*; Kelley, *Freedom Dreams*; Singh, *Black Is a Country*; Feldstein, "'I Don't Trust You Anymore'"; Joseph, "Introduction: Toward a Historiography of the Black Power Movement."

8. Cobb and Fowler, eds., *Beyond Red Power*.

9. Cobb, "Philosophy of an Indian War"; Cobb, "'Us Indians Understand the Basics.'"

10. Hoikkala, "Feminists or Reformers?"

11. Makofsky, "Tradition and Change in the Lumbee Indian Community of Baltimore."

12. "Planned Conference on Indian Relocation Problems," *Talking Leaf*, 15 November 1967; "LA County Supervisor on Warpath," *Talking Leaf*, 15 December 1967.

13. Miller, "Involvement in an Urban University."

14. Boyer, "Reflections of Alcatraz"; Forbes, "The Native Struggle for Liberation."

15. "American Indian Educational Opportunities at UCLA," *UCLA Native American* [publication of the University of California, Los Angeles, American Indian Students Association], Spring 1970, 5.

16. "High Potential Program at UCLA," *UCLA Native American*, Fall 1969, 4.

17. Tafoya interview.

18. "High Potential Program at UCLA."

19. Castillo, "A Reminiscence of the Alcatraz Occupation."

20. "About Us," *American Indian Studies Center*, http://www.aisc.ucla.edu (accessed 1 September 2011).

21. Castillo, "A Reminiscence of the Alcatraz Occupation"; Talbot, "Indian Students and Reminiscences of Alcatraz"; Kemnitzer, "Personal Memories of Alcatraz, 1969."

22. Johnson, *Occupation of Alcatraz*; Johnson, Nagel, and Champagne, "American Indian Activism and Transformation"; Forbes, "The Native Struggle for Liberation," quotation on p. 133.

23. Banks interview.

24. "In Support of Wounded Knee [flyer]," Wounded Knee Legal Defense/Offense Committee Folder, Organizational Files, Southern California Library.

25. "Break the Blockade of Wounded Knee [flyer]," Wounded Knee Legal Defense/Offense Committee Folder, Organizational Files, Southern California Library.

26. "For the Struggle at Wounded Knee [flyer]," Wounded Knee Legal Defense/Offense Committee Folder, Organizational Files, Southern California Library.

27. Banks interview.

28. Edmonds interview.

29. "Benefit: Wounded Knee [flyer]," Wounded Knee Legal Defense/Offense Committee Folder, Organizational Files, Southern California Library.

30. "Wounded Knee Trials Continue [flyer]," Wounded Knee Legal Defense/Offense Committee Folder, Organizational Files, Southern California Library.

31. "Victory Party for Wounded Knee Defendants [flyer]," Wounded Knee Legal Defense/Offense Committee Folder, Organizational Files, Southern California Library.

32. Forbes, "The Native Struggle for Liberation: Alcatraz," 134–35; Oppelt, *Tribally Controlled Indian Colleges*, 69–73.

33. "Chicano Indian Study Center of Oregon" [promotional letter], 1971, Multnomah County Library.

34. Ibid.; *Northwest Native American News*, 1972.

35. Deloria, *Behind the Trail of Broken Treaties*, 43–62.

36. Spence interview; "Chicano Indian Study Center of Oregon"; "Indian Occupation Plan Aired," *Oregon Journal*, 22 November 1972, p. 2.

37. Stone interview.

38. Spence interview.

39. *Northwest Native American News.*

40. "100 Indians Protest, Museum Pledges to Remove 3 Exhibits," *Los Angeles Times*, 21 December 1970, sec. 1, pp. 1, 3.

41. Robert Kistler, "Director, Indians Clash Again on Museum Display," *Los Angeles Times*, 28 December 1970, sec. 1, pp. 3, 27.

42. David Shaw, "12 Protestors Arrested at Southwest Museum," *Los Angeles Times*, 13 January 1971, sec. 1, p. 21.

43. LaGrand, *Indian Metropolis*, 229–45.

44. Johnson, Nagel, and Champagne, "American Indian Activism and Transformation," 32.

45. Miller interview.

46. Arlene Poemoceah interview.

47. Elmer Poemoceah interview.

48. Trillin, "New Group in Town."

49. Ibid.

50. "Indian Panel Falls Victim to Group Strife," *Oregonian*, 30 August 1971, sec. 2, p. 8; "Indians Disband Council," *Oregon Journal*, 31 August 1971, p. 6; Steve Neal, "Portland's Indians Still Looking for Identity in Solving Own Problems," *Oregon Journal*, 30 September 1971, p. 12.

51. Amerman, "'Let's Get In and Fight!,'" 609.

52. Tom Knifechief interview.

53. Adamson interview.

54. "A Sampling of Local Reactions to Wounded Knee," *Talking Leaf*, February 1973, 10.

55. Tafoya interview.

56. Edmonds interview.

57. Bad Horse interview.

58. Jean Murphy, "Wanted: Slice of the American Dream," *Los Angeles Times*, 23 March 1970, sec. 4, pp. 1, 8, 9.

59. Sorkin, *Urban American Indian*, 47–55.

60. UCLA School of Public Health, *The Health Problems Among Native Americans in Central Los Angeles*; UCLA School of Public Health, *Los Angeles Area Indian Population*.

61. Ragni L. Griffin, "Indian Free Clinic—Like 'Family,'" *Los Angeles Times*, 4 January 1976, sec. 8, pp. 1, 4, 7.

62. Amos interview; Griffin, "Indian Free Clinic"; UCLA School of Public Health, *The Health Problems Among Native Americans in Central Los Angeles*; UCLA School of Public Health, *Los Angeles Area Indian Population*.

63. Sorkin, *Urban American Indian*, 56–63.

64. Morton Spence, "'Native' Center Organized," *Oregon Journal*, 8 September 1970, quotation on p. 7; Stone interview; Spence interview.

65. Wannassay interview.

66. "Indian Triumphs in Fight Against Alcohol," *Tribal Spokesman* [publication of the Intertribal Council of California, Sacramento, Calif.], June/July 1971, 5; Chiloquin interview; DuPoint interview; Seabay interview.

67. Chiloquin interview.

68. Olivas interview.

69. DuPoint interview.

70. "Indian Triumphs in Fight Against Alcohol"; Chiloquin interview; Olivas interview; DuPoint interview; Seabay interview.

71. "American Indian Free Clinic—Vital to Urban American Indians," *Newsletter: American Indian Culture Center at the University of California Los Angeles*, Fall 1974; "Compton Indian Free Clinic Moves," *Talking Leaf*, June 1974, 3; Amos interview.

72. Rambeau interview; Amos interview.

73. Sorkin, *Urban American Indian*, 95–103; Fixico, *Urban Indian Experience in America*, 147–49.

74. LaGrand, *Indian Metropolis*, 245.

75. Amos interview; "Tribal American Preschool," *Talking Leaf*, October–November 1972, 9; Long, Canyon, and Churchman, "A Tribal American Preschool"; "Parents and Toddlers," *TACC Messenger* [publication of the Tribal American Consulting Corporation, City of Commerce, Calif.], January 1978, 5; "TACC Education," *TACC Messenger*, February 1978, 3; "Profiles in CETA," *TACC Messenger*, February 1978, 3–4.

76. *Moccasin Telegraph* [publication of the American Indian Education Commission, Los Angeles, Calif.], November/December 1979.

77. "Do You Want to Go to College," *Indian Newsletter* [publication of Access, Pala, Calif.], July 1972.

78. "Article from Jack Allen," *Newsletter: American Indian Culture Center at the University of California Los Angeles*, September 1970.

79. "Campus Activities: A Curriculum Report," *Newsletter: American Indian Culture Center at the University of California Los Angeles*, June 1972; "Progress of AICC Library," *Newsletter: American Indian Culture Center at the University of California Los Angeles*, Winter/Spring 1974.

80. "UCLA Academic Advancement Program," *Newsletter: American Indian Culture Center at the University of California Los Angeles*, Winter/Spring 1974.

81. "For Graduate Students," *Newsletter: American Indian Culture Center at the University of California Los Angeles*, June 1972; "Indian Masters," *Newsletter: American Indian Culture Center at the University of California Los Angeles*, Spring/Summer 1973; "Native American Librarian Training Program," *Newsletter:*

American Indian Culture Center at the University of California Los Angeles, Fall 1974.

82. "Campus Activities," *Newsletter: American Indian Culture Center at the University of California Los Angeles*, Fall 1973.

83. "American Indian Student Association Report," *Newsletter: American Indian Culture Center at the University of California Los Angeles*, Fall 1973.

84. "UCLA Indian Culture Week," *Newsletter: American Indian Culture Center at the University of California Los Angeles*, Spring/Summer 1973.

85. Ellen S. Rodman, "UCLA Indian Cultural Center Seeks Relevant Curriculum," *Los Angeles Times*, 4 January 1971, sec. 4, pp. 2, 14.

86. Monroe interview.

87. "Indian Center Evaluation Underway," *Talking Leaf*, July/August 1972, 4.

88. "Annual Staff Reports," *Talking Leaf*, July/August 1972, 5; "Grand Opening," *Talking Leaf*, July/August 1972, 15; "Indian Center, Inc.," *Talking Leaf*, January 1973, 18.

89. "IC West," *Talking Leaf*, September 1973, 2; "SE Indian Center," *Talking Leaf*, April 1973, 2; "Indian Center West Activities," *Talking Leaf*, April 1973, 2.

90. "Indian Center Periled by Auction Failure," *Talking Leaf*, April 1974, 1.

91. "ICI Education Department to Continue Under Grant," *Talking Leaf*, May 1974, 11.

92. "Indian Center Gets CETA Grant," *Talking Leaf*, October 1974, 1.

93. "Executive Director's Message," *Talking Leaf*, October 1975, 1.

94. "ICI New Facilities Best in 20 Years," *Talking Leaf*, December/January 1975, 1; "San Gabriel Valley Center Opens," *Talking Leaf*, June 1975, 4.

95. "Center Extends Services with Opening of Bell Gardens Branch," *Talking Leaf*, November 1976, 5.

96. *Talking Leaf* was published monthly or bimonthly from 1972 through the remainder of the decade.

97. "Silversmithing at ICW," *Talking Leaf*, August/September 1973, 10; "Boxing Club Formed for Youngsters at IC West," *Talking Leaf*, February 1974, 7; "Indian Center West Activities."

98. "SE Indian Center," *Talking Leaf*, April 1973, 2; "SE Indian Center," *Talking Leaf*, September 1973, 2.

99. "Career Day Set at SE Center," *Talking Leaf*, April 1975, 7; "Career Day Attracts Students," *Talking Leaf*, May 1975, 7.

100. "SE Indian Center Offers Indian Dance Classes," *Talking Leaf*, July 1974, 7; "Southeast Receives $20,000 Special Grant from GLACAA Council," *Talking Leaf*, June 1975, 4.

101. "Victor Hill Finds New Life at the Lodge," *Talking Leaf*, February/March 1975, 5.

102. "Gloria Sanborn: Turning Worlds into Money," *Talking Leaf*, March 1976, pp. 4, 7.

103. Tafoya interview.

104. Stone interview.

CONCLUSION

1. M. M. interview; "American Indian Resource Center," *County of Los Angeles Public Library*, *http://www.colapublib.org/services/ethnic/indian.php4* (accessed 1 September 2011).

2. M. M. interview.

3. Exceptions have been especially helpful as I have thought through these points: Yu, "Los Angeles and American Studies in a Pacific World of Migrations"; Gabaccia, "Is Everywhere Nowhere?"; Delgado, "In the Age of Exclusion"; McKeown, *Chinese Migrant Networks and Cultural Change*; Ngai, *Impossible Subjects*.

4. Works on wage labor are among the few studies in American Indian history whose authors think outside the boundaries of Indian reservations and other institutions. See Hosmer, *American Indians in the Marketplace*; Hosmer and O'Neill, eds., *Native Pathways*; O'Neill, *Working the Navajo Way*; and Bauer, *We Were All Like Migrant Workers Here*. Also see Fisher, *Shadow Tribe*, for an innovative study of off-reservation communities in the Pacific Northwest. Another especially insightful and creative study for thinking about Native people's movements is Ramirez, *Native Hubs*. Focusing on California's Silicon Valley in the 1990s, Ramirez highlights the "unbound connections to tribal homeland and urban spaces," through the development of what she calls "Native hubs," or places in cities where people from many different indigenous backgrounds come together to establish communities, develop new identities, and advocate for change.

5. "American Indian Complete Count Committee of Los Angeles and Orange Counties" [flyer], in author's possession.

6. Gwen Carr, "Urban Indians: The Invisible Minority," *News From Indian Country*, 30 April 1996, p. 7A.

7. "Report Notes 'Crisis' Facing Urban Indian Youth," *Indianz.Com*, http://www.indianz.com/News/archives/002846.asp (accessed 1 September 2011).

8. Sam Lewin, "Urban Indians: More at Risk than Anyone," *Native American Times* (Tulsa, Okla.), 24 March 2004, p. 7.

9. Examples can be found in Ahhaitty interview; Amos interview; Edmonds interview; M. M. interview; Rambeau interview; Spence interview; Stone interview; Tafoya interview; Wannassay interview; and Jacquelyn Ross, "Profile: Laura Williams, M.D., M.P.H.," *News from Native California* 14 (December 2000): 28.

10. Weibel-Orlando, *Indian Country L.A.*, 23–31.

11. Amos interview.

12. Kara Briggs, "PSU Center for Native Americans a Landmark," *Oregonian*, 24 October 2003, p. A1.

13. "About Us," *American Indian Studies Center*, http://www.aisc.ucla.edu (ac-

cessed 1 September 2011). Much of this evidence is based on the author's personal experience as a graduate student at UCLA.

14. "The Urban Indian Program" [promotional flyer], Commissioner Jordan Series, Collected Reports and Studies, Box: Law Enforcement, Energy, and Social Services, File: Urban Indian Program Progress Report, Stanley Parr Archives and Record Center; Robert Olmos, "Portland Begins to Recognize Plight of Urban Indians," *Oregonian*, 16 September 1973, p. 18; Eleanor Boxx, "Indian Urban Program Grows by Leaps and Bounds," *Oregon Journal*, 9 November 1974, sec. B, p. 2; James Duncan, "Cutting Out White Tape," *Willamette Week* (Portland, Ore.), 22 December 1975, p. 1, 9; "Free Clinic Expands Indian Medical Care," *Oregon Journal*, 6 November 1976, p. 3; Phil Adamsak, "Portland Indian Agency to Serve as Model," *Oregon Journal*, 30 July 1979, p. 9; Alan K. Ota, "Indian Health Clinic Gets Federal Grant," *Oregonian*, 19 December 1979, sec. C, p. 1; Wannassay interview; King, "NARA, the Center of Indian Community in Portland, Oregon." For Reaganomics and its effects on Indian peoples, see Jorgensen, "Federal Policies, American Indian Politics and the 'New Federalism'"; and Morris, "Termination by Accountants."

15. Amos interview; "Rift Draws Huge Turnout," *Talking Leaf*, February/March 1979, 14; "Charges CETA Funds Squandered," *Talking Leaf*, October/November 1979, 4; "Message to Our Readers, *Talking Leaf*, June 1987, 2; "LA Briefly," *Talking Leaf*, September/October 1987, 2.

16. Spence interview; Stone interview; Wannassay interview; King, "NARA," 196–200.

17. "President's Message," *Southern California Indian Center, Inc.* [Los Angeles, Calif.], January/February 1993, 1; Amos interview.

18. Sam Howe Verhovek, "Budget-Cutting Endangers Indian Clinics," *Los Angeles Times*, 2 May 2006, p. A6.

19. Felicia Fonseca, "Health Care Commission to Advocate on Behalf of Urban Indians," *Albuquerque Journal*, 23 February 2008. Also see "Urban Indians Complaint About Health Care Funding Cuts," *Associated Press State and Local Wire*, 6 August 2005; Angie Wagner, "Urban Indians Fear Loss of Native-friendly Health Clinics Under Bush Budget," *Associated Press State and Local Wire*, 24 March 2006; Julie Anderson, "Indian Clinic Budget Cuts Disastrous, Director Says," *Omaha World-Herald*, 28 March 2006.

20. Carr, "Urban Indians."

21. Bog Egelko, "American Indian Sues Over County Welfare Process; Single Mother Says She Was Told to Seek Tribal Aid," *San Francisco Chronicle*, 25 November 2002, p. A12.

22. For additional recent struggles to fund urban Indian services, see Paulette Bleam, "American Indian Center Struggles to Save Itself," *Inside Bay Area* [California], 10 March 2007; and Georgia Pabst, "A Home for the Great Spirit: American Indian Parish Fights Closure," *Milwaukee Journal Sentinel*, 17 October 2008.

23. Edmonds interview.

24. Brenda Norrell, "Families and Identity are the Focus of New Coalition to Assist Urban Indians," *Indian Country Today*, 11 February 2005.

25. "The Seamless Indian Community: Reservation to City and Back Again," *Indian Country Today*, 17 February 2005.

26. See *Tribal TANF Today* [Thermal, Calif.], a publication of the Torrez Martinez tribe.

27. "Navajo President Suggests Albuquerque Navajo Chapter," *Associated Press State and Local Wire*, 22 March 2006.

28. Erny Zah, "Navajos Can Vote in Phoenix, Albuquerque This Weekend," *Navajo Times*, 10 February 2011.

29. "Tsa-La-Gi LA," available online at http://losangeles.cherokee.org (accessed 1 September 2011).

30. For a more in-depth discussion of the patterns outlined in the remainder of this chapter, see Chapter 7 in Rosenthal, "Re-imagining Indian Country," 228–59.

31. "Football Schedule," *Sherman Bulletin*, 2 October 1936, 4; "Handball," *Sherman Bulletin*, 11 December 1936, 4; "Cross Country Team Wins," *Sherman Bulletin*, 24 December 1936, 6; "Boxing," *Sherman Bulletin*, 24 December 1936, 6; "Leather Slingers Break Even," *Sherman Bulletin*, 19 February 1937, 4; "Sherman Grapplers in Match," *Sherman Bulletin*, 5 March 1937, 4; "Boxing and Wrestling," *Sherman Bulletin*, 19 March 1937, 4; "Handball Team in AAU Meet," *Sherman Bulletin*, 19 March 1937, 4; "Handball Team Victorious," 2 April 1937, 4; "Sherman Cross Country Activities," *Sherman Bulletin*, 14 May 1937, 6.

32. *Warm Springs Reservation Tomahawk* [publication of the Confederated Tribes of the Warm Springs Reservation, Warm Springs, Ore.], 14 November 1963, 4 August 1966, 9 February 1963, 18 March 1965, 7 August 1964, 3 June 1965, 3 March 1964, 1 September 1965, 2 September 1970, 8 March 1970.

33. "Tom-Tom Booms at Indian Rights Powwow," *Los Angeles Examiner*, 27 September 1954, sec. 1, p. 5; "Orange Show Again Honoring Indians," *Indian Reporter*, March-April 1964; "4th Annual Indian Show Set," *Indian Trader* [La Mesa, Calif.], September 1970; "American Indian and Western Relic Show," *Indian Trader*, September 1971; "American Indian and Western Relic Show," *Indian Trader*, February 1973; "Announcing," *Talking Leaf* [publication of Los Angeles (Calif.) Indian Center], January/February 1972, 11; "4th Annual All American Indian Week," *Indian Trader*, September 1970; "All American Indian Week Enjoyed by Thousands," *Indian Trader*, December 1970; "Successful 1971 Indian Show Season Closes," *Indian Trader*, November 1971; "Sports," *Talking Leaf*, July/August 1972, 12–14; "Los Angeles 11th All Indian Softball Tournament Results," *Take Ten* [publication of the San Diego (Calif.) Indian Center], September/October 1976.

34. *Tribal Council News* (Warm Springs, Ore.), 23 November 1973; *Weekly News Release* [publication of the Confederated Tribes of the Warm Springs Reservation,

Warm Springs, Ore.], 13 May 1976, 4 August 1977, 23 March 1978; "32nd NCAI Convention to be Held in Portland," *Yakima Nation Review* (Yakima, Wash.), 12 October 1975, p. 4; "Warm Springs Testimony Heard in Portland," *Spilyay Tymoo* [Coyote News] (Warm Springs, Ore.), 10 January 1978, p. 12; "Affiliated Tribes Meet in Portland," *Spilyay Tymoo*, 10 December 1976, p. 1; *Confederated Umatilla Journal*, April 1980; July 1980.

35. For a more in-depth discussion of tribal gaming, see Rosenthal, "The Dawn of a New Day?"

36. Christopher Reynolds, "Betting on their Heritage," *Los Angeles Times*, 7 April 2002, sec. F, p. 8.

37. Jeffrey Rabin and Jean Merl, "Mayoral Campaign Stirred by Indians' Last-Minute Ads Against Villaraigosa," *Los Angeles Times*, 7 April 2001, sec. B, p. 7; "Indians to Spend $100,000 to Support James Hahn," *Associated Press State and Local Wire*, 26 May 2001; James Rainey and Jeffrey L. Rabin, "Hahn Backers Sought Tribal Funds for Ads," *Los Angeles Times*, 31 May 2001, sec. A, p. 1; Tom Gorman and Dan Morain, "Backers of Indian Casino Measure Double War Chest," *Los Angeles Times*, 29 February 2000, sec. A, p. 12; Lance Williams, "In Sacramento, Tribes Have Become Bigger Players than Power Companies," *Sacramento Bee*, 12 March 2010; "Local Tribes' Political Spending Ranks High," *Press-Enterprise* (Riverside, Calif.), 14 March 2010.

38. "Cabazons Support Community Endeavors," *Cabazon Circle* [publication of the Cabazon Tribe of Mission Indians, Indio, Calif.], January 2000, 2; "Cabazons Support Community Endeavors," *Cabazon Circle*, February 2000, 9; "Cabazons Sponsor First Americans Arts Awards," *Cabazon Circle*, April 2000, 7; "Cabazons Celebrate Diversity Awards," *Cabazon Circle*, December 2000, 14; "Fantasy Springs Knows How to Entertain," *Cabazon Circle*, April 2001, 18; "University of California Puts on a Class Act," *Cabazon Circle*, May 2001, 13; Doug Hoagland, "Tribe Donates $10M to Library, *Fresno Bee*, 15 December 2006; Suzanne Muchnic, "Southwest Museum Receives New Offer," *Los Angeles Times*, 30 May 2001, sec. 6, p. 1; Suzanne Muchnic, "Southwest Museum Seeks Ways to Break out of Box," *Los Angeles Times*, 2 June 2001, sec. 6, p. 1; Christopher Reynolds, "Are They Pardners No More?," *Los Angeles Times*, 2 February 2002, sec. 6, p. 1; Reynolds, "Betting on their Heritage"; Christopher Reynolds, "Pechangas Delay Pact with L.A. Museum," *Los Angeles Times*, 20 May 2002, sec. B, pp. 1, 6; "L.A.'s Southwest Museum Merging with Autry Museum," Associated Press and Local Wire, 11 December 2002.

39. Stone interview.

BIBLIOGRAPHY

PRIMARY SOURCES

Manuscript Collections

Autry National Center, Los Angeles, Calif.
    Braun Research Library Collections
        Frederic Webb Hodge Collection (MS 7)
        Talking Leaf Bound File
        Richard Davis Thunderbird Collection (MS 641)
        Institute for the Study of the American West Collections
Chicago Historical Society, Chicago, Ill.
    Church Federation of Greater Chicago Collection
    Graphics Collection
Henry H. Huntington Library, San Marino, Calif.
    William H. Weinland Collection
Los Angeles Natural History Museum, Los Angeles, Calif.
    Seaver Center for Western History Research
        William S. Hart Collection
Multnomah County Library, Portland, Ore.
National Archives and Records Administration, Pacific Alaska Region,
        Seattle, Wash.
    Record Group 75, Portland Area Office
        Administrative Records of the Relocation and Employment
            Assistance Branch, 1958–1966
        Grande Ronde/Siletz Decimal Files
        Individual Case Files for Relocation, Training and Employment, 1955–68
National Archives and Records Administration, Pacific Region, Riverside, Calif.
    "Census Roll of the Indians of California under the Act of May 18, 1928"
    Federal Manuscript Census, Los Angeles County, 1900
    Federal Manuscript Census, Los Angeles County, 1910

Federal Manuscript Census, Los Angeles County, 1920
Federal Manuscript Census, Los Angeles County, 1930
Record Group 75
 Branch of Relocation Services Administrative Files
 Los Angeles Field Employment Assistance Office
 Central Classified Files, 1948–62
 Mission Indian Agency
 Central Classified Files, 1870–1953
 Education Field Agent, General Correspondence, 1932–46
 Sherman Institute
 Records of the Superintendent, Central Classified Files, 1907–1939
 Student Case Files, 1903–1980
Newberry Library, Chicago, Ill.
 Bureau of Indian Affairs Relocation Records
Southern California Library for Social Studies and Research, Los Angeles, Calif.
 Organizational Files
Stanley Parr Archives and Record Center, Portland, Ore.
 Commissioner Jordan Series
University of California, Davis, Shields Library
 Jack Forbes Collection
University of Iowa, Iowa City
 Special Collections
 Redpath Chautauqua Collection

Uncollected Interviews

Ahhaitty, Glenda. Interview, by the author. Cerritos, Calif., 21 September 2005.

Amos, Glenna J. Interview by the author. Los Angeles, Calif., 7 May 2004.

Banks, Mark. Interview by the author. Chatsworth, Calif., 5 May 2004.

Brown, H. Interview by the author. North Hollywood, Calif., 21 April 2004.

Edmonds, Randy. Interview by the author. San Diego, Calif., 13 October 2005.

M., M. Interview by the author. Huntington Park, Calif., 22 April 2004.

Rambeau, Dave. Interview by the author. Los Angeles, Calif., 11 October 2005.

Skyhawk, Sonny. Interview by Frank J. King III and Lise Balk-King. Los Angeles, Calif., October 2004.

Spence, John. Interview by the author. Salem, Ore., 14 July 1999.

Stone, Sidney (Brown). Interview by the author. Aloha, Ore., 21 July 1999.

Tafoya, Dennis. Interview by the author. Los Angeles, Calif., 6 May 2004.

Wannassay, Vincent. Interview by the author. Portland, Ore., 21 July 1999.

Collected Interviews

California State University, Fullerton. Oral History Collection. Indian
Urbanization Project.

Adamson, Wanda Big Canoe. Interview by Nancy Callaci. La Mirada, Calif.,
7 April 1971.

Bad Horse, Mahonta. Interview by Marian Ryan. Los Angeles, Calif.,
22 June 1971.

Bowen, Carole. Interview by Kathy Bie. Corona, Calif., 9 December 1970.

Bruner, Charles. Interview by Helen Amgwerd. Westminster, Calif.,
25 October 1971.

Charley, Fern and Priscilla. Interview by Clare Engle. Santa Ana, Calif.,
25 October 1970.

Chiloquin, Melvin. Interview by Nancy Callaci. Los Angeles, Calif.,
5 May 1971.

Cody, Iron Eyes. Interview by Georgia Brown. Los Angeles, Calif., 6 April 1971.

Costo, Martina. Interview by Georgia Brown. Norwalk, Calif., 31 May 1971.

DuPoint, Frank. Interview by Nancy Callaci. Los Angeles, Calif., 5 May 1971.

Edmunds [sic], Randy. Interview by Marian Ryan. Hollywood, Calif.,
4 June 1971.

Fixico, Hannah. Interview by M. J. Zarek. Compton, Calif., 14 June 1971.

Gabouri [sic], Frances. Interview by Georgia Brown. Burbank, Calif.,
5 April 1971.

Gibbs, Richard. Interview by Christine Valenciana. Fullerton, Calif., 30 March
1971.

Haberman, Lena. Interview by Georgia Brown. La Mirada, Calif., 12 May 1971.

Jeppsen, Grace. Interview by Nancy Callaci. Los Angeles, Calif., 23 April 1971.

Knifechief, John and Lois. Interview by Clare Engle. Stanton, Calif.,
29 October 1970.

Knifechief, (Tom E). Interview by Christine Valenciana. Santa Ana, Calif., 10
May 1971.

Lester, A. David. Interview by Nancy Callaci. Los Angeles, Calif., 5 May 1971.

Miller, Wayne. Interview by Georgia Brown. Long Beach, Calif., 15 November
1970.

Monroe, James. Interview by Helen Amgwerd. Los Angeles, Calif., 19 October
1971.

Olivas, Edward. Interview by Nancy Callaci. Los Angeles, Calif., 5 May 1972.

Peters, Ernie. Interview by Georgia Brown. Valindo, Calif., 10 April 1971.

Pinto, Sam. Interview by Clare Engle. Santa Ana, Calif., 29 October 1970.

Poemoceah, Arlene. Interview by Christine Valenciana. Garden Grove, Calif.,
22 April 1971.

Poemoceah, Elmer. Interview by Christine Valenciana. Garden Grove, Calif.,
    8 December 1970.

Seabay, Joseph. Interview by Mary Jane DeCarlo. Los Angeles, Calif.,
    24 August 1971.

Wills, Patricia Mae. Interview by Georgia Brown. Long Beach, Calif., 2 May 1971.

Yackitonipah, Howard. Interview by Marian Ryan. Los Angeles, Calif.,
    20 November 1970.

Yackitonipah, Kenneth and Greta. Interview by Marian Ryan. Los Angeles,
    Calif., 2 November 1970.

Young, Glover. Interview by Christine Valenciana. La Mirada, Calif.,
    27 April 1971.

Newberry Library, Chicago, Ill. Chicago American Indian Oral History Project.

Fastwolf, Phyllis. Interview by Pat Tyson, Chicago, Ill., 8 May 1983.

Forcia, Floria. Interview by Peggy Desjarlait. Chicago, Ill., 25 March 1983.

Penn, Cornelia. Interview by Mae Chevalier. Chicago, Ill., 3 September 1983.

Skenandore, Amy. Interview by Peggy Desjarlait. Chicago, Ill., 31 March 1983.

Strouse, Marlene. Interview by Mae Chevalier. Chicago, Ill., 18 June 1984.

Published Interviews

De Rockbraine, Andre. Interview by Steve Plummer. Bullhead, S.D., 26 June 1972.
    University of South Dakota American Indian Oral History Research Project.
    Glen Rock, N.J.: Microfilming Corp. of America, 1975.

Rainwater, Purcell. Interview by Joseph H. Cash. Mile Camp, Nebr., Summer
    1967. *University of South Dakota American Indian Oral History Research
    Project.* Glen Rock, N.J.: Microfilming Corp. of America, 1975.

Rogoff, Ethel. In *Urban Voices: The Bay Area American Indian Community*,
    ed. Susan Lobo, 8. Tucson: University of Arizona Press, 2002.

Underwood, Brenda. Interview by Sam Myers. St. Louis, Mo., 10 September 1973.
    In New York Times Oral History Program, *Listening to Indians.* New York:
    New York Times, 1978.

Community, Tribal, and Institutional Publications

These are ephemeral publications housed at various repositories.

American Indian Advocate [Tepee Order]

American Indian Magazine [Society of American Indians]

American Indian Registry for the Performing Arts [Los Angeles, Calif.]

American Indians of Today [Portland (Ore.) American Indian Center]

Bo's'ns Whistle (Oregon Shipyard Edition) [Oregon Shipbuilding Corporation,
    Portland, Ore.]

Cabazon Circle [Cabazon Band of Mission Indians, Indio, Calif.]

Chemehuevi Newsletter [Chemehuevi Tribe, Los Angeles, Calif.]

Confederated Umatilla Journal [Confederated Tribes of the Umatilla Reservation, Umatilla, Ore.]

First People [American Friends Service Committee, Pacific Southwest Region, Pasadena, Calif.]

Indian [Mission Indian Federation, Riverside, Calif.]

Indian Newsletter [Access, Pala, Calif.]

Indian Reporter: The Newspaper of the Southern California Indian [Hemet, Calif.]

Indian Trader [La Mesa, Calif.]

Many Smokes: The Voice of the American Indian [Los Angeles, Calif.]

Masterkey [Southwest Museum of the American Indian, Los Angeles, Calif.]

Mission Indian [Mission Indian Agency, Office of Indian Affairs, Riverside, Calif.]

Moccasin Telegraph [American Indian Education Commission, Los Angeles, Calif.]

The Moravian [Northern Province of the Moravian Church in America, Bethlehem, Pa.]

Newsletter: American Indian Culture Center at the University of California Los Angeles

Northwest Native American News [Native American Rehabilitation Association, Portland, Ore.]

Okeh: Official Publication of the American Indian Progressive Association [Los Angeles, Calif.]

Purple and Gold [Sherman Institute, Riverside, Calif.]

Quarterly Journal of the Society of American Indians [Society of American Indians]

SCL Heritage [Southern California Library for Social Studies and Research, Los Angeles, Calif.]

Sherman Bulletin [Sherman Institute, Riverside, Calif.]

Smoke Signals [Colorado River Indian Tribes, Parker, Ariz.]

Southern California Indian Center, Inc. [Los Angeles, Calif.]

Spilyay Tymoo [Confederated Tribes of the Warm Springs Reservation, Warm Springs, Ore.]

TACC Messenger [Tribal American Consulting Corporation, City of Commerce, Calif.]

Take Ten [San Diego (Calif.) Indian Center]

Talking Leaf [Los Angeles (Calif.) Indian Center]

Tipi News [Portland (Ore.) American Indian Center]

Tribal Spokesman [Inter-Tribal Council of California (Sacramento)]

Tribal TANF Today [Thermal, Calif.]

UCLA Native American [University of California, Los Angeles, American Indian Students Association]

UIDA Reporter [Urban Indian Development Association, Los Angeles, Calif.]

Government Publications

"American FactFinder." *U.S. Census Bureau.* http://factfinder.census.gov (accessed 1 September 2011).

American Indian Policy Review Commission. *Report on Urban and Rural Non-Reservation Indians.* Washington, D.C.: GPO, 1976.

National Council on Indian Opportunity. *Public Forum before the Committee on Urban Indians in Los Angeles, CA.* Washington, D.C.: GPO, 1969.

U.S. Bureau of Indian Affairs. *The Bureau of Indian Affairs Voluntary Relocation Service Program.* Washington, D.C.: GPO, 1958.

———. *Handbook: Relocation Services: A Guide for All Employees of the Branch of Relocation Services.* Washington, D.C.: GPO, 1956.

U.S. Bureau of the Census. *1950 Census of Population: Volume II, Characteristics of the Population; Part I: U.S. Summary.* Washington, D.C.: GPO, 1953.

———. *1950 Census of Population: Volume II, Characteristics of Population, Part 5: California.* Washington, D.C.: GPO, 1952.

———. *1960 Census of Population: Volume I, Characteristics of the Population; Part I: U.S. Summary.* Washington, D.C.: GPO, 1961.

———. *1960 Census of Population: Volume I, Characteristics of the Population; Part 6: California.* Washington, D.C.: GPO, 1961.

———. *1960 Census of Population: Volume I, Characteristics of the Population; Part 7: Colorado.* Washington, D.C.: GPO, 1961.

———. *1960 Census of Population: Volume I, Characteristics of the Population; Part 15: Illinois.* Washington, D.C.: GPO, 1961.

———. *1960 Census of Population: Volume I, Characteristics of the Population; Part 25: Minnesota.* Washington, D.C.: GPO, 1961.

———. *1960 Census of Population: Volume I, Characteristics of the Population; Part 33: New Mexico.* Washington, D.C.: GPO, 1961.

———. *1960 Census of Population: Volume I, Characteristics of the Population; Part 34: New York.* Washington, D.C.: GPO, 1961.

———. *1960 Census of Population: Volume I, Characteristics of the Population; Part 38: Oklahoma.* Washington, D.C.: GPO, 1961.

———. *1960 Census of Population: Volume I, Characteristics of the Population; Part 49: Washington.* Washington, D.C.: GPO, 1961.

———. *1970 Census of Population: Volume I, Characteristics of the Population; Part I: U.S. Summary.* Washington, D.C.: GPO, 1973.

———. *1970 Census of the Population: Volume 1, Characteristics of the Population; Part 6: California.* Washington, D.C.: GPO, 1973.

———. *1970 Census of the Population: Volume 1, Characteristics of the Population; Part 7: Colorado.* Washington, D.C.: GPO, 1973.

———. *1970 Census of the Population: Volume 1, Characteristics of the Population; Part 15: Illinois.* Washington, D.C.: GPO, 1973.

———. *1970 Census of the Population: Volume 1, Characteristics of the Population; Part 25: Minnesota.* Washington, D.C.: GPO, 1973.

———. *1970 Census of the Population: Volume 1, Characteristics of the Population; Part 33: New Mexico.* Washington, D.C.: GPO, 1973.

———. *1970 Census of the Population: Volume 1, Characteristics of the Population; Part 34: New York.* Washington, D.C.: GPO, 1973.

———. *1970 Census of the Population: Volume 1, Characteristics of the Population; Part 38: Oklahoma.* Washington, D.C.: GPO, 1973.

———. *1970 Census of the Population: Volume 1, Characteristics of the Population; Part 49: Washington.* Washington, D.C.: GPO, 1973.

———. *1980 Census of Population: Volume I, Characteristics of the Population; Chapter C: General Social and Economic Characteristics; Part I: U.S. Summary.* Washington, D.C.: GPO, 1982.

———. *1980 Census of Population: Volume I, Characteristics of the Population; Chapter B: General Population Characteristics; Part 6: California.* Washington, D.C.: GPO, 1983.

———. *1980 Census of Population: Volume I, Characteristics of the Population; Chapter B: General Population Characteristics; Part 7: Colorado.* Washington, D.C.: GPO, 1983.

———. *1980 Census of Population: Volume I, Characteristics of the Population; Chapter B: General Population Characteristics; Part 15: Illinois.* Washington, D.C.: GPO, 1983.

———. *1980 Census of Population: Volume I, Characteristics of the Population; Chapter B: General Population Characteristics; Part 25: Minnesota.* Washington, D.C.: GPO, 1983.

———. *1980 Census of Population: Volume I, Characteristics of the Population; Chapter B: General Population Characteristics; Part 33: New Mexico.* Washington, D.C.: GPO, 1983.

———. *1980 Census of Population: Volume I, Characteristics of the Population; Chapter B: General Population Characteristics; Part 34: New York.* Washington, D.C.: GPO, 1983.

———. *1980 Census of Population: Volume I, Characteristics of the Population; Chapter B: General Population Characteristics; Part 38: Oklahoma.* Washington, D.C.: GPO, 1983.

———. *1980 Census of Population: Volume I, Characteristics of the Population; Chapter B: General Population Characteristics; Part 49: Washington.* Washington, D.C.: GPO, 1983.

———. *1990 Census of Population; General Population Characteristics: Urbanized Areas.* Washington, D.C.: GPO, 1992.

———. *1990 Census of Population; General Population Characteristics: United States.* Washington, D.C.: GPO, 1992.

———. *Sixteenth Census of the United States: 1940, Population, Volume II, Characteristics of Population, Part I: United States Summary and AL–D.C.* Washington, D.C.: GPO, 1943.

———. *2000 Census of Population and Housing, United States: 2000, Summary Population and Housing Characteristics.* Washington, D.C.: GPO, 2002.

U.S. Department of the Interior. *Annual Report of the Secretary of the Interior.* Washington, D.C.: GPO, 1945.

———. *Annual Report of the Secretary of the Interior.* Washington, D.C.: GPO, 1951.

———. *Annual Report of the Secretary of the Interior.* Washington, D.C.: GPO, 1952.

———. *Annual Report of the Secretary of the Interior.* Washington, D.C.: GPO, 1958.

Newspapers

Albuquerque Journal

Associated Press State and Local Wire

Christian Science Monitor

Copley News Service

Daily News (Los Angeles)

Desert Sun (Palm Springs, Calif.)

Independent Press Telegram (Long Beach, Calif.)

Indian Country Today

Inside Bay Area (California)

Los Angeles Evening Mirror News

Los Angles Examiner

Los Angeles Herald-Examiner

Los Angeles Times

Milwaukee Journal Sentinel

New York Herald Tribune

New York Times

Omaha World-Herald

Oregonian (Portland, Ore.)

Oregon Journal (Portland, Ore.)

Press-Enterprise (Riverside, Calif.)

San Diego Union-Tribune

San Francisco Chronicle

Wall Street Journal

Willamette Week (Portland, Ore.)

SECONDARY SOURCES

Abbott, Carl. *Portland: Planning, Politics and Growth in a Twentieth Century City.* Lincoln: University of Nebraska Press, 1983.

"About Us." *American Indian Studies Center.* http://www.aisc.ucla.edu (accessed 1 September 2011).

Alamillo, José M. *Making Lemonade out of Lemons: Mexican American Labor and Leisure in a California Town, 1880–1960.* Urbana: University of Illinois Press, 2006.

Albon, Joan. "Relocated American Indians in the San Francisco Bay Area." *Human Organization* 24 (1964): 296–304.

"American Indian Relocation: Problems of Dependency and Management in the City." *Phylon* 26 (1965): 362–71.

"American Indian Resource Center." *County of Los Angeles Public Library*. *http://www.colapublib.org/services/ethnic/indian.php4* (accessed September 2011).

Amerman, Stephen Kent. "'Let's Get In and Fight!': American Indian Political Activism in an Urban Public School System, 1973," *American Indian Quarterly* 27 (2003): 607–38.

———. *Urban Indians in Phoenix Schools, 1940-2000*. Lincoln: University of Nebraska Press, 2010.

Anderson, Reynaldo. "Practical Internationalists: The Story of the Des Moines, Iowa, Black Panther Party." In *Groundwork: Local Black Freedom Movements in America*, ed. Jeanne Theoharis and Komozi Woodard, 282–99. New York: New York University Press, 2005.

Arnold, David. "Work and Culture in Southeastern Alaska: Tlingits and the Salmon Fisheries." In *Native Pathways: American Indian Culture and Economic Development in the Twentieth Century*, ed. Brian Hosmer and Colleen O'Neill, 156–83. Boulder: University of Colorado Press, 2004.

Austin, Leonard. *Around the World in San Francisco: A Guide Book to the Racial and Ethnic Minorities of the San Francisco-Oakland District*. San Francisco: Abbey Press, 1955.

Balshofer, Fred J., and Arthur C. Miller. *One Reel A Week*. Berkeley: University of California Press, 1967.

Barrera, Mario. *Race and Class in the Southwest: A Theory of Racial Inequality*. Notre Dame, Ind.: University of Notre Dame Press, 1979.

Bataille, Gretchen M., and Charles L. P. Silet, eds. *The Pretend Indians: Images of Native Americans in the Movies*. Ames: Iowa State University Press, 1980.

Bauer, William J., Jr. *We Were All Like Migrant Workers Here: Work, Community, and Memory on California's Round Valley Reservation, 1850-1941*. Chapel Hill: University of North Carolina Press, 2010.

———. "'We Were All Migrant Workers Here'": Round Valley Indian Labor in Northern California, 1850–1929," *Western Historical Quarterly* 37 (2006): 43–63.

———. "Working for Identity: Race, Ethnicity, and the Market Economy in Northern California, 1875–1936." In *Native Pathways: American Indian Culture and Economic Development in the Twentieth Century*, ed. Brian Hosmer and Colleen O'Neill, 238–57. Boulder: University of Colorado Press, 2004.

Beck, David. "The Chicago American Indian Community." In *Native Chicago*, ed. Terry Straus and Grant P. Arndt, 170–72. Chicago: Native Chicago, 1999.

Bell, James Ruben. "The Rules and Regulations of Aggression and Violence among the American Indian Men of Skid Row, Los Angeles." *California Anthropologist* 9 (1979): 1–28.

Berryhill, Peggy. "Memories of Growing Up in the Oakland Community, circa 1952–66." In *Urban Voices: The Bay Area American Indian Community*, ed. Susan Lobo, 28–31. Tucson: University of Arizona Press, 2002.

Black, Liza. "Picturing Indians: American Indians in Movies, 1941–1960." Ph.D. diss., University of Washington, 1999.

Blackhawk, Ned. "'I Can Carry On From Here': The Relocation of American Indians to Los Angeles." *Wicazo Sa Review* 11, no. 2 (Fall 1995): 16–30.

Blauner, Robert. *Racial Oppression in America*. New York: Harper and Row, 1972.

Bohanan, Lyndon Earl. "The Urban Indian Program in Portland, Oregon." M.A. thesis, Portland State University, 1974.

Boyer, LaNada. "Reflections of Alcatraz." In *American Indian Activism: Alcatraz to the Longest Walk*, ed. Troy Johnson, Joane Nagel, and Duane Champagne, 88–103. Urbana: University of Illinois Press, 1997.

Bramstedt, Wayne Glenn. "Corporate Adaptations of Urban Migrants: American Indian Voluntary Associations in the Los Angeles Metropolitan Area." Ph.D. diss., University of California, Los Angeles, 1977.

Brooks, James F. *Captives and Cousins: Slavery, Kinship, and Community in the Southwest Borderlands*. Chapel Hill: University of North Carolina Press/ Omohundro Institute of Early American History and Culture, 2002.

Brown, Dee. *Bury My Heart at Wounded Knee: An Indian History of the American West*. Thirtieth Anniversary Edition. New York: Henry Holt, 2001.

Brownlow, Kevin. *The War, the West, and the Wilderness*. New York: Knopf, 1978.

Buffalo Tiger and Harry A. Kersey Jr. *Buffalo Tiger: A Life in the Everglades*. Lincoln: University of Nebraska Press, 2002.

Bunting, Wade Adair. "The Effect of Social Adaptation on the Semantic Structure of the Conceptual Domain of Occupation Names Among Navajo Migrants to the Los Angeles Urban Area." Ph.D. diss., University of California, Los Angeles, 1973.

Burt, Larry W. "Roots of the Native American Urban Experience: Relocation Policy in the 1950s." *American Indian Quarterly* 10 (1986): 85–99.

Calloway, Colin G. *One Vast Winter Count: The Native American West Before Lewis and Clark*. Lincoln: University of Nebraska Press, 2003.

———, ed. *After King Philip's War: Presence and Persistence in Indian New England*. Hanover, N.H.: University Press of New England, 1997.

Carrico, Richard L., and Florence C. Shipek, "Indian Labor in San Diego County, California, 1850–1900." In *Native Americans and Wage Labor*, ed. Alice Littlefield and Martha C. Knack, 198–217. Norman: University of Oklahoma Press, 1996.

Castillo, Edward D. "A Reminiscence of the Alcatraz Occupation." In *American Indian Activism: Alcatraz to the Longest Walk*, ed. Troy Johnson, Joane Nagel, and Duane Champagne, 119–28. Urbana: University of Illinois Press, 1997.

Cattelino, Jessica R. "Casino Roots: The Cultural Production of Twentieth-Century Seminole Economic Development." In *Native Pathways: American Indian Culture and Economic Development in the Twentieth Century*, ed. Brian Hosmer and Colleen O'Neill, 66–90. Boulder: University Press of Colorado, 2004.

Chance, John K. *Race and Class in Colonial Oaxaca*. Stanford, Calif.: Stanford University Press, 1978.

"Charles Stevens (I)." *Internet Movie Database*. http://www.imdb.com/name/nm0828314 (accessed 1 September 2011).

"Chief Standing Bear." *Internet Movie Database*. http://www.imdb.com/name/nm0822052 (accessed 1 September 2011).

"Chief Thunderbird." *Internet Movie Database*. http://www.imdb.com/name/nm0862083 (accessed 1 September 2011).

"Chief Yowlachie." *Internet Movie Database*. http://www.imdb.com/name/nm0950385 (accessed 1 September 2011).

Churchill, Ward. *Fantasies of the Master Race: Literature, Cinema, and the Colonization of American Indians*. Monroe, Me.: Common Courage Press, 1992.

Churchill, Ward, Mary Anne Hill, and Norbert S. Hill Jr. "Examination of Stereotyping: An Analytical Survey of Twentieth-Century Indian Entertainers. In *The Pretend Indians: Images of Native Americans in the Movies*, ed. Gretchen M. Bataille and Charles L. P. Silet, 35–48. Ames: Iowa State University Press, 1980.

City Club of Portland. "Special Issue: Report on the Urban Indian in Portland." *City Club of Portland Bulletin* 56 (27 October 1975): 61–64.

Clark, Christopher. *The Roots of Rural Capitalism: Western Massachusetts, 1780–1860*. Ithaca, N.Y.: Cornell University Press, 1990.

Clarkin, Thomas. *Federal Indian Policy in the Kennedy and Johnson Administrations, 1961–1969*. Albuquerque: University of New Mexico Press, 2001.

Cobb, Daniel M. *Native Activism in Cold War America: The Struggle for Sovereignty*. Lawrence: University Press of Kansas, 2008.

———. "Philosophy of an Indian War: Indian Community Action in the Johnson Administration's War on Indian Poverty, 1964–1968." *American Indian Culture and Research Journal* 22, no. 2 (Spring 1998): 71–102.

———. "'Us Indians Understand the Basics': Oklahoma Indians and the Politics of Community Action, 1964–1970." *Western Historical Quarterly* 33 (2002): 41–66.

Cobb, Daniel M., and Loretta Fowler, eds. *Beyond Red Power: American Indian Politics and Activism since 1900*. Santa Fe: School for Advanced Research Press, 2007.

Cody, Iron Eyes, as told to Colin Perry. *Iron Eyes, My Life as a Hollywood Indian*. New York: Everest House, 1982.

Cohen, Lizbeth. *A Consumers' Republic: The Politics of Mass Consumption in Postwar America*. New York: Knopf, 2003.

Cowie, Jefferson, and Joseph Heathcott, eds. *Beyond the Ruins: The Meanings of Deindustrialization*. Ithaca, N.Y.: Cornell University Press, 2003.

Danziger, Edmund Jefferson. *Survival and Regeneration: Detroit's American Indian Community*. Detroit: Wayne State University Press, 1991.

Davis, Clark. *Company Men: White-Collar Life and Corporate Culture in Los Angeles, 1892–1941*. Baltimore: Johns Hopkins University Press, 2000.

Delgado, Grace. "In the Age of Exclusion: Race, Region and Chinese Identity in the Making of the Arizona-Sonora Borderlands, 1863–1943." Ph.D. diss., University of California, Los Angeles, 2000.

Deloria, Philip J. *Indians in Unexpected Places*. Lawrence: University Press of Kansas, 2004.

———. *Playing Indian*. New Haven, Conn.: Yale University Press, 1998.

Deloria, Vine, Jr. *Behind the Trail of Broken Treaties: An Indian Declaration of Independence*. Austin: University of Texas Press, 1985.

———. "This Country Was a Lot Better Off When the Indians Were Running It." In *Red Power: The American Indians' Fight for Freedom*, ed. Alvin M. Josephy Jr., 240–41. New York: American Heritage Press, 1971.

Dittmer, John. *Local People: the Struggle for Civil Rights in Mississippi*. Urbana: University of Illinois Press, 1994.

Dobyns, Henry F., Richard W. Stoffle, and Kristine Jones. "Native American Urbanization and Socio-Economic Integration in the Southwestern United States." *Ethnohistory* 22 (1975): 155–79.

Drown, D. Bartlet. "Indian Grape Pickers in California." *Overland Monthly* 65 (1915): 554–58.

Eargle, Dolan H., Jr. *Native California Guide*. San Francisco: Trees Company Press, 2000.

Ehrheart, William J. "Chief Luther Standing Bear II: Activist, Author, Historian." *Persimmon Hill* 25, no. 3 (August 1997): 44–46.

Einhorn, Arthur C. "The Indians of New York City." In *American Indian Urbanization*, ed. Jack O. Waddell and O. Michael Watson, 90–99. Lafayette, Ind.: Purdue Research Foundation, 1973.

———. "The Warriors of the Sky: The Iroquois Iron Workers." *European Review of Native American Studies* 13, no. 1 (1999): 25–34.

Eisler, Kim Isaac. *Revenge of the Pequots: How a Small Native American Tribe Created the World's Most Profitable Casino*. New York: Simon & Schuster, 2001.

Ellis, Clyde. "Five Dollars a Week to Be 'Regular Indians': Shows, Exhibitions, and the Economics of Indian Dancing, 1880–1930." In *Native Pathways: American Indian Culture and Economic Development in the Twentieth Century*, ed. Brian Hosmer and Colleen O'Neill, 184–208. Boulder: University Press of Colorado, 2004.

Escobar, Edward. *Race, Police and the Making of a Political Identity: Mexican Americans and the Los Angeles Police Department, 1900–1945*. Berkeley: University of California Press, 1999.

Fairbanks, Douglas, Jr. *The Salad Days*. New York: Doubleday, 1988.

Feldstein, Ruth. "'I Don't Trust You Anymore': Nina Simone, Culture, and Black Activism in the 1960s." *Journal of American History* 91 (2005): 1349–79.

Fisher, Andrew H. *Shadow Tribe: The Making of Columbia River Indian Identity*. Seattle: University of Washington Press, 2010.

Fiske, Shirley. "Intertribal Perspectives: Navajo and Pan-Indianism." *Ethos* 5 (1977): 358–75.

———. "Rules of Address: Navajo Women in Los Angeles." *Journal of Anthropological Research* 34 (1978): 72–79.

———. "Urban Indian Institutions: A Reappraisal from Los Angeles." *Urban Anthropology* 8 (1979): 149–72.

Fixico, Donald L. *Termination and Relocation: Federal Indian Policy, 1945–1960*. Albuquerque: University of New Mexico Press, 1986.

———. *The Urban Indian Experience in America*. Albuquerque: University of New Mexico Press, 2000.

Fogelson, Robert M. *The Fragmented Metropolis: Los Angeles, 1850–1930*. Berkeley: University of California Press, 1967.

Forbes, Jack D. *Native Americans and Nixon: Presidential Politics and Minority Self-Determination, 1969–1972*. Los Angeles: American Indian Studies Center, 1981.

———. "The Native Struggle for Liberation: Alcatraz." In *American Indian Activism: Alcatraz to the Longest Walk*, ed. Troy Johnson, Joane Nagel, and Duane Champagne, 129–35. Urbana: University of Illinois Press, 1997.

———. "The Urban Tradition Among Native Americans." *American Indian Culture and Research Journal* 22 (1998): 15–42.

Fortunate Eagle, Adam. *Alcatraz! Alcatraz! The Indian Occupation of 1969–1971*. Berkeley, Calif.: Heyday Books, 1992.

Foster, Morris. *Being Comanche: A Social History of an American Indian Community*. Tucson: University of Arizona Press, 1991.

Fowler, Loretta. *Shared Symbols, Contested Meanings: Gros Ventre Culture and History, 1778–1984*. Ithaca, N.Y.: Cornell University Press, 1987.

Friar, Ralph E., and Natasha A. Friar. *The Only Good Indian . . . The Hollywood Gospel*. New York: Drama Book Specialists, 1972.

Gabaccia, Donna R. "Is Everywhere Nowhere? Nomads, Nations, and the Immigrant Paradigm of United States History." *Journal of American History* 86 (1999): 1115–34.

Gabourie, Fred Whitedeer. *Justice and the American Indian*. Sherman Oaks, Calif.: Merdler and Gabourie, 1971.

Garbarino, Merwyn S. "The Chicago American Indian Center: Two Decades." In *American Indian Urbanization*, ed. Jack O. Waddell and O. Michael Watson, 169–205. Lafayette, Ind.: Purdue Research Foundation, 1973.

Garcia, Matt. *A World of Its Own: Race, Labor, and Citrus in the Making of Greater Los Angeles, 1900–1970*. Chapel Hill: University of North Carolina Press, 2001.

Gardner, Richard E. "The Role of a Pan-Indian Church in Urban Indian Life." *Anthropology* 1 (1969): 14–26.

Gerstle, Gary. "Liberty, Coercion, and the Making of Americans." *Journal of American History* 84 (1997): 524–58.

Gleach, Frederic W. "Pocahontas at the Fair: Crafting Identities at the 1907 Jamestown Expedition." *Ethnohistory* 50 (2003): 419–61.

Glenn, Evelyn Nakano. "From Servitude to Service Work: Historical Continuities in the Racial Division of Paid Reproductive Labor." *Signs* 18 (1992): 1–43.

Goodvoice, Ed. "Relocation: Indian Life on Skid Row." In *Native Chicago*, ed. Terry Strauss and Grant P. Arndt, 128–45. Chicago: Native Chicago, 1998.

Graves, Theodore D. "Drinking and Drunkenness Among Urban Indians." In *The American Indian in Urban Society*, ed. Jack O. Waddell and O. Michael Watson, 275–311. Boston: Little, Brown, 1971.

Gregory, James N. *American Exodus: The Dust Bowl Migration and Okie Culture in California*. New York: Oxford University Press, 1989.

Gridley, Marion E. *Indians of Today*. 4th ed. Chicago: Indian Council Fire, 1971.

Guillemin, Jeanne. *Urban Renegades: The Cultural Strategy of American Indians*. New York: Columbia University Press, 1975.

Guilmet, George Michael. "The Nonverbal American Indian Child in the Urban Classroom." Ph.D. diss., University of California, Los Angeles, 1976.

Gutiérrez, David G. *Walls and Mirrors: Mexican Americans, Mexican Immigrants, and the Politics of Ethnicity*. Berkeley: University of California Press, 1995.

Haas, Lisbeth. *Conquests and Historical Identities in California, 1769–1936*. Berkeley: University of California Press, 1995.

Hansen, Karen Tranberg. "Ethnic Group Policy and the Politics of Sex: The Seattle Indian Case." *Urban Anthropology* 8 (1979): 29–48.

Harmon, Alexandra. "American Indians and Land Monopolies in the Gilded Age." *Journal of American History* 90 (2003): 106–33.

———. *Indians in the Making: Ethnic Relations and Indian Identities around Puget Sound*. Berkeley: University of California Press, 1998.

———. *Rich Indians: Native People and the Problem of Wealth in American History*. Chapel Hill: University of North Carolina Press, 2010.

Hiryabashi, James, William Willard, and Luis Kemnitzer. "Pan-Indianism in the Urban Setting." In *The Anthropology of Urban Environments*, ed. Thomas Weaver and Douglas White, 177–87. Boulder, Colo.: Society for Applied Anthropology, 1972.

Hoikkala, Päivi. "Feminists or Reformers? American Indian Women and Political Activism in Phoenix, 1965–1980." *American Indian Culture and Research Journal* 22 (1998): 163–85.

Hosmer, Brian. *American Indians in the Marketplace: Persistence and Innovation Among the Menominees and Metlakatlans, 1870–1920*. Lawrence: University Press of Kansas, 1999.

Hosmer, Brian, and Colleen O'Neill, eds. *Native Pathways: American Indian Culture and Economic Development in the Twentieth Century.* Boulder: University Press of Colorado, 2004.

Hoxie, Frederick E. "Exploring a Cultural Borderland: Native American Journeys of Discovery in the Early Twentieth Century." *Journal of American History* 79 (1992): 969–95.

———. *A Final Promise: The Campaign to Assimilate the Indian, 1880–1920.* Lincoln: University of Nebraska Press, 1984.

———. "Introduction: American Indian Activism in the Progressive Era." In *Talking Back to Civilization: Indian Voices from the Progressive Era*, ed. Frederick E. Hoxie, 1–28. Boston: Bedford/St. Martin's, 2003.

———. *Parading Through History: The Making of the Crow Nation in America, 1805–1935.* New York: Cambridge University Press, 1995.

Hurtado, Albert. "'Hardly a Farm House—A Kitchen Without Them': Indian and White Households on the California Borderland Frontier in 1860." *Western Historical Quarterly* 13 (1982): 245–70.

Hyer, Joel R. *"We Are Not Savages": Native Americans in Southern California and the Pala Reservation, 1840–1920.* East Lansing: Michigan State University Press, 2001.

Imada, Adria L. "Aloha America: Hawaiian Entertainment and Cultural Politics in the United States Empire." Ph.D. diss., New York University, 2003.

———. "Hawaiians on Tour: Hula Circuits through the American Empire." *American Quarterly* 56 (2004): 111–49.

Iverson, Peter. "American Indians in the Twentieth Century." In *A Companion to the American West*, ed. William Deverell, 329–45. Malden, Mass.: Blackwell, 2004.

———. *Diné: A History of the Navajos.* Albuquerque: University of New Mexico Press, 2002.

———. *"We Are Still Here": American Indians in the Twentieth Century.* Wheeling, Ill.: Harlan Davidson, 1998.

"James Young Deer." *Internet Movie Database.* http://www.imdb.com/name/ nm0949220 (accessed 1 September 2011).

Jennings, Francis. *The Invasion of America: Indians, Colonialism, and the Cant of Conquest.* Chapel Hill: University of North Carolina Press, 1975.

Johnson, Troy R. *The Occupation of Alcatraz Island: Indian Self-Determination and the Rise of Indian Activism.* Urbana: University of Illinois Press, 1996.

Johnson, Troy, Joane Nagel, and Duane Champagne, eds. *American Indian Activism: Alcatraz to the Longest Walk.* Urbana: University of Illinois Press, 1997.

———. "American Indian Activism and Transformation: Lessons from Alcatraz." In *American Indian Activism: Alcatraz to the Longest Walk*, ed. Troy Johnson, Joane Nagel, and Duane Champagne, 9–21. Urbana: University of Illinois Press, 1997.

Jones, Patrick. "'Not a Color, but an Attitude'": Father James Groppi and Black Power Politics in Milwaukee." In *Groundwork: Local Black Freedom Movements in America*, ed. Jeanne Theoharis and Komozi Woodard, 259–81. New York: New York University Press, 2005.

Jorgensen, Joseph G. "Federal Policies, American Indian Politics and the 'New Federalism.'" *American Indian Culture and Research Journal* 10 (1986): 1–13.

Joseph, Peniel E. "Introduction: Toward a Historiography of the Black Power Movement." In *The Black Power Movement: Rethinking the Civil Rights-Black Power Era*, ed. Peniel E. Joseph, 1–25. New York: Routledge, 2006.

Kelley, Robin D. G. *Freedom Dreams: The Black Radical Imagination*. Boston: Beacon Press, 2002.

———. *Race Rebels: Culture, Politics, and the Black Working Class*. New York: Free Press, 1994.

Kemnitzer, Luis S. "Personal Memories of Alcatraz, 1969." In *American Indian Activism: Alcatraz to the Longest Walk*, ed. Troy Johnson, Joane Nagel, and Duane Champagne, 113–18. Urbana: University of Illinois Press, 1997.

Keshena, Rita. "The Role of American Indians in Motion Pictures." In *The Pretend Indians: Images of Native Americans in the Movies*, ed. Gretchen M. Bataille and Charles L. P. Silet, 106–11. Ames: Iowa State University Press, 1980.

Kessler-Harris, Alice. *In Pursuit of Equity: Women, Men, and the Quest for Economic Citizenship in 20th-Century America*. New York: Oxford University Press, 2001.

Kilpatrick, Jacquelyn. *Celluloid Indians: Native Americans and Film*. Lincoln: University of Nebraska Press, 1999.

King, Richard. "NARA, the Center of Indian Community in Portland, Oregon: A Possible Model for Chicago." In *Native Chicago*, ed. Terry Straus and Grant P. Arndt, 196–200. Chicago: Native Chicago, 1998.

Knack, Martha C. "Nineteenth-Century Great Basin Indian Wage Labor." In *Native Americans and Wage Labor: Ethnohistorical Perspectives*, ed. Alice Littlefield and Martha C. Knack, 144–76. Norman: University of Oklahoma Press, 1996.

Knight, Rolf. *Indians at Work: An Informal History of Native Indian Labor in British Columbia, 1858-1930*. Vancouver: New Star Books, 1978.

Kotlowski, Dean J. "Alcatraz, Wounded Knee, and Beyond: The Nixon and Ford Administrations Respond to Native American Protest." *Pacific Historical Review* 72 (2003): 201–27.

Kramer, Josea B., and Judith C. Barker. "Homelessness Among Older American Indians, Los Angeles, 1987–1989." *Human Organization* 55 (1996): 396–408.

LaGrand, James B. *Indian Metropolis: Native Americans in Chicago, 1945-1975*. Urbana: University of Illinois Press, 2002.

Lamore-Choate, Yvonne. "My Relocation Experience." In *Urban Voices: The Bay Area American Indian Community*, ed. Susan Lobo, 38–41. Tucson: University of Arizona Press, 2002.

Lane, Ambrose I., Sr. *Return of the Buffalo: The Story Behind America's Indian Gaming Explosion.* Westport, Conn.: Bergin and Garvey, 1995.

Lawson, Steven F. "Freedom Then, Freedom Now: The Historiography of the Civil Rights Movement." *American Historical Review* 96 (1991): 456–71.

Lemke-Santangelo, Gretchen. *Abiding Courage: African American Migrant Women and the East Bay Community.* Chapel Hill: University of North Carolina Press, 1996.

———. "Deindustrialization, Urban Poverty and African American Community Mobilization in Oakland, 1945 through the 1990s." In *Seeking El Dorado: African Americans in California,* ed. Lawrence B. De Graaf, Kevin Mulroy, and Quintard Taylor, 343–76. Seattle: University of Washington Press, 2001.

Liebow, Edward D. "Urban Indian Institutions in Phoenix: Transformation from Headquarters City to Community." *Journal of Ethnic Studies* 18 (1991): 1–27.

Limerick, Patricia Nelson. *The Legacy of Conquest: The Unbroken Past of the American West.* New York: W. W. Norton, 1987.

Lipsitz, George. *Dangerous Crossroads: Popular Music, Postmodernism, and the Poetics of Place.* London: Verso, 1994.

Littlefield, Alice, and Martha Knack, eds. *Native Americans and Wage Labor: Ethnohistorical Perspectives.* Norman: University of Oklahoma Press, 1996.

Lobo, Susan, and Kurt Peters. *American Indians and the Urban Experience.* Walnut Creek, Calif.: Altimira Press, 2001.

Lomawaima, K. Tsianina. *They Called It Prairie Light: The Story of Chilocco Indian School.* Lincoln: University of Nebraska Press, 1994.

Long, John, Lena Canyon, and David Churchman. "A Tribal American Preschool." *Journal of American Indian Education* 13, no. 1 (October 1973): 7–13.

"Looking Back: Noted Director Tells How He Made His Start in Motion Pictures." *Moving Picture World,* 10 March 1917, 1506.

Lynch, Lawrence. "In the Urban Spirit." *Westways* 67:3 (March 1975): 22–25, 70.

MacKenzie, Kent, dir. *The Exiles.* Film, 1961.

Magliari, Michael. "Free Soil, Unfree Labor: Cave Johnson Couts and the Binding of Free Workers in California, 1850–1867." *Pacific Historical Review* 73 (2004): 349–90.

Makofsky, Abraham. "Tradition and Change in the Lumbee Indian Community of Baltimore." *Maryland Historical Magazine* 75 (1980): 55–71.

Margon, Arthur. "Indians and Migrants: A Comparison of Groups New to the City." *Journal of Ethnic Studies* 4 (1977): 17–28.

McBride, Bunny. *Molly Spotted Elk: A Penobscot in Paris.* Norman: University of Oklahoma Press, 1995.

McCoy, Tim, with Ronald McCoy. *Tim McCoy Remembers the West: An Autobiography.* Garden City, N.Y.: Doubleday, 1977.

McDonnell, Janet A. *The Dispossession of the American Indian, 1887–1934.* Bloomington: Indiana University Press, 1991.

McGirr, Lisa. *Suburban Warriors: The Origins of the New American Right.* Princeton, N.J.: Princeton University Press, 2001.

McKeown, Adam. *Chinese Migrant Networks and Cultural Change: Peru, Chicago, Hawaii, 1900–1936.* Chicago: University of Chicago Press, 2001.

McWilliams, Carey. *Southern California: An Island on the Land.* Salt Lake City: Peregrine Smith Books, 1946.

Means, Russell, with Marvin J. Wolf. *Where White Men Fear to Tread: The Autobiography of Russell Means.* New York: St. Martin's Press, 1995.

Meeks, Eric V. "The Tohono O'odham, Wage Labor, and Resistant Adaptation, 1900–1930." *Western Historical Quarterly* 34 (2003): 469–89.

"Memoirs of Thomas H. Ince," *Exhibitor's Herald*, 20 December 1934, 31–32.

Meriam, Lewis. *The Problem of Indian Administration.* New York: Johnson Reprint Corp., 1971.

Meyer, Melissa L. *The White Earth Tragedy: Ethnicity and Dispossession at a Minnesota Anishinaabe Reservation, 1889–1920.* Lincoln: University of Nebraska Press, 1994.

Meyerowitz, Joanne. "Beyond the Feminist Mystique: A Reassessment of Postwar Mass Culture, 1946–1958." *Journal of American History* 79 (1993): 1455–82.

Meyn, Susan Labry. "Cincinnati's Wild West: The 1896 Rosebud Sioux Encampment." *American Indian Culture and Research Journal* 26 (2002): 1–20.

Miles, Tiya. *Ties That Bind: The Story of an Afro-Cherokee Family in Slavery and Freedom.* Berkeley: University of California Press, 2005.

Miller, Frank C. "Involvement in an Urban University." In *The American Indian in Urban Society*, ed. Jack O. Waddell and O. Michael Watson, 312–40. Boston: Little, Brown, 1971.

Miller, Nancy Brown. "Utilization of Services for the Developmentally Disabled by American Indian Families in Los Angeles." Ph.D. diss., University of California, Los Angeles, 1978.

Mitchell, Joseph. "The Mohawks in High Steel." In *Apologies to the Iroquois*, ed. Edmund Wilson and Joseph Mitchell, 3–36. New York: Farrar, Straus and Cudahy, 1959 [1949].

Morris, Patrick C. "Termination by Accountants: The Reagan Indian Policy." In *Native Americans and Public Policy*, ed. Fremont J. Lyden and Lyman H. Legters, 63–84. Pittsburgh: University of Pittsburgh Press, 1992.

Moses, L. G. *Wild West Shows and the Images of American Indians, 1883–1933.* Albuquerque: University of New Mexico Press, 1996.

Nash, Gerald D. *The American West Transformed: The Impact of the Second World War.* Bloomington: Indiana University Press, 1985.

Nash, Philleo. "Relocation." In *Indian Self-Rule: First-Hand Accounts of Indian-White Relations from Roosevelt to Reagan*, ed. Kenneth R. Philp, 164–69. Salt Lake City: Howe Brothers, 1986.

Nesper, Larry. "Simulating Culture: Being Indian for Tourists in Lac du Flambeau's Wa-Swa-Gon Indian Bowl." *Ethnohistory* 50 (2003): 447–72.

Ngai, Mae M. *Impossible Subjects: Illegal Aliens and the Making of Modern America*. Princeton, N.J.: Princeton University Press, 2004.

Nicolaides, Becky. *My Blue Heaven: Life and Politics in the Working-Class Suburbs of Los Angeles, 1920–1965*. Chicago: University of Chicago Press, 2002.

Nixon, Richard M. "Message to Congress on Indian Affairs." In *Red Power: The American Indians' Fight for Freedom*, ed. Alvin M. Josephy Jr., 211–30. New York: American Heritage Press, 1971.

O'Brien, Jean M. *Dispossession by Degrees: Indian Land and Identity in Natick, Massachusetts, 1650–1790*. Cambridge: Cambridge University Press, 1997.

Office of Indian Affairs. *Proceedings of the Conference for the Indians of Southern California, Held at Riverside, California, March 17 and 18, 1934, to discuss the Wheeler-Howard Indian Bill*. Washington, D.C.: GPO, 1934.

O'Neill, Colleen. *Working the Navajo Way: Labor and Culture in the Twentieth Century*. Lawrence: University of Kansas Press, 2005.

Oppelt, Norman T. *The Tribally Controlled Indian Colleges: The Beginnings of Self Determination in American Indian Education*. Tsaile, Ariz.: Navajo Community College Press, 1990.

Ortiz, Simon J. "Foreword." In *Urban Voices: The Bay Area American Indian Community*, ed. Susan Lobo, xvii–xviii. Tucson: University of Arizona Press, 2002.

Oropeza, Lorena. *¡Raza Sí! ¡Guerra No!: Chicano Protest and Patriotism During the Viet Nam War Era*. Berkeley: University of California Press, 2005.

Ostler, Jeffrey. *The Plains Sioux and U.S. Colonialism from Lewis and Clark to Wounded Knee*. New York: Cambridge University Press, 2004.

Owens, Louis. *Mixedblood Messages: Literature, Film, Family, Place*. Norman: University of Oklahoma Press, 1998.

Parman, Donald L. *Indians and the American West in the Twentieth Century*. Bloomington: Indiana University Press, 1994.

Patterson, Michelle Wick. "'Real' Indian Songs: The Society of American Indians and the Use of Native American Culture as a Means of Reform." *American Indian Quarterly* 26 (2002): 44–65.

Patterson, Victoria D. "Indian Life in the City: A Glimpse of the Urban Experience of Pomo Women in the 1930s." In *Urban Voices: The Bay Area American Indian Community*, ed. Susan Lobo, 6–17. Tucson: University of Arizona Press, 2002.

Payne, Charles M. *I've Got the Light of Freedom: the Organizing Tradition and the Mississippi Freedom Struggle*. Berkeley: University of California Press, 1995.

Pescador, Juan Javier. "Vanishing Woman: Female Migration and Ethnic Identity in Late-Colonial Mexico City." *Ethnohistory* 42 (1995): 617–26.

Peters, Kurt M. "Continuing Identity: Laguna Pueblo Railroaders in Richmond, California." *American Indian Culture and Research Journal* 22, no. 4 (1998): 187–91.

Philips, George Harwood. "Indians in Los Angeles, 1781–1875: Economic Integration, Social Disintegration." *Pacific Historical Review* 49 (1980): 427–51.

Philp, Kenneth. "Stride Toward Freedom: The Relocation of Indians to Cities, 1952–1960." *Western Historical Quarterly* 16 (1985): 175–90.

Pitti, Stephen. *The Devil in Silicon Valley: Northern California, Race, and Mexican Americans*. Princeton, N.J.: Princeton University Press, 2003.

Powers, Karen Vieira. *Andean Journeys: Migration, Ethnogenesis, and the State in Colonial Quito*. Albuquerque: University of New Mexico Press, 1995.

Price, John A. "The Migration and Adaptation of American Indians to Los Angeles." *Human Organization* 27 (1968): 168–75.

———. "U.S. and Canadian Indian Ethnic Institutions." *Urban Anthropology* 4 (Spring 1975): 35–52.

Prins, Harald E. L. "Tribal Network and Migrant Labor: Mi'kmaq Indians as Seasonal Workers in Aroostook's Potato Fields, 1870–1980." In *Native Americans and Wage Labor: Ethnohistorical Perspectives*, ed. Alice Littlefield and Martha C. Knack, 25–65. Norman: University of Oklahoma Press, 1996.

Prucha, Francis Paul. *The Great Father: The United States Government and the American Indians*. Lincoln: University of Nebraska Press, 1984.

Raheja, Michelle. "Screening Identity: Beads, Buckskin, and Redface in Autobiography and Film." Ph.D. diss., University of Chicago, 2001.

Raibmon, Paige. *Authentic Indians: Episodes of Encounter from the Late-Nineteenth Century Northwest Coast*. Durham, N.C.: Duke University Press, 2005.

———. "Theatres of Contact: The Kwakwaka'wakw Meet Colonialism in British Columbia and at the Chicago World's Fair." *Canadian Historical Review* 81 (2000): 157–90.

Ramirez, Renya K. *Native Hubs: Culture, Community, and Belonging in Silicon Valley and Beyond*. Durham, N.C.: Duke University Press, 2007.

Red Bird, Aileen, and Patrick Melendy. "Indian Child Welfare in Oregon." In *The Destruction of American Indian Families*, ed. Steven Unger, 43–46. New York: Association on American Indian Affairs, 1977.

Red Fox, Chief. *The Memoirs of Chief Red Fox*. New York: McGraw-Hill, 1971.

"Red Wing (I)." *Internet Movie Database*. http://www.imdb.com/name/nm934969 (accessed 1 September 2011).

"Report Notes 'Crisis' Facing Urban Indian Youth." *Indianz.Com*. http://www.indianz.com/News/archives/002846.asp (accessed 1 September 2011).

Reyes, Lawney L. *Bernie Whitebear: An Urban Indian's Quest for Justice*. Tucson: University of Arizona Press, 2006.

Richter, Daniel K. "Whose Indian History?" *William and Mary Quarterly* 50 (1993): 378–93.

Rollins, Peter C., and John E. O'Connor, eds. *Hollywood's Indian: The Portrayal of the Native American in Film*. Lexington : University Press of Kentucky, 1998.

Ronda, James P. "Generations of Faith: The Christian Indians of Martha's Vineyard." *William and Mary Quarterly* 398 (1980): 369–94.

Rosenthal, Nicolas G. "American Indian Day." In *Encyclopedia of American Holidays and National Days: A Historical Guide*, ed. Len Travers, 364–76. Westport, Conn.: Greenwood Press, 2006.

————. "Beyond the New Indian History: Recent Trends in Historiography on the Native Peoples of North America." *History Compass* 4 (September 2006).

————. "The Dawn of a New Day?: Notes on Indian Gaming in Southern California." In *Native Pathways: Economic Development and American Indian Culture in the Twentieth Century*, ed. Brian Hosmer and Colleen O'Neill, 91–111. Boulder: University Press of Colorado, 2004.

————. "Re-imagining Indian Country: American Indians and the Los Angeles Metropolitan Area." Ph.D. diss., University of California, Los Angeles, 2005.

————. "Repositioning Indianness: Native American Organizations in Portland, Oregon, 1959–1975." *Pacific Historical Review* 71 (2002): 415–38.

————. "'Walk Across the Bridge . . . An' You'll Find Your People': Native Americans in Portland, Oregon, 1945–1980." M.A. thesis, University of Oregon, 2000.

Rosier, Paul C. *Rebirth of the Blackfeet Nation, 1912–1954*. Lincoln: University of Nebraska Press, 2001.

————. *Serving Their Country: American Indian Politics and Patriotism in the Twentieth Century*. Cambridge, Mass.: Harvard University Press, 2009.

————. "'They Are Ancestral Homelands': Race, Place, and Politics in Cold War Native America, 1945–1961." *Journal of American History* 92 (2006): 1300–1326.

Ross, Jacquelyn. "Profile: Laura Williams, M.D., M.P.H." *News from Native California* 14 (December 2000): 28.

Ryckman, John W. *Story of an Epochal Event in the History of California: The Pacific Southwest Exposition, 1928*. Long Beach, Calif.: Long Beach Chamber of Commerce, 1929.

Sanchez, George J. *Becoming Mexican American: Ethnicity, Culture, and Identity in Chicano Los Angeles, 1900–1945*. New York: Oxford University Press, 1995.

Sando, Joe S. *Pueblo Profiles: Cultural Identity through Centuries of Change*. Santa Fe: Clear Light Publishers, 1998.

Scott, James C. *Domination and the Arts of Resistance: Hidden Transcripts*. New Haven, Conn.: Yale University Press, 1990.

Self, Robert O. *American Babylon: Race and the Struggle for Postwar Oakland*. Princeton, N.J.: Princeton University Press, 2003.

Shipek, Florence Connolly. *Pushed into the Rocks: Southern California Land Tenure, 1769–1986*. Lincoln: University of Nebraska Press, 1988.

Shoemaker, Nancy. *American Indian Population Recovery in the Twentieth Century.* Albuquerque: University of New Mexico Press, 2000.

———. *A Strange Likeness: Becoming Red and White in Eighteenth-Century North America.* New York: Oxford University Press, 2004.

———. "Urban Indians and Ethnic Choices: American Indian Organizations in Minneapolis, 1920–1950." *Western Historical Quarterly* 19 (1988): 431–47.

Sides, Josh. *L.A. City Limits: African American Los Angeles from the Great Depression to the Present.* Berkeley: University of California Press, 2003.

Silverheels, Jay. "Lo! The Image of the Indian!!!." *Indians Illustrated* 1, no. 6 (July 1968): 8–9.

Singer, Beverly R. *Wiping the War Paint off the Lens: Native American Film and Video.* Minneapolis: University of Minnesota Press, 2001.

Singh, Nikhil Pal. *Black Is a Country: Race and the Unfinished Struggle for Democracy.* Cambridge, Mass.: Harvard University Press, 2004.

Sitton, Tom, and William Deverell, eds. *Metropolis in the Making: Los Angeles in the 1920s.* Berkeley: University of California Press, 2001.

Smith, Andrew Brodie. *Shooting Cowboys and Indians: Silent Western Films, American Culture, and the Birth of Hollywood.* Boulder: University Press of Colorado, 2003.

Smith, Paul Chaat, and Robert Allen Warrior. *Like a Hurricane: The Indian Movement from Alcatraz to Wounded Knee.* New York: New Press, 1996.

Sorkin, Alan. *The Urban American Indian.* Lexington, Mass.: Lexington Books, 1978.

Spencer, Jon Michael. *The New Negroes and Their Music: The Success of the Harlem Renaissance.* Knoxville: University of Tennessee Press, 1997.

"Spotted Elk." *Internet Movie Database.* http:www.imdb.com/name/nm0819492 (accessed 1 September 2011).

Standing Bear, Luther. *Land of the Spotted Eagle.* Lincoln: University of Nebraska Press, 1934.

———. *My Indian Boyhood.* Lincoln: University of Nebraska Press, 1988.

———. *My People, the Sioux.* Boston: Houghton Mifflin, 1928.

———. *Stories of the Sioux.* Lincoln: University of Nebraska Press, 1933.

Straus, Terry, and Grant P. Arndt. *Native Chicago.* Chicago: Native Chicago, 1999.

Straus, Terry, and Debra Valentino. "Retribalization in Urban Indian Communities." *American Indian Culture and Research Journal* 22, no. 4 (1998): 103–15.

Street, Richard Steven. *Beasts of the Field: A Narrative History of California Farmworkers, 1769–1913.* Stanford, Calif.: Stanford University Press, 2004.

Sugrue, Thomas J. "Affirmative Action From Below: Civil Rights, the Building Trades, and the Politics of Racial Equality in the Urban North, 1945–1969." *Journal of American History* 91 (2004): 145–73.

———. *The Origins of the Urban Crisis: Race and Inequality in Postwar Detroit.* Princeton, N.J.: Princeton University Press, 1996.

Svensson, Frances. *The Ethnics in American Politics: American Indians.* Minneapolis: Burgess Publishing Company, 1973.

Talbot, Steve. "Indian Students and Reminiscences of Alcatraz." In *American Indian Activism: Alcatraz to the Longest Walk,* ed. Troy Johnson, Joane Nagel, and Duane Champagne, 104–12. Urbana: University of Illinois Press, 1997.

Theoharis, Jeanne, and Komozi Woodard, eds. *Groundwork: Local Black Freedom Movements in America.* New York: New York University Press, 2005.

Thorne, Tanis. "The Indian Beverly Hillbillies: The Migration of Oklahoma's Wealthy Indians to Southern California in the 1920s." Paper presented at the Annual Western History Association Conference. Colorado Springs, Colo., October 16–19, 2002.

Thrush, Coll. *Native Seattle: Histories from the Crossing-Over Place.* Seattle: University of Washington Press, 2008.

Trillin, Calvin. "New Group in Town," *New Yorker,* 18 April 1970, 92–104.

"Tsa-La-Gi LA." Available online at http://losangeles.cherokee.org (accessed 1 September 2011).

Tuska, Jon. *The Filming of the West.* Garden City, N.Y.: Doubleday, 1976.

Tygiel, Jules. "Metropolis in the Making: Los Angeles in the 1920s." In *Metropolis in the Making: Los Angeles in the 1920s,* ed. Tom Sitton and William Deverell, 1–10. Berkeley: University of California Press, 2001.

UCLA School of Public Health. *The Health Problems Among Native Americans in Central Los Angeles.* Los Angeles: UCLA School of Public Health, 1974.

———. *Los Angeles Area Indian Population: Health Care Needs and Resources.* Los Angeles: UCLA School of Public Health, 1975.

Urban Indian Development Association. *American Indian Business Directory.* Los Angeles: Urban Indian Development Association, 1972.

Usner, Daniel H., Jr. "American Indians on the Cotton Frontier: Changing Economic Relations with Citizens and Slaves in the Mississippi Territory." *Journal of American History* 72 (1985): 297–317.

———. *Indians, Settlers, and Slaves in a Frontier Exchange Economy: The Lower Mississippi Valley before 1783.* Chapel Hill: University of North Carolina Press, 1992.

Vicenti-Carpo, Myla Thyrza. "'Let Them Know We Still Exist': Indians in Albuquerque." Ph.D. diss., Arizona State University, 2001.

Von Eschen, Penny M. *Race Against Empire: Black Americans and Anticolonialism, 1937–1957.* Ithaca, N.Y.: Cornell University Press, 1997.

Waddell, Jack O., and O. Michael Watson, eds. *The American Indian in Urban Society.* Boston: Little, Brown, 1971.

———. *American Indian Urbanization.* Lafayette, Ind.: Purdue Research Foundation, 1973.

Wallis, Michael. *The Real Wild West: The 101 Ranch and the Creation of the American West*. New York: St. Martin's Press, 1999.

Watkins, Mel. *Stepin Fetchit: The Life and Times of Lincoln Perry*. New York: Pantheon, 2005.

Weibel-Orlando, Joan. *Indian Country L.A.: Maintaining Ethnic Community in a Complex Society*. Revised ed. Urbana: University of Illinois Press, 1999.

White, Richard. *"It's Your Misfortune and None of My Own": A New History of the American West*. Norman: University of Oklahoma Press, 1991.

———. *The Middle Ground: Indians, Empires, and Republics in the Great Lakes Region, 1650–1815*. New York: Cambridge University Press, 1991.

Wightman, Ann M. *Indigenous Migration and Social Change: The Forasteros of Cuzco, 1570–1720*. Durham, N.C.: Duke University Press, 1990.

Wild, Mark. *Street Meeting: Multiethnic Neighborhoods in Early Twentieth-Century Los Angeles*. Berkeley: University of California Press, 2005.

"William Eagle Shirt." *Internet Movie Database*. http://www.imdb.com/name/nm/0794405 (accessed 1 September 2011).

Williams, Rhonda Y. "Black Women, Urban Politics, and Engendering Black Power." In *The Black Power Movement: Rethinking the Civil Rights-Black Power Era*, ed. Peniel E. Joseph, 79–103. New York: Routledge, 2006.

Yellow Bird, Michael. "What We Want to Be Called: Indigenous Peoples' Perspectives on Racial and Ethnic Identity Labels." *American Indian Quarterly* 23 (Spring 1999): 1–21.

Yellow Eagle, Glen. "Oral History: Glen Yellow Eagle." In *Urban Voices: The Bay Area American Indian Community*, ed. Susan Lobo, 33. Tucson: University of Arizona Press, 2002.

Yu, Henry. "Los Angeles and American Studies in a Pacific World of Migrations." In *Los Angeles and the Future of Urban Cultures*, ed. Raúl Homero Villa and George J. Sánchez, 33–46. Baltimore: John Hopkins University Press, 2005.

Zulawski, Ann. "Social Differentiation, Gender, and Ethnicity: Urban Indian Women in Colonial Bolivia, 1640–1725." *Latin American Research Review* 25 (1990): 93–113.

American Indian Student Association,
UCLA, 149

American Indian Study Center,
Baltimore, 132

Americanization, 50–51, 74; of Native
Americans, 50, 51, 59–61, 62

Amos, Glenna, 66, 72, 119–20, 125,
147, 159–60

Amos, Will, 66

Angelo, Nellie, 107

Anishinaabe Indians, 135

Anpo, 143, 144

Apache Indians, 16, 39, 98

Arapaho Indians, 38

Arizona, 15, 16, 19, 21, 24, 27, 39, 81, 150

Arkansas, 21, 24

Arquero, J. S., 116

Askenette, Steve, 143

Assimilation, 50, 52. *See also*
Americanization

Bad Horse, Mahonta, 63–64, 140

Banks, Dennis, 135

Banks, Mark, 135

Bartlett, Mira Frye, 111, 124

Battle of the Red Men, The (movie, 1912),
37

Bear Don't Walk, Marjorie, 162

Becenti, Bessie, 80

Becenti, Richard, 80

Beck, Dale, 82

Begay, Andrew, 80

Begay, Bobby, 116, 117

Begay, George, 67–68

Bergie, Joe, 26

Bernstine, Daniel, 160

Berryhill, Peggy, 91–92

Billedeaux, Lincoln, 151

Birth of a Nation (movie, 1915), 39

Bison 101, 37, 39

Bison Life Motion Pictures Company, 37

Blackfeet Indians, 44, 98, 112–13, 136,
137, 149

Blackfeet Reservation, 137, 149, 168

Bowen, Carole, 85

Boyer, LaNada, 66

Bradley, Tom, 86

Brando, Marlon, 135

British Columbia, 36, 62

Brown, H., 85, 86

Brown, Jerry, 95

Bruner, Charles, 38–39

Bulin, Amabel, 110

Burbee, Carolina, 23

Burbee, Charles, 23

Bureau of American Ethnology, 40

Bureau of Indian Affairs (BIA), *59,*
90, 151; Chicago office, 60, 61, 69,
70, 137; Native American activism
and, 136, 137; relocation services,
1, 49–74, *57, 58,* 82. *See also* Adult
Vocational Training; Los Angeles
Field Relocation Office; Native
American boarding schools; Portland
Area Office of BIA

Bush, George W., 162

Caddo Indians, 91, 163

Cahuilla Indians, 13, 17, 24, 133, 164

Cahuilla Reservation, 14, 17

California Indian Rights Association,
110

California Savings and Loan, 95

California State Health Department,
142

California State University, Long Beach
(CSULB), 148

California State University, Los Angeles,
88, 139

California Urban Indian Health
Council, 142

Campadona, Juana, 21

Campbell, Noel, 83

Campo Reservation, 15, 17

Canada, 36, 62, 95

Carlisle Indian School, 26, 40, 41, 107

Cash, Warren, 110

Castillo, Edward D., 133, 134

and, 57, 58–59, 181 (n. 28). *See also* Sherman Institute

Native American Committee, 137

Native American culture, 6, 7, 8; alcoholism treatment and, 144; American fascination with, 31–33, 104–5; early twentieth-century urban Indian groups and, 105–11; Indian Day and, 45, 103, 108–10, 165; in Los Angeles, 2, 31, 41–42, 69, 103, 105–11, 114–19, 155–56, 161–62, 165; performances, 2, 33–36, 39, 40, 41, 92, 93–95, 152; powwows in Los Angeles and, 44–45, 69–70, 117–19, 122–24, 152, 160; rise of, post–World War II, 103–4, 111–27, 189 (n. 3); sign language, 42, 44, 122; traditional foods, 118; Wild West shows, 34–35, 37, 39, 40, 41

Native American federal initiatives, 1960s and 1970s, 130, 167; budget cuts to, 1980s and 1990s, 161; Indian centers and, 149–50; Indian education and, 146–47; Indian health care and, 98, 141–42; Los Angeles Indian Center and, 97, 125–26, 129, 150–51; War on Poverty and, 95, 97, 132

Native American Rehabilitation Association (NARA), 143, 144, 145, 161

Native Americans: assimilation, 50, 52; deindustrialization and, 76, 77, 82–83, 89, 185–86 (n. 5); education and, 95, 97, 98–99, 159, 160, 161; federal government and, 3–4, 7, 104; movies with, 31–34, 37–40; naming of, 169–70 (n. 3); new scholarship about, 4, 6, 34, 156–57, 170 (n. 5), 178 (n. 38), 189 (n. 3), 198 (n. 4); pan-Indian identity and, 117–18, 119; slavery and, 13; stereotyping, 7, 8, 46–47, 85, 104–5; World War II and, 24–30, 49, 80

— in cities: 1920s to 1940s, 2, 17–18, 19–30, 31–47; 1950s to 1980s, 2, 78–80, *78*; 1980s to 2000s, 157–66,

158; health of, 91, 141–43, 157, 159, 162; poverty of, 64–65, 85, 87–89, 90, 124, 157, 159, 162, 164; prior to and early years of 1900s, 11, 12–13, 16–17, 171 (nn. 4, 8); racism and, 6, 7, 8, 64, 83–84, 85–87, 162–63; today, 167–68

— work for: as actors, 6, 7, 31–34, 40–48, 117, 118, 131, 176 (n. 4); in cities, 11, 12, 19, 20–21, 22–23, 24, 25–26, 75, 76, 81–82, 173 (n. 54); as performers, 2, 33–36, 40, 41, 92, 93–95; racism and, 64, 83–84, 85; near reservations, 15–18

See also Alcohol; Chicago; Federal relocation program; Los Angeles; Migration; Minneapolis; Native American culture; Native American federal initiatives, 1960s and 1970s; Native American tribal affiliations; Native American women; Portland, Ore.; Reservations

Native American Student Alliance, 148

Native American tribal affiliations: Agua Caliente, 23, 24; Anishinaabe, 135; Apache, 16, 39, 98; Arapaho, 38; Blackfeet, 44, 98, 112–13, 136, 137, 149, 168; Caddo, 91, 163; Cahuilla, 13, 14, 17, 24, 133, 164; Campo, 15, 17; Cherokee, 21–22, 40, 52, 66, 119, 147, 159, 164; Cheyenne, 31, 38, 40, 46, 137, 140; Chippewa, 69, 107, 110, 131; Choctaw, 66; Chumash, 12, 85, 90, 145; Colville, 68; Comanche, 21–22, 26, 27, 49, 95, 98, 120, 123, 138; Cree, 162; Creek, 84, 91; Cupeño, 13; Dakota, 110; Delaware, 115, 134; Gabrielino, 13; Gros Ventre, 137; Ho-Chunk, 16; Hopi, 52; Hualapai, 16; Kaw, 108; Kickapoo, 111; Kiowa, 82, 84, 91, 98, 135, 145, 163; Klamath, 27, 80, 144; Kumeyaay, 13; Kwakwa̲ka'wakw, 36; Luiseño, 133; Lumbee, 132; Makah, 68, 98; Maliseet, 16; Menominee, 16, 80,

143; Miccosukee, 36; Mi'kmaw, 16; Mission, 13, 14, 17, 25; Mohawk, 19, 100, 134; Mojave, 15–16; Muscogee, 38; Nez Perce, 66; Ojibwa/Ojibway, 39, 107, 110, 111; Oneida, 81; Pala, 13, 17; Papago, 24; Passamaquoddy, 16; Pauite, 23, 107; Pawnee, 1, 2, 35, 139; Pechanga, 16, 23, 166; Penobscot, 16, 39; Pima, 65; Pomo, 84, 108; Powhatan, 115, 134; Quechan, 98; San Luiseño, 13; Seminole, 36, 140; Seneca, 85, 95, 109; Serrano, 13; Shasta, 144; Sin-Aikst, 86; Stockbridge Mohican, 80; Tohono O'odham, 15, 81, 139; Umatilla, 25, 26, 62, 144; Ute, 38; Winnebago, 23, 63, 64, 84, 85, 155; Wintu, 85; Yakama, 40, 45, 149, 160. *See also* Navajo Indians; Pueblo Indians; Sioux Indians

Native American women: alcohol and, 145; cultural organizations, 109, 112–13; migrating from reservations to cities, 80, 81, 84; relocation program and, 55–57, *57*, 61–62, 63–64, 65, 68, 69; work for, in cities, 19, 20, 22; working as actors/performers, 39, 40; World War II and, 25, 28, 29, 80

Navajo Club, 121

Navajo Indians, 15, 117, 164; culture of, 118, 119, 121, 122, 152; in Los Angeles, 80, 81–82, 83, 90, 95, 100, 153; relocation program and, 52, *58*, *59*, 64, 67–68

Navajo Reservation, 2, 15, 26, 67–68, 78, 95, 153

Nebraska, 41, 64, 84, 150

Nelson, Molly. *See* Spotted Elk, Molly

New Mexico, *79*, 92, 117, *158*, 164; Indians in Los Angeles from, 19, 20, 21, 23, 27, 65–67, 80, 81, 93–95, *96–97*, 120

New York City, 19, 36, 39, 41, *79*, 80, 110, 138, *158*

New York state, 19, 100, *158*

Nez Perce Indians, 66

Nixon, Richard M., 73, 97, 141

Noonan, Joe, 100

Noonan, Nunny, 100

North American Aviation, Inc. (NAA), 58, 82

Northern Aircraft, 91

Notah, Luke, *58*

Oakes, Richard, 134

Oakland, 92, 99, 108, 150, *158*. *See also* San Francisco

Office of Economic Opportunity (OEO), 73, 125, 132, 141, 144, 149, 150

Office of Indian Affairs (OIA), 13, 19, 20, 173 (n. 56)

Office of Native American Programs, 142

Oglala Sioux Indians, 28, 84

Ojibwa/Ojibway Indians, 39, 107, 110, 111

Oklahoma, 21, 22, 24, 26, 92; Indian movie actors from, 40; Indian population, 1980s to 2000s, *158*; Indians in Los Angeles from, 1, 23, 82, 91, 95, 98, 119, 121, 122–23, 138, 140, 163; Indians "relocating" from, 49, 66, 69; as Indian Territory, 35, 38–39

Olivas, Edward, 85, 90, 145

Oneida Indians, 81

O'Neill, Colleen, 15

Orange County Indian Center, 2, 69, 98, 123, 161

Oregon, 25–26, 114, 136–37, 143–44

Orpheum Vaudeville Circuit, 40

Ortega, Paul, 149

Ortiz, Simon J., 21, 29

Osawa, Sandra, 98

Owen, Charles, 100

Pacific Palisades, 37

Pacific Southwest Exposition of 1928, 40

Paisano, Ferris, 27

Pala Reservation, 13, 17

163–64, 166–67, 168; Indians in cities and, 98, 112, 113, 116, 164–66; migrating from reservations to cities, post–World War II, 80, 81, 84; racism and, 84; recruitment of Indians for movies from, 37–38, 42, 116; relocation program and, 52, 53, 62, 65, 66, 68, 69, 74; in Southern California, 11, 13, 14–18, 19–20, 25, 27; work for Indians near, 15–18. *See also specific reservations*

Rincon Reservation, 16

Riverside, 11, 13, 17, 20, 25, 26, 45, 81, 165, 166, 167. *See also* Sherman Institute

Roach Society, 122

Road Runners, 2, 69, 123

Rogoff, Ethel, 20

Romero, Rick, 100

Rosebud Reservation, 29, 41, 63, 80, 82, 87

Ross, Ann, 40

Ross, John, 40

St. Regis Mohawk Indian Reservation, 100

Sanborn, Gloria, 153

San Carlos Reservation, 16

San Diego, 18, 150, 165, 166; Indian gaming and, 163–64, 167; Indians near, early twentieth century, 15, 16, 17; World War II and, 25, 27

San Francisco, 19, 92, 98–99, 134, 150, 163; Indian population, *79*, 112, *158*; relocation program and, 66, 69

San Francisco State University (SFSU), 133, 134

San Luiseño Indians, 13

Santa Clara Pueblo Indians, 65, 83, 93–94, 133

Santa Fe Railway, 16, 19

Santa Monica, 27, 29

Santa Ynez Canyon, 37, 176 (n. 15)

Santo Domingo Pueblo Indians, 116

Sarracino, Etta, 23

Scott, James C., 6

Screen Actors' Guild, 44

Seattle, 26, 64, *79*, 150, *158*

Seattle Indian Health Board, 159

Self, Robert O., 76

Seminole Indians, 36, 140

Seneca, Martin, 88

Seneca Indians, 85, 95, 109

Serrano Indians, 13

Shasta Indians, 144

Sherman Institute, 11, 20, 81–82, 83, 181 (n. 28); founding of, 13; Los Angeles Indians and, 45, 108, 116, 165; World War II and, 26–28

Shirley, Joe, Jr., 164

Shoemaker, Nancy, 107

Sides, Josh, 77

Silent Enemy, The (movie, 1930), 39

Silent Lie, The (movie, 1917), 39

Sin-Aikst Indians, 86

Sioux Indians, 16, 29, 75, 82, 110–11, 129; culture of, 41–42, 123; Dakota, 110; Hollywood movies and, 37, 39, 43, 116; Lakota Sioux Indians, 35, 143; Lower Sioux Reservation, 63; Oglala Sioux Indians, 28, 84; relocation program and, 63; Wounded Knee occupation and, 134–35

Six Nations Reserve, 95

Skenandore, Amy, 80

Sloan's Drycleaners and Laundry, 100

Smith, Bob, 81

Smith, Nelson, 24

Smithsonian Institute, 137

Soboba Reservation, 15, 16–17

Society of American Indians (SAI), 105, 109

Solar Aircraft Company, 27, 28

South Dakota, 16, 35; Indians from, in Chicago, 84, 92; Indians from, in Los Angeles, 28–29, 75, 80, 84; movie actors from, 37, 38; Wounded Knee occupation, 134–35

Universal Studios, 31
University of California, Berkeley, 98, 133, 134, 148
University of California, Los Angeles (UCLA): Academic Advancement Program, 148–49; American Indian Cultural Center, 148; American Indian Student Association, 149; High Potential Program, 133, 139, 140; Native Americans and, 42, 133–34, 139, 140, 148–49, 153, 159, 160, 176 (n. 4)
University of Minnesota, 132
University of Southern California, 135
Urban Indian Development Association (UIDA), 72, 74, 91, 98, 99, 121
Urban Indian Program (UIP), 160–61
Utah, 57, 58
Ute Indians, 38

Vasquez, Joe, 124, 125, *126*
Verdugo, Ella, 20
Verdugo, Jalino, 20
Vietnam War, 80, 90, 98, 135, 136
Voice of the American Indian Association (VAIA), 112–13, 124

Waano Gano, Joe, 100
Wampum Club, 124
Wannassay, Vincent, 144
Warm Springs Reservation, 56, 68, 165
Warm Springs Reservation Tomahawk, The, 165
Warner Brothers, 37
War on Poverty, 95, 97, 132, 152
War on the Plains (movie, 1912), 37, 39
War Paint Club, 44
Warren, Earl, 110
Washington, 40, 68, 86–87, 89, 98, 138
Watchman, Raymond, 68
Wells, Harvey, 139

Westerman, Floyd, 135, 149
Western movies, 8, 31–33, 37–40, 41, 131; stereotyping of Indians in, 42–43, 46, 47
White, Aletha, 26, 92
White, Bernard, 92
White, Edmund, 81–82
White, Jeanette, 81–82
Whitebear, Bernie, 86–87, 89
White Bird, 45
White Earth Reservation, 107
Whiteman, Charlie, 38
Wigwam Club, 45, 108–9, 110
Wild, Mark, 22
Wild West shows, 34–35, 37, 39, 40, 41
Wills, Patricia Mae, 28–29
Wind River Reservation, 37–38
Winnebago Indians, 23, 63, 64, 84, 85, 155
Winnebago Reservation, 63, 84
Wintu Indians, 85
Wisconsin, 23, 80, 81
Women, Infants, and Children (WIC) Nutritional Program, 142
Women's Auxiliary Corps (WACS), 25, 29
World War II, 1, 24–30, 49, 52, 80
Wounded Knee, 85, 134–35, 139
Wyoming, 37–38

Yackitonipah, Greta, 123
Yackitonipah, Howard, 49–50, 120–21
Yackitonipah, Kenneth, 123
Yackitonipah, Kimmy, 123
Yakama Indians, 45, 149, 160
Yakama Reservation, 40
Yellow Eagle, Glen, 69
Yellow Eagle, Irmlee, 69
Young, Glover, 75–76
Yowlachie, Daniel, 40, 45
Yu, Henry, 5